CW00503181

THE SHORT PRAJNĀPĀRAMITĀ TEXTS

PERFECT WISDOM

The Short Prajñāpāramitā Texts

Translated by

Edward Conze

Buddhist Publishing Group

Buddhist Publishing Group
Sharpham North, Ashprington,
Totnes, Devon TQ9 7UT, England.

First published by Luzac & Co Ltd London 1973.

© Edward Conze 1973

© Muriel Conze 1993

ISBN 0-946672-28-8

A catalogue record for this book is available
from the British Library.

Printed and bound in Great Britain
by The Cromwell Press.

TABLE OF CONTENTS

TABLE OF CONTENTS (CONTINUED)

PREFACE

The corpus of the Prajñāpāramitā literature falls into three parts, comprising respectively the large, medium and short versions.

The large version, i.e. No. (1) to (4) of my *The Prajñāpāramitā Literature*, 1960[1] consists of the recensions in 100,000, 25,000, 18,000 and 10,000 *ślokas*. It has been translated in my *The Large Sutra on Perfect Wisdom* (I 1960, II and III 1964, 1966), which is being republished in one volume by the University of California Press.

The medium version is No. (5), *The Perfection of Wisdom in Eight Thousand Lines*, of which my translation first appeared in Calcutta in 1958 in the Bibliotheca Indica (reprinted 1970), and which has been republished, together with its Verse Summary, the "Verses on the Accumulation of Precious Qualities" (originally printed in 1962) by the Four Seasons Foundation of Bolinas, California.

The short versions are No. (6) to (40). Of these we have translated in this volume the bulk, i.e. nineteen, No. (6) to (9), (11) to (13), (17) to (26), and (32). What has been omitted are I. most of those which exist in Chinese only, i.e. No. (10), (12) except for a few brief extracts, (12a), (13) except for a summary, (14) to (16), and II. most of those which have a highly Tantric character, i.e. No. (27) to (31), and (33) to (40). The first have to wait until competent scholars of Chinese Buddhism come round to studying and eventually translating them. As for the Tantric texts, they employ a highly technical vocabulary which has so far been insufficiently explored and which, when translated, rarely yields anything that is readily comprehensible. The warning against those who promise bread and in fact give stones has so far applied to nearly all the translations we have had from the Tantras. A few propagandistic and edifying texts are quite readable, perhaps. As for the essence of the matter, it is intentionally esoteric, and thus remains inaccessible to the profane multitude.

Larger Texts

The *version in 2,500 Lines* (6) is the latest in time of the full-scale P.P. texts. It must be earlier than A.D. 625 since Candrakīrti quotes it in his *Mādhyamakāvatāra*.[2] In addition to the Sanskrit we have one

[1]Abbreviated as PPL. This book gives the bibliographical data as well as a short description of each text. There is no point in repeating here what was said there.

[2]L. de la Vallée Poussin, *Le Muséon* VIII, 1907, p. 265. The quotation is from Chapter 1, folio 16b.

Chinese and one Tibetan translation. The alternative title names the Bodhisattva *Su-vikrānta-vikrāmin,* i.e. "one who is quite courageous and displays valour". The text re-states P.P. doctrine on a very high level of ratiocination and does not deserve the neglect into which it has fallen in the past. The page references in brackets give the folios of the unique Cambridge Ms.

The *version in 700 Lines* (7), or *Saptaśatikā,* is older than A.D. 500. My translation of only the first part is reliable. It is based on the excellent text which J. Masuda established in 1930. For the second part we so far have only G. Tucci's 1923 transcript of the very faulty Cambridge Ms. Add 868, though I have sporadically corrected the text from the Tibetan, especially at 24a–b, 25b, 26b, 27a, 32b–33a, 38b–39a and 40a–41b. The page references of the first part are those of Masuda's edition, while those of the second are the folio numbers of the Cambridge Ms.

The *version in 500 Lines* (7a) is preserved only in Tibetan. The scholarly investigation of the Tibetan language has not yet gone very far. Except for Professor Tucci no living white scholar has ever been to Tibet. Few objective standards are at present generally agreed upon. The reader must therefore be warned that my translation is here less accurate and reliable than in the case of the Sanskrit Sutras. The text used is that of Narthang, *Sher phyin Sna ṭshogs* 170a–196. To help matters I have added a good number of Tibetan terms in the notes, together with their Sanskrit equivalents taken from the many vocabularies now at our disposal.

Summaries

Six of our texts are summaries of the doctrine, designed to act as pocket-size editions of the *Prajñāpāramitā.*

Two of these, the *Diamond Sutra* (8) and the *Heart Sutra* (11) are in a class by themselves and deservedly renowned throughout the world of Northern Buddhism. Both have been translated into many languages and have often been commented upon. The title *Vajracchedikā prajñāpāramitā* means "the perfection of wisdom which cuts like the thunderbolt" (of Indra). "Diamond Sutra" has gained currency in the West on the unwarranted assumption that *vajra* means "diamond". I have translated this text twice, once quite literally (Rome 1957, reprinted 1973), and once with greater regard for English idiom (London 1958, reprinted 1972). It is the second which I reprint here. The *Heart Sutra* exists in two recensions, (a) one long (25 *ślokas*) and (b) one short (14 *ślokas*). In the latter I have introduced the sub-divisions which should help the reader to study this superb spiritual masterpiece and to meditate on it. The short version is the earlier of the two. It is attested by the translations of Kumārajīva (ca 400) and Hsüan-tsang (649), the transliteration from Tun-huang (before 600) and the Ms. in the Horyūji Temple (609), whereas the long text makes its first appearance with Dharmacandra's Chinese translation of A.D. 741.

For the "Diamond Sutra" we have three commentaries which can be read in English. One is my own, in *Buddhist Wisdom Books*, 1958, pp. 21–74. Another is that of Asaṅga (ca A.D. 400), "Seventy Verses on the Perfection of Wisdom in Three Hundred Lines", translated by G. Tucci in *Minor Buddhist Texts* I, 1956, pp. 93–128, who also summarizes the sub-commentary of Vasubandhu on pp. 131–171. This is a fine example of a commentary of the Yogācāra school which re-interprets obscure and uncongenial sayings by revealing their "hidden meaning". Thirdly we have Han Shan (A.D. 1616), translated by Ch.Luk in *Ch'an and Zen Teaching*, First Series, 1960, pp. 149–206. This is based on Vasubandhu's commentary, but gives it a special Ch'an twist, by regarding the Sutra as a successive self-revelation of the true original nature of all living beings; it departs still further from the text of the Sutra, though not necessarily from its spirit.

For the "Heart Sutra" we have my commentary in *Buddhist Wisdom Books*,[1] on pages 77–107, as well as the article of 1948 reprinted in *Thirty Years of Buddhist Studies*, 1967, pp. 148–167. Apart from this there are three Zen commentaries, by Han Shan (pp. 209–233), D. T. Suzuki[2] and the Abbot Obora.[3] The indigenous Indian tradition is preserved in seven commentaries found in Tibetan translation in the Tanjur. They should be made accessible fairly soon. To make a start I plan to bring out a study of Praśāstrena's *ṭīkā* (cy 4) in the near future.

The Perfection of Wisdom in Very Few Words (18) (*sv=su, alpa+akṣara*) is a kind of counterpart to the *Heart Sutra*. It is addressed to the mass of dull and foolish people, whereas the *Heart Sutra* was intended for the spiritual élite. The Tantric element is also more pronounced than in the *Heart Sutra*.[4] The translation is done from the Sanskrit Calcutta Ms. and I have noted the main variations of the Chinese (A.D. 900) and Tibetan translations.

[1]This contains a few errors, of which the most horrifying is the assertion on p. 106 that *gate* is a *feminine* locative. This howler has given so much joy to my detractors that I am almost glad to have made it.

[2]In: *Essays in Zen Buddhism* III, 1934, pp. 187–206.

[3]In: T. Leggett, *The Tiger's Cave*, 1964, pp. 15–125.

[4]For further comments I refer to my PPL, pp. 81–82.

Five brief, simple and unpretentious treatises on P.P. subjects, (20) to (24), are preserved only in Tibetan, and belong into the Tantric period, i.e. after A.D. 750. They are associated with five Bodhisattvas who form a cycle in the system of the Tantras. Their names, translated, would be "Womb of the Sun", "Womb of the Moon", "All-round Auspicious", "The Holder of the Thunderbolt" (see page VII) and "The Adamantine Banner". It is noteworthy that exalted Bodhisattvas like Sūryagarbha and Candragarbha are considered as laymen, and are addressed as "sons of good family". The text is again from the Narthang Kanjur.

Three texts, (9), (10) and (19), finally condense the teaching by way of *compilation.* They represent the very nadir of inspiration, and their Chinese translations, all by Dānapāla ca A.D. 1000, are very late. Two of them may suffice.[1]

The *version in 50 Lines* (9) has been translated from the Tibetan. The Chinese agrees in general, but is much shorter, especially towards the end. It consists of a few stock phrases from traditional P.P. texts. The exhortation to practise is from *A* i 6–7; the list of wholesome dharmas is constantly reiterated in the Large Sutra; and the difficulties of fathoming the P.P. are derived from *A* viii 185.

As to No. (19), *Kauśika,* the tutelary deity of the brahminic clan of the Kuśika, is the Buddhist name for the Hindu god Indra. He is considered to be none too intelligent, and so the level of instruction is on a pretty elementary level. The Sanskrit text found in Central Asia and the Chinese translation are longer than the Tibetan version which I have followed here. All that the Tibetan misses out are twelve additional mantras, which in any case cannot be translated into English. Section I is a definition of the P.P. by way of negations, to which *Suv.* iii 36a–b provides a close parallel; II is taken from *A* xxx 525–6, the "demonstration of the P.P." by the Bodhisattva Dharmodgata; III is untraced; IV is a traditional list of eighteen kinds of emptiness, explained in *P* 195–8; V is ch. 32a of the "Diamond Sutra"; VII are the two first verses of Nāgārjuna's *Mādhyamakakārikā* (when he says that the Buddha "has demonstrated" the first six lines he means to say that in fact they are a literal quotation from an actual *Prajñāpāramitā* text[2]). The mantra of VI, or something very much like it, is the mantra of the P.P. also in the *Mahāvairocanasūtra* (the six-armed form) and in *sādhanas*

[1]No. (10), "The P.P. Sutra which gives the direct meaning", has been left out as altogether too boring.

[2]See page 189 of my Rome edition of *abhisamayas* VI–VIII of the Gilgit Ms. of the *Aṣṭādaśasāhasrikā.*

153 and 157 of the *Sādhanamālā* (the yellow two-armed form). *Dhī* is a Sanskrit word for "wisdom", and *dhīḥ* is often the germ syllable used for conjuring up a figure of the Prajñāpāramitā; *śrī* means "majesty"; *śruti smṛti mati gati* refers to stages of the realization of the P.P., as "heard, remembered, understood and arrived at"; *vijaye* means "victorious, invincible" (vocative); *svāhā* normally ends mantras addressed to feminine deities.

Special Texts

The two special texts from the Chinese, which we include at least in part, are of some interest as applying the principles of P.P. thought to social affairs. The *Questions of Nāgaśrī* (12) were translated first by A.D. 420 as "The Sūtra on the Bodhisattva Mañjusrī's highest pure act of seeking for alms", and apply the basic conceptions of the P.P. to the various aspects of begging for alms, eating, etc. The present extracts, about one-tenth of the total text, are those chosen by the editor of the *Hōbōgirin* in his article *Bunne* (pp. 164–166) and have been translated anew by Professor L. Lancaster. Each of the extracts is very brief, as can be seen by comparing the Taishō text.[1] The few pages give a tantalizing glimpse into the way in which the Hinayana attitude of mindfulness, with which the Vinaya used to hedge in the subject of begging for alms, is subjected to destructive criticism.[2]

The P.P. Sūtra which explains how benevolent kings may protect their countries (13) is more important and is our main source for the social attitudes and ideals of P.P. Buddhism.[3] It is extant in two translations, the first by Kumārajīva, A.D. 401 and the second by the Tantric master Amoghavajra, A.D. 765. My summary is based on the account of M. W. de Visser, *Ancient Buddhism in Japan* I, 1928, pp.

[1]Section I=T 234–740c: 10–13; T 220(8)–974c: 8–10. II=741b: 11–19; 974c: 10–15. III=743b: 17–22; 977a: 1–5. IV=743b: 24. V=744c: 6–8. VI=744c: 20–22. VII=745b: 9–16. VIII=745: 18–23. IX=745b: 26c: 1. X=745c: 3–4. XI=745c: 18–26. XII=745c: 28–29. XIII=745c: 29–746a: 8. XIV=746a: 13–22. XV=747a: 22–29. XVI=747b: 6–8. XVII=747b: 9–11. XVIII=747b: 14-c: 5. XIX=747c: 15–16. XX=747c: 19–21. XXI=747c: 22–23.

[2]Compare, for instance, section III with the famous *Satipatthānasutta*. It is interesting to compare this Mahayana metaphysical moonshine with the strictly clinical meditations on food and eating which were prescribed to Theravādins; see Buddhaghosa, *Visuddhimagga*, ed. H. C. Warren, 1950, XI 1–26 (English summary in my *Buddhist Meditation*, 1956, pp. 100–103.

[3]Paul Mus was the first to grasp that a doctrine of society was an integral part of Asian Buddhism—cf. *Présence du Bouddhisme*, France Asie, XVI, 1959, pp. 189–200. I have written about the problem in "Dharma as a Spiritual, Social and Cosmic Force", in *The Concept of Order*, ed. P. G. Kuntz, 1968, pp. 239–252. Important also is H. Bechert, *Buddhismus, Staat und Gesellschaft in den Laendern des Theravāda-Buddhismus*, 3 vols, 1966, 1967, 1973.

116–189, who in general follows Amoghavajra. The terminology has, however, been brought in line with that observed elsewhere in these translations. For a large part of chapters 2 and 3 I owe a rough translation to Professors R. Robinson (formerly of Wisconsin) and L. Lancaster (of Berkeley).

Tantric Texts

We now come to the purely Tantric works. The very tentative translation of *The Perfection of Wisdom in 150 Lines* (17) is based on the Sanskrit and Tibetan text edited by S. Toganoo in *Rishukyō no kenkyū*, 1930. I have also consulted E. Leumann's German translation of the Khotanese version of the "Anpreisungen"[1] (which I have marked with an A), but have made no use of the Khotanese itself or of the six Chinese translations. This translation was first published in *Studies of Esoteric Buddhism and Tantrism*, edited by Koyasan University, 1965, pp. 101–115. The Sutra is likely to have been composed before A.D. 600. Candrakīrti (ca 625) quotes it[2] and in A.D. 660 it was first translated into Chinese.

Some people write because they wish to reveal their thoughts, others because they desire to conceal them. This Sūtra abounds in "esoteric" words, i.e. in terms that by their very definition require an explanation which only a qualified teacher gives only to his initiated disciples. Being uninitiated myself, I have had no choice but to translate mechanically with the help of dictionaries, and I have marked them off by capital letters. The total result is rather weird, and reminds one of Dr. Johnson's comment on hearing a woman preach, i.e. "what is surprising is not that it was done badly, but that it was done at all". The alternative would have been to either rely on my own guesses, or to scan fashionable Western philosophers for suitable equivalents which in the nature of things are unlikely to exist there. Priests of the Shingon school, or some among the Tibetan refugees, may have preserved an oral tradition behind these esoteric teachings.

The 108 Names of Perfect Wisdom (25) are one of the many litanies which Tantrists composed in honour of their deities. It is instructive to compare it with the well-known hymn enumerating the 108 Names of the Holy Tārā.[3] The word *mtshan* of the Tibetan

[1]Die nordarischen Abschnitte der Adhyardhaśatikā Prajñāpāramitā, Text und Uebersetzung mit Glossar. *Taishō Daigaku Gakuhō*, 1930, pp. 47–87.

[2]Chapter 7 is quoted in *Prasannapadā*, 238, 8; cf. xxii, 445, 504, 7. Chapter 15 is, incidentally, quoted (about A.D. 770) in *AAA* 132 as *etad uktam*.

[3]Translated in E. Conze, ed. *Buddhist Texts*, 1954, pp. 196–202.

title which I have rendered as "names" may also mean "marks", "attributes". The numbering of the 108 items has been inserted from Fa-hsien's Chinese translation of A.D. 982.

The 25 Doors to Perfect Wisdom (26) have in a different recension occurred previously as No. XV B of the version in 150 Lines. The Vajrapāṇi who plays a prominent part in it is the "Master of the Mysteries" (*guhyakādhipati*) of the Vajrayāna, a direct emanation of the supreme being, and quite different from the Vajrapāṇi of both Hīnayāna and Mahāyāna.[1]

Our final text, *The Perfection of Wisdom in One Letter* (32), is preserved only in Tibetan and is included to show the lower limit of the compression of P.P. thought. The idea behind it is the doctrine of the Mahāsanghika school who maintained that the Buddha has taught everything by emitting just one single sound.[2] The auditors hear it each one according to their own needs and in this way the one syllable A[3] is transmitted in the minds of people into all the sermons on Prajñāpāramitā, and on spiritual topics in general all over the world.

These translations were first completed in 1954. For 18 years they have been kept alive through the efforts of Mrs. Frances Hunt and of Mrs. Alma Bevan supported by the Buddhist Society of London who indefatigably distributed the typescripts. Some translations have been printed before, and I am happy to thank B. Cassirer of Oxford (7), G. Allen & Unwin (8), E. J. Brill (13) and Koyasan University (17) for permission to reprint.

Sherborne, Dorset

October 1972

[1]E. Lamotte, Vajrapāni en Inde, *Mélanges de Sinologie offerts a M. P. Demiéville*, 1966, pp. 113–159.

[2]A. Bareau, *Les sectes bouddhiques du petit véhicule*, 1955, p. 58. See the excellent note 52 on pp. 109–110 of E. Lamotte, *L'enseignement de Vimalakīrti*, 1962. The Sanskrit is *eka-ghoṣa-udāhāra* at Dbh. 79. Elsewhere *eka-svara* is used.

[3]See the article A in *Hobogirin*, pp. 1–5.

ABBREVIATIONS

A	... ...	Aṣṭasāhasrikā
AAA	... ...	Abhisamayālaṅkārāloka by Haribhadra, ed. Wogihara, 1935
Adhy	... ...	Adhyardhaśatikā
Am	... ...	Amoghavajra
Dbh	... ...	Daśabhūmikasūtra, ed. J. Rahder
Gv	... ...	Gaṇḍavyūha
Ku	... ...	Kumārajīva
Hikata	... ...	ed. Suv, 1958
MDPL	... ...	Materials for a Dictionary of the Prajñāpāramitā Literature, by E. Conze, 1967
P	... ...	Pañcaviṃśatisāhasrikā prajñāpāramitā
PDc	... ...	Pali Dictionary
P.P.	... ...	Prajñāpāramitā
PPL	... ...	The Prajñāpāramitā Literature, by E. Conze, 1960
Sa	... ...	Saptaśatikā
Suv	... ...	Suvikrāntavikrāmiparipṛcchā
Sv	... ...	Svalpakṣarā
T	... ...	Taishō Issaikyō
V	... ...	Vajracchedikā
V.R.	... ...	Variant Reading

THE QUESTIONS OF SUVIKRĀNTAVIKRĀMIN

CHAPTER I: INTRODUCTION

Introduction

Thus have I heard at one time. The Lord dwelt at Rājagṛha in the Bamboo Grove, in the place where one makes oblations to squirrels, together with a great gathering of monks, with 1,250 monks and with immeasurable and countless Bodhisattvas, great beings, assembled from different Buddha-fields, bound to one more birth only. At that time again the Lord, surrounded and revered by an assembly consisting of many hundreds of thousands, (3a) demonstrated Dharma. Thereupon a Bodhisattva, a great being, *Suvikrāntavikrāmin* was present and seated in that assembly. He rose from his seat, put his upper robe over one shoulder, placed his right knee on the earth, bent forth his folded hands towards the Lord and said to the Lord:

"I would like to ask the Lord, the Tathagata, the Arhat, the fully Enlightened One, for some definition of the doctrine (*pradeśa*) if the Lord, when asked, gives an opportunity for the questions to be answered."

When this had been said, *the Lord* said to the Bodhisattva Suvikrāntavikrāmin, the great being: "Do ask the Tathagata, the Arhat, the fully Enlightened One, whatever you may desire (or are in doubt about), with regard to that I will gladden your heart through my explanation of the question."

Suvikrāntavikrāmin: One speaks, O Lord, of "perfect wisdom", "perfect wisdom". Because of what does one speak of the perfection of wisdom of the Bodhisattvas, the great beings? (3b). How does the Bodhisattva, the great being, course in the perfection of wisdom? How does the development of perfect wisdom, on the part of a Bodhisattva who courses in the perfection of wisdom go to fulfilment? How does Mara, the Evil One, not gain entry to a Bodhisattva, a great being, who develops the perfection of wisdom and how can one recognize all the deeds of Mara? And, which are the other dwellings in perfect wisdom, dwelling in which a Bodhisattva, a great being, quickly arrives at the fulfilment of the dharma of all-knowledge?

The Lord: Well said, well said, Suvikrāntavikrāmin, you who question the Tathagata for the sake of the Bodhisattvas, the great beings, you who have progressed for the sake of the welfare of many people, you who want to spread light for the happiness of many people, out of pity for the world, for the sake of a great body of people, for the welfare and happiness of gods and men (4a), and of the Bodhisattvas, the great beings who have not come here.

The Worthy Audience

Thereupon *the Lord*, although he knew the answer, asked Suvikrāntavikrāmin, the Bodhisattva, the great being: "As a result of which sequence of thought do you question the Tathagata about that matter?"

Suvikrāntavikrāmin: We question the Tathagata about this matter for the sake of all beings, for the welfare of all beings, out of pity for all beings. And why? The perfection of wisdom comprises all dharmas, i.e. the dharmas of Disciples, of Pratyekabuddhas, of Bodhisattvas and of fully enlightened Buddhas. Therefore, O Lord, do expound the sphere of a Tathagata, the cognition of a Tathagata! When they have heard it, beings who are fixed on the Disciple-vehicle will quickly realize the stage which is without outflows. Those who are fixed on the vehicle of the Pratyekabuddhas will go forth quickly by means of the Pratyekabuddha-vehicle. Those who have set out for the utmost, right and perfect enlightenment (4b) will quickly fully know the utmost, right and perfect enlightenment. But those who have not yet entered on any certainty about the road by which they will win salvation, who are not fixed on any of the three levels, will raise their heart to the utmost, right and perfect enlightenment.[1] And much merit will be created for all beings by the Tathagata's reply to this question about the perfection of wisdom.

We do not question the Tathagata for the sake of beings of inferior resolve, nor for those with weak hearts or poor minds, who are lazy or overcome by sloth, who have sunk into the mud of false views, who are caught in Mara's snare, who discredit the doctrine by their deeds,[2] who dread austerities, who are confused and not mindful, bewildered in their hearts, or immersed in the mire of sensuous pleasures, who are dishonest and deceitful, or without gratitude, who desire evil and habitually do it, whose morality has gone wrong, whose morality is not perfectly pure, whose views have gone wrong, who course in Mara's range, who exalt themselves and deprecate others, who attach weight to gain and honour, or are bent on food and robes[3]—cheats, (5a) boasters, hinters, bullies, keen on

[1]Or: will produce the thought of the supreme enlightenment (of a Buddha).

[2]Ch: who lack any shame and are without dread of blame.

[3]The following five items represent the usual list of the wrong ways in which a monk may get a living: he extracts gifts from his patrons (1) by trickery or hypocrisy, (2) by boasting of his own spiritual stature, (3) by hinting at desire for a particular gift, (4) by extortion or threats, and (5) by referring to a gift received from others.

making a profit. We do not question the Tathagata for the sake of beings of that kind.

But we question him for the sake of beings who strive after the cognition of the all-knowing, the non-attached cognition, the cognition of the Self-Existent, the unequalled cognition, the utmost cognition; for the sake of Bodhisattvas, of great beings who cannot exalt themselves or deprecate others because they apprehend neither themselves nor others, who have slain all pride, who are like bulls with their horns sawn off, Bodhisattvas whose stings (of craving, etc.) have been pulled out, lowly in mind, modest like the children of outcasts, with their minds level like the earth, or like water, fire, air or space. They do not apprehend even dharma, or feel inclined towards it, how much less that which is wrong (*a-dharma*). Their resolutions are pure, they are free from dishonesty, upright, even-minded in their hearts, (5b) full of pity for all beings and desirous of their welfare. They instigate others to good actions, incite and encourage them. They carry the great burden, have mounted on the great vehicle, live for the great task, possess the great compassion and bring benefits and happiness to all beings, as their guides, conductors and leaders. They dwell unsupported by all dharmas, do not care for any of the places of rebirth, they have escaped all the snares of Mara, are zealous, vigorous and vigilant, attain to the highest perfection in all dharmas and have great skill in removing all kinds of uncertainty. For the sake of such beings, O Lord, of Bodhisattvas, of great beings, do we question the Tathagata. For the sake of those who put their minds not even to the cognition of a Buddha, do not settle down in it, do not adopt any inclination for it, who have completely transcended all mindings, are established on the Path, have progressed along it and point it out to others.

We question the Tathagata in the interest of the welfare of all beings, for their benefit, happiness and pacification, (6a) bearing in mind the happiness of all beings, the utmost happiness, the supreme happiness, the happiness of Nirvana, the happiness of the Buddhas, the unconditioned happiness. We therefore question the Tathagata in order to remove the uncertainties of all beings. We ourselves, O Lord, want to be freed from uncertainty and then, freed from uncertainty, we want to demonstrate the Dharma to all beings, so that they also might lose their uncertainties. For all beings, O Lord, want happiness and are averse from suffering. All beings are desirous of happiness, but outside wisdom we do not see, O Lord, any happiness for any being. Outside the vehicle of the Bodhisattvas, the great beings, there is nowhere any happiness for any being.

Thereupon, considering this sequence of thought, we who want to bear in mind the happiness of beings, ask about the perfection of wisdom, and seeing this advantage to the Bodhisattvas have we asked the Tathagata about this matter.

The Lord: Well said, well said, Suvikrāntavikrāmin. It is not easy to reach the full extent of your meritorious deeds, you who question the Tathagata about the perfection of wisdom, (6b) out of pity for a great body of people. Therefore then, Suvikrāntavikrāmin, listen and attend well, I will teach you!

Suvikrāntavikrāmin: So be it, O Lord! and listened in silence to the Lord.

The Perfection of Wisdom

The Lord: As, Suvikrāntavikrāmin, you say, "one speaks, O Lord, of 'perfect wisdom, perfect wisdom' ". Because of what does one speak of the perfection of wisdom of the Bodhisattvas, the great beings? For the perfection of wisdom cannot be expressed by any dharma, since it has transcended all speech and one cannot say about the perfection of wisdom: this is the perfection of wisdom, he has the perfection of wisdom, through that is the perfection of wisdom, from that is the perfection of wisdom. A non-perfection is this of all dharmas, therefore is it called "perfection of wisdom". Even wisdom has the Tathagata not seized or apprehended, how then can he apprehend a perfection of wisdom?

"Wisdom" (*pra-jñā*), the perfect knowledge (*ā-jñā*)[1] of all dharmas is that, the perfect cognizing (*ā-jānanā*) of all dharmas—therefore is it called "wisdom". And what (7a) is the perfect cognizing of all dharmas? Otherwise are all those dharmas, as otherwise they are talked about, but they are not quite set free from talk. Yet the perfect knowledge and perfect cognizing of all dharmas cannot be expressed in words, but, as having been cognized by beings, is it called "wisdom". It is also called verbal intimation (*pra-jñap-tir*)—therefore is it called "wisdom". But all dharmas are incapable of being intimated; they do not proceed, they cannot be explained and they are imperceptible: this kind of non-cognizing is called their "perfect cognizing". "Wisdom", that is not knowledge, nor non-knowledge, nor both knowledge and non-knowledge—therefore is it called "wisdom". It is not the range of cognition, nor the range of non-cognition, not the sphere of non-cognition, nor also the sphere of cognition; for it is a cognition without an (objective) sphere. If

[1]Here and throughout this passage I follow the Chinese and Tibetan translations against our unique Cambridge Ms of the Sanskrit text.

there were an objective sphere in non-cognition, that would be a non-cognition. Nor is cognition from non-cognition, nor non-cognition from cognition, nor is cognition non-cognition, nor non-cognition cognition; not is it through non-cognition that "cognition" is so called, nor is it through cognition that that "cognition" is so called. For it is through non-cognition that "cognition" is so called, but again there is nowhere a non-cognition which one could show up (in a mirror, by saying:) (7b) "This is that cognition, or he has that cognition, or, by that is that cognition". Therefore that cognition does not exist by means of a state of cognizing, nor also has that cognition been established through a real entity, nor also is non-cognition called "cognition". If one would speak of "cognition" by way of non-cognition, then all foolish common people would become cognizers. But, because neither cognition nor non-cognition have been apprehended, there is a comprehension of cognition–non-cognition as it really is and just that is called "cognition"—but again cognition is not so as one speaks of it. And why? For cognition is not something that can be expressed in words, nor is cognition the sphere of anything, for cognition is something that has transcended all spheres and it is not a sphere. This is the exposition of cognition, as without a place, without a locality. It is through this cognition that this "cognition of the cognizers" comes to be styled thus and thus the exercise of wisdom (*pra-jānanā*), the understanding, the perfect cognizing, that is called "wisdom".

Supramundane Wisdom

Such reunion and realization, that is called supramundane wisdom, but again the "supramundane wisdom" is not so as one speaks of it. And why? Even the world is not apprehended, how much less the wisdom which transcends the world. How much less still (8a) he who completely rises above the world with the help of supramundane wisdom. And why? For she does not apprehend the world, therefore there is not anything which she does not rise above and in that sense is she called "supramundane wisdom". "World", a verbal concept that is called, but a verbal concept is not something that can completely transcend the world; but on the contrary, one speaks of the "supramundane" as of that which has completely transcended all verbal concepts. Moreover, the supramundane is not a matter of rising above, but a matter of not rising above is the supramundane. And why? In relation to it even the least dharma does not exist which one should rise above, or by which one should rise above—therefore is it called "supramundane". For in relation to the supramundane the world does not exist, and so it cannot be said to be above the world; where the unsurpassed is concerned, there is no further possibility of surpassing anything—therefore is it called "supramundane". This is called the exposition of supramundane wisdom. But "supramundane wisdom" is not so as one speaks of it. And why? For what is supramundane, that cannot be expressed in words; and therefore it has (definitely) crossed over (into a world totally different from ours); there is in it not anything that should any further cross over. Therefore is it called "supramundane wisdom".

Penetrating Wisdom[1]

Here, as to penetrating (*nirvedhikā*) wisdom, what does that wisdom penetrate (*nirvidhyati*)? There is nothing that should be penetrated. (8b) If there were anything that should be penetrated, one would (be able to) intimate, "this is that wisdom, she who penetrates". It does not pierce (*vidhyate*) or probe (*āvidhyate*) with anything and one cannot apprehend anything other which would be pierced. "It penetrates", but there is not anything which pierces or is pierced, which probes or is probed. It is in that sense that one says that "it penetrates". It reaches no end or middle—in that sense one says "it penetrates". One says that "penetrating wisdom penetrates", but though he penetrates there is nothing that could move,[2] move away from, or move towards.[3] In that sense one speaks of it as "penetrating". Moreover, "penetrating wisdom"—what does it penetrate? Whatever is visible, all that it penetrates. Whereby does it penetrate? With wisdom it penetrates. How then does it penetrate with wisdom? It penetrates to it (saying that), "it has the mark of being a verbal concept". "But what has the mark of being a verbal concept, all that has no mark; no mark has that which has the mark of being a verbal concept." One who, endowed with suchlike wisdom, pierces, he pierces what belongs to the triple world. How does he pierce? He penetrates (to the conviction that) "what belongs to the triple world that belong to no world". (9a) Because he does not pierce any world,[4] he penetrates (to the conviction that) "that which belongs to the triple world belongs to no world". When he has

[1]This section largely relies on a play on Sanskrit words which cannot be reproduced in English. Some of it I do not even understand in the Sanskrit.

[2]run, travel, advance.

[3]runs through, spends time.

[4]or element; *dhātu*.

thus penetrated[1] the triple world, then one calls him "someone who is endowed with penetrating wisdom". And how is he endowed with penetrating wisdom? None of his penetrations[2] is unwholesome, but they are all wholesome, (and that is why) he transcends (everything) with the help of penetrating wisdom. And thus he is endowed with penetrating wisdom; whatever he sees, hears, smells, tastes, touches, or discerns, all that he penetrates.[3]

Truth of Ill

How does he become disgusted with it? Because it is impermanent, ill, a boil, a disease, a thorn (*śalya*), empty, a misfortune, a slaughter house, foreign, disturbing, by its very nature a disturbance, shaky, brittle, not-self, unproduced, not stopped, without mark—that is called the "cool freedom from grief" (*viśalya*). Just as a kind of medicine, called "freedom from thorns", if it is placed somewhere takes away (*apanayati*) and cleanses away (*nirvidhyati*) all thorns from there, thus, endowed with suchlike dharmas, a monk is freed from thorns (*viśalya*), cool, endowed with penetrating wisdom, (9b) one who dwells beyond the extremes of birth-and-death, wise with penetrating wisdom, free from passion, one who has transcended all that belongs to the triple world and all Mara's snares. Just as a thunderbolt penetrates everything wherever it may be hurled for the purpose of penetrating something (*nirvedhana*)[4]; just so, whatever monk's adamantine (*vajropama*) concentration takes hold of through his penetrating wisdom wherein he may place it, or what he may frequent,[5] all that he penetrates. Endowed with penetrating wisdom, unstained as a result of the supramundane going to the right extinction of suffering, he is called "one who has the triple knowledge" (*traividya*).[6] "Knowledge" (*vidyā*), of the appeasing of ignorance is that a synonym; "the comprehension of ignorance", of the appeasing of the mass of ill is that a synonym. Just as if a learned doctor (*vaidya*) handsome and intelligent, were endowed with skill in diagnosis and skilled in all remedies, skilled in the (knowledge of the) origin of all diseases, a liberator from all ill, and

[1] *nirviddham*; also: *nirbiddham*, become disgusted with; cf. *nibbidā*.

[2] or: none of the objects of his penetration; *nirveddhayyam*; or: become disgusted with.

[3] or: becomes disgusted with.

[4] or: smashing. Ch: boring a hole in things (as a firestick).

[5] roams about in.

[6] The three knowledges are in fact three of the six super-knowledges, i.e. (1) the recollection of previous births, (2) the knowledge of the rise and fall of beings, (3) the knowledge of the extinction of the outflows.

whichever disease he would treat, that he would just liberate from. And why? Because he is one who is skilled in all remedies, skilled in the (knowledge of the) origin of all diseases, one who frees from all sickness. (10a) Just so the third knowledge[1] is conducive to the appeasing of all ignorance, conducive to the removal of all suffering, conducive to the appeasing of all decay, death, sorrow, lamentation, pain, sadness and despair. This is called the supramundane wisdom which leads to penetration (*nirvedha*).

Truth of Origination

And this, Suvikrāntavikrāmin, has been said by me in a hidden sense:

"Wisdom is the best thing in the world, she is the one who leads to penetration,
And through her he rightly comprehends the complete extinction of birth and becoming."

"The complete extinction of birth and becoming", of what is that a synonym? It is a synonym for the penetration (*prativedha*) into rise and disappearance. And what is the penetration into rise and disappearance? "Whatever is doomed to originate, all that is doomed to stop," thus he penetrates to origination and disappearance. "Origination," of production is that a synonym; "disappearance", of stopping is that a synonym. But again rise and disappearance are not so as they are spoken of. An origination (*samudaya*) does not dharmically involve an arising (*udaya-dharmaḥ*). And why? For there is no arising (*udayo*) of what is the same (*samasya*) (with that from which it arises), nor does that appear (*samudāgacchati*),[2] but it is just in accord with (*anuyāta*) sameness; therefore is it called "origination". "In accord with sameness," therein not anything does arise (*udayati*) or appear; the own-being of that is not brought into being by itself; it is stopping, but in it there is no stopping of anything; there is nothing between origination and stopping. Where there is no production, there is also no stopping; and that is (the true meaning of) stopping. Thus as to the penetration into origination and disappearance, the penetration into disappearance takes place for the sake of non-production and non-stopping; this is why one speaks of "penetration into origination and disappearance".

"Penetration," a comprehension of conditioned co-production is that. Conditioned by what a dharma is produced, conditioned by just that that dharma does not exist; this is called the penetration to

[1]i.e., the knowledge of the extinction of the outflows.

[2]also: arrive at full knowledge, or enlightenment.

conditioned co-production. And that comprehension of conditioned co-production, that is the state of reality as it truly is; it is indicated by means of non-production; for non-production is conditioned co-production, (always?) the same (*sama*) is non-production (*anutpāda*), therefore is it called "conditioned co-production" (*pratītyasamutpāda*).

Truth of Stopping

Where there is no production, how can there be stopping? Taking non-stopping as stopping, (11a) that is an understanding of conditioned co-production. As a non-co-production is "conditioned co-production" so called; what is non-co-production that is non-production; what is non-production, that is not past, future or present, the stopping of that cannot possibly exist. That of which the stopping does not exist, that is called the "cognition of non-production". And that through which non-production has been cognized, that does no longer cause anything to be produced, nor does it realize stopping. What does not produce, that does not stop; for only where there is production can stopping be conceived. Where one does not produce, there as just stopped are all dharmas cognized, seen, penetrated, realized—therefore one speaks of (the fact that) "stopping has been realized".

As to the "cognition of extinction"—extinct is non-cognition, that is why one speaks of "cognition of extinction". Extinct through what? Extinct through non-extinctness; one cannot review its extinction; it is (just) the departure of non-cognition, therefore is it called "the cognition of extinction". It is the comprehension of a non-cognition and therefore the extinction of non-cognition is called the "cognition of extinction", since non-cognition is neither extinction nor non-extinction. But it will be cognized as a departure and it is in that sense that one speaks of (11b) "cognition of extinction". It is a comprehension of that which really is and that is why one speaks of the "departure" (of the veil with which ignorance covers true reality). Nothing else is here apprehended—this is "that departure of non-cognition". Even cognition is not apprehended, how much less the non-cognition the extinction of which would lead to emancipation; in that sense one speaks of the "cognition of extinction". But again also this is not so as one speaks of it. That (object) to which the cognition of extinction refers, of that there is no conventional expression; in fact one just engages in verbal play[1] when one speaks of "extinction of non-cognition" or "cognition of

[1]This is rather free for *api tu nirdeśa*.

extinction". This is the investigation of the cognition of both extinction and non-extinction with regard to all dharmas. When one has understood it, one is free from the cognition of extinction and has reached the limit of non-extinction—a no-limit which is the limit of Nirvana; but again not so as one speaks of it. For without limit are all dharmas, with Nirvana for their limit. The cutting off of all limits is called the "Nirvana-limit"; but again not so as one speaks of it. For inexpressible is Nirvana,[1] and all conventional expressions are there completely cut off. This is the exposition of the Nirvana-element, but again it is not so as it is expounded; for the Nirvana-element is something that cannot be expounded, it has completely transcended all expositions; the Nirvana-element is something which has completely cut off all expositions—this is called the exposition through the supramundane penetrating wisdom (12a), and that is what this "Nirvana-element" is. But the Nirvana-element is not placed in any spot or place (*deśastho*; *pradeśastaḥ*). This is its exposition (*nirdeśa*).

Perfection

What then is the perfection of wisdom? With regard to the perfection of wisdom there is nothing on this (*āram*) or on yonder shore (*pāram*). If one could, with regard to the perfection of wisdom, apprehend this or yonder shore, the Tathagata would explain this or yonder shore of the perfection of wisdom; since, however, this shore of the perfection of wisdom cannot be apprehended, one cannot explain its beyond either. Moreover the "perfection of wisdom" (*prajñā-pāramitā*) that is the beyond (*pāram*) of all dharmas, whether they be objects of cognition or deeds; it is in that sense that one speaks of "perfection of wisdom"; but again it is not so as one speaks of it. For the perfection of wisdom has not been set up by speech or by deed and that is why it cannot be explained.

Enlightenment

It is the understanding of all dharmas, but that understanding is non-obstruction. And why? For nothing is here understood or penetrated, since enlightenment is the sameness of penetration and understanding and one speaks of enlightenment because all dharmas (12b) are understood. And what is the understanding of all dharmas? There is here no enlightenment (*bodhi*) nor understanding (*anubodha*). And why? If one could apprehend enlightenment, then enlighten-

[1]V.R.: the Nirvana-limit.

ment could be seized in enlightenment; but there exists no enlightenment in enlightenment; it is thus that this enlightenment should be fully known. Because of non-understanding, because of non-penetration does one speak of "one who has understood", but again it is not so as one speaks of it; for all dharmas are not understood, not penetrated. And again a dharma does not exist by way of having the own-being of a non-dharma; when this is understood, one speaks of "enlightenment". For the Tathagata has not apprehended any enlightenment, nor has he intimated any enlightenment, for enlightenment cannot be intimated, cannot be a subject of wise instruction. Nor has the Tathagata known or generated enlightenment; for enlightenment is not born nor reproduced. Nor is enlightenment the (objective) sphere of anything, nor is there in enlightenment any being or concept of a being; wherein there is neither a being nor the concept of a being, how can one say "this is an enlightenment-being (*bodhi-sattva*)", "this is the perfection of wisdom of an enlightenment-being". For in enlightenment there is no enlightenment, nor is there in enlightenment any (13a) being; quite transcendent is that enlightenment, non-produced is that enlightenment, unreproducable is that enlightenment, unmarked is that enlightenment; and in it no being exists or can be apprehended. Enlightenment cannot be conceived through its relationship to a being; to understand the absence of beings (everywhere) that is called "enlightenment".

Enlightenment-being

Enlightenment is not being (*asattva*); one who has cognized that, he is called a "Bodhi-being" (*bodhi-sattva*). And why? For it is not by the perception of a being that a Bodhi-being has been brought about, but, on the contrary, it is because of the meditational annihilation of the notion of a being that he is called an "enlightenment-being"; but again it is not so as one speaks of it. And why? Because a Bodhisattva is inexpressible; a Bodhi-being is without the own-being of a being, and enlightenment is without the notion of a being. One who has thus cognized enlightenment, he is called an "enlightenment-being". And how has enlightenment been cognized? Quite transcendent is that enlightenment and there is nothing to be done about it. Because it is non-production and non-stopping. Enlightenment does not instruct about enlightenment, nor can enlightenment be conveyed by instructions. One speaks of enlightenment as unconveyable by instructions, as unteachable by verbal intimations, as unreproducable. Someone is a "Bodhisattva" if he has understood and penetrated it, as quite indiscriminate, because all thought-constructions have been completely cut off; but again he is not so as one speaks of him. And why? (13b) Because there is here no (living) being. If one could apprehend a Bodhi-being, then enlightenment could be seized upon (in the sense that:) "this is that enlightenment, in it there is this being". Because of the understanding that there is no being, that a being is non-existent, that there is the absence of a being, does one speak of a "Bodhi-being". Because of the non-existence of a being, because of the annihilation (by meditation) of the notion of a being (because of the annihilation (by meditation) of the notion of a no-being)[1] does one speak cf a "Bodhi-being". And why? "The world[2] of beings", of the state of the absence of a being is that a synonym; for no being is found (or exists) in a being, because the world of beings does not exist. If there were a being in a being, one would not speak of "the world of beings". A definition of a no-world is that, i.e. "the world of beings", for the world of beings is not something that belongs to a world. If there were a world of beings in the world of beings, then it would be (true that) "what is the soul that is the body". But the world is set free from the world of beings,[3] for the world of beings is not something that belongs to a world, a world finds conventional expression by way of agreed symbols. For no world exists in the world of beings, nor does a world of beings exist outside the world of beings; for all dharmas are such that they do not belong to a world. And I have taught this in a hidden sense when I have said of the world of beings no deficiency or completion is conceived. And why? Because of the absence of a being in the world of beings, (14a) because of the isolatedness of the world of beings. And as of the world of beings, so also of all dharmas no deficiency or completion is conceived. For there is not any accomplishment (*parinispatti*)[4] of all dharmas through which they would have a deficiency or completion. To understand all dharmas thus, that is called the "understanding of all dharmas". And I have taught this in a hidden sense when I have said that "as of the world of beings, so of all dharmas also no deficiency or completion can be conceived". The non-deficiency and non-completion of all dharmas results from the absence of accomplishment in them, and just that is also the non-deficiency and non-

[1]Omitted in Ch. and Tib.

[2]*dhātu*, also element, realm, etc. The following argumentation relies on the ambiguity of this technical term for its effects and cannot be reproduced in English.

[3]Ch. and Tib. add: and the soul would be one thing and the body another.

[4]This is a very difficult term which occurs frequently in later Yogācārin-influenced Buddhist ontology.

completion of the Buddha-dharmas. In that way the non-deficiency and non-completion of the Buddha-dharmas follows from the understanding of all dharmas, and the Buddhadharmas are because of the non-deficiency and non-completion of all dharmas. Therefore that is a synonym for the Buddhadharmas, for it is not possible that anyone could make the Buddhadharmas deficient or complete. And why? Such is the understanding of all dharmas. In it there is no deficiency or completion of any dharma. "All dharmas", of the realm of Dharma[1] is that a synonym; (14b) but there can be no deficiency or completion of the realm of Dharma. And why? For the realm of Dharma is infinite. For one cannot apprehend any differentiation between the realm[2] of beings and the realm of Dharma, nor can one apprehend any deficiency or completion in either the realm of beings or the realm of Dharma, nor does there exist one in them. To understand it thus, that is called "enlightenment". Therefore it is said that "of the Buddhadharmas no deficiency or completion can be conceived". "Non-deficiency, non-completion," that is a synonym of the vision according to the reality of that which in its real existence is indiscriminate. Nothing can here be added or subtracted. To understand it thus, that is called "enlightenment". "Enlightenment", that is the mark of the Buddha. How is it the mark of the Buddha? The marks of all dharmas are a no-mark and that is the Buddha-mark; for enlightenment is without mark, in its own-being it has turned back on marks. To understand it thus, that is called "enlightenment", but it is not so as one speaks of it. For one speaks of a "Bodhi-being" because he has understood these dharmas. For if anyone, without wisely knowing, without understanding these dharmas, (15a) asserts of himself that he is a "Bodhisattva", far is the Bodhisattva-stage from that Bodhisattva, far away are the dharmas of a Bodhisattva, he fails to keep his word to the world with its gods, men and asuras when he claimed the name of a Bodhisattva. If, on the other hand, he were a Bodhisattva merely by way of speech, then all beings would likewise be Bodhisattvas. "The stage of a Bodhisattva," that is not mere speech, nor can one through speech fully know the supreme enlightenment. For it is not by a deed of speech that one can attain enlightenment or the dharmas of a Bodhisattva. All beings course to enlightenment, though they neither cognize nor understand and so they are not called "enlightenment-beings". And why? For they do not wisely know beings as

[1] *dharmadhātu*, also "dharma-element".
[2] *dhātu*, or world, or element.

"non-beings".[1] If they were to cognize this they would by the practices of self become Bodhisattvas; perverted beings, however, do not wisely know their own course, their own sphere, their own range. If they were wisely to know the course of their self, they would no longer course in any discrimination whatever. It is through their coursings in discrimination that all the foolish common people course in an unreal objective support. Even of enlightenment they think[2] (15b) by having made it into an objective support. Since they have coursed in objective supports and in discrimination, how can they have enlightenment, how can they have the dharmas of an enlightenment-being? They who thus wisely know the dharma, they no longer course in an unreal objective support, they no longer think of[3] any dharma; therefore one speaks of the "coursing of a Bodhisattva", which is a no-coursing. Bodhisattvas course in neither thought-construction nor in discrimination. Where there is no thought-construction or discrimination, there is also no course; and where there is non-discrimination, therein there is no coursing of anyone. All the coursings of Buddhas and Bodhisattvas are "coursings in non-discrimination". All minding is with-object.[4] One who thus wisely knows all dharmas, he no longer courses (*carati*) or wanders (*vicarati*) in objective support or in discrimination; this is the course of the Bodhisattvas, by way of no-coursing. It is thus that the Bodhisattvas course in the Bodhisattva-course. Because they thus understand and awaken to dharmas, therefore are they called Bodhisattvas.

"No-being," that is a synonym for an enlightenment-being. For he has annihilated (in meditation) the omniscient beings.[5] And why? For he has cognized all beings as unreal, (and he knows that) "all beings are no-beings", they are beings who result from perverted views, (16b) imagined beings, beings with an unreal objective support, beings who have lost their own course, beings fashioned together by ignorance. And why? The dharmas of all beings do not exist, but they have manufactured them. Therefore one says that "all beings are beings who have been fashioned together by ignorance". Which dharma does not exist? One speaks of "I" or "mine", or "I am", but no dharmic fact corresponds to this. If "I" or "mine", or "I am" were dharmic facts, then beings would be real. But

[1]So Ch., Tib. Sanskrit Ms as "beings".
[2]mind
[3]mind
[4]Tib. without object.
[5]Ch. Tib.: beings with all their perceptions?

because there is no such dharma as "I", or "mine", or "I am", therefore one says that "all beings are unreal, fashioned together by ignorance". For no dharma called being exists at all, with regard to which "I", or "mine", or "I am" would be (a fact); and because it does not exist, therefore (16b) "beings" are called "unreal". "Unreal," of no-beings that is a synonym. In so far as they have settled down in the notion of an unreal being, in so far are they called "unreal beings". "Unreal," in it there is nothing that is real or that has come into being, for all dharmas are unreal and have not come into being. Beings, however, who are bent on the unreal are put into bondage, therefore they are called "beings with an unreal objective support". Not wisely knowing that own-course of theirs, they are called "unreal beings". But theirs is a non-awakening. Because of the understanding of that course one is called a "Bodhisattva".

One who thus understands dharmas, he is called a "Bodhisattva". "Bodhisattva," of a being who has understood is that a synonym: he has fully known (*buddhā*) and cognized all dharmas. How cognized? As unreal (*abhūtā*), as not come into being, as false, as not so as they are imagined by the foolish common people, or seized upon by them—therefore are they called "Bodhisattvas". And why? They are not discriminated. For enlightenment (*bodhi*) is not imagined, not discriminated, not fabricated and without basis and (17a) the Tathagata has not seized upon enlightenment. One speaks of "enlightenment" because all dharmas are not met with and are without basis. It is thus that one speaks of "the enlightenment of a Buddha", but again it is not so as one speaks of it. When, (thinking) "we will raise this thought to enlightenment", they raise their thought to that enlightenment, then they mind enlightenment (i.e. they think that) "there is this enlightenment to which we shall raise our thought". They are not called "Bodhisattvas", they are called "beings who have been produced". And why? Because, having settled down in production, having settled down in thought, they settle down in enlightenment. Those who raise their thought to enlightenment are called "beings who have settled down in the thought of enlightenment". Because they manufacture (fictitious entities), therefore do they raise their thought to enlightenment. Therefore are they called "beings who manufacture", and they are not enlightenment-beings. And why? They are called beings who have been produced. For it is not possible to raise thought to enlightenment, because enlightenment is non-production and no-thought. Just the produced they settle down in, (17b) and they do not wisely know non-production. What again is the sameness of production, that is the real sameness; what is the real sameness that is the sameness of thought; and what is the sameness of thought that is enlightenment and in that there is the state of that which is truly real, but there is no discrimination in it. Again they, having discriminated, having settled down in thought and in enlightenment, raise their thought to a dual enlightenment. For thought is not one thing and enlightenment another. Nor is enlightenment in thought, nor also thought in enlightenment. But what is enlightenment and what is thought, that is the state of true reality, the state of reality as it actually is.

Great Being

There is here no enlightment and no thought. Nor has enlightenment been apprehended. It is not production nor non-production. Therefore is he called a "Bodhisattva", a "truly real being", a "great being". And why? For what is unreality, that he has cognized. And how is that unreality? All this world is unreal, included in the unreal is this our establishment in the world, it is unreal and has not come into being. What is the possible origin of the unreal? There is no possible origin for the unreal, for what is unreal that has not come into being, therefore it is said that "all dharmas are without own-being, unreal". One who has cognized thus, he is called a "truly real being". (18a) He does not get attached to the real in the real, therefore is he called a "truly real being". But again he is not so as one speaks of him. And why? For in the truly real there is not any being or great being. For one is called a "great being" if he plunges into the great vehicle.

The Great Vehicle

And what is the great vehicle? All cognition is the great vehicle. And what is all cognition? Whatever (there) is (by way of) conditioned cognition, unconditioned cognition, worldly cognition, supramundane cognition. Therefore is he called a "great being". And why? For he has been freed from the great (false) notion of a being; therefore is he called a "great being". He has been freed from the great mass of ignorance; therefore is he called a "great being". He has been freed from the great mass of karma-formations; therefore is he called a "great being". He has been freed from the great mass of non-cognition; therefore is he called a "great being". He has been freed from the great mass of ill; therefore is he called a "great being". For those who have censured the notion of a (great)[1] being, and who yet do not apprehend a thought, nor the dharmas which constitute thought and who wisely know the essential original nature of thought, but do not apprehend an enlightenment, nor the dharmas which are the wings of enlightenment and who wisely know the essential original nature of enlightenment, they do not with an uncognized (18b) thought see enlightenment: they do not see a thought either outside or inside enlightenment, nor do they see enlightenment inside a thought. Those who annihilate (by meditation), they do neither develop (their meditation) nor undo it. They also do not apprehend meditational development, do not mind it, do not settle down in it. For they raise their thought to enlightenment. But those who thus raise thought to enlightenment, they are called "true[2] Bodhisattvas", and they do not turn away from enlightenment. And why? Because they are established in enlightenment, they who do not review any differentiation between enlightenment and thought, between production and stopping. For here no one reviews, no one settles down, no one performs a discrimination. Those who thus produce a thought full of the resolve to win emancipation, they are called "true Bodhisattvas". But those who, while they have a notion of thought and a notion of enlightenment, raise their thought to enlightenment, they are far from enlightenment and not at all near it. But again those who do not consider whether they are far from enlightenment, or near it, (19a) they are near to enlightenment and they have raised their thought to enlightenment. And I have pointed this out with a hidden meaning: one who wisely knows himself (*ātmānam*) as non-dual, he wisely knows both Buddha and Dharma. And why? He develops a personality (*ātmabhāva*) which consists of all dharmas. His non-dual comprehension comprehends all dharmas; for all dharmas are fixed on the self in their own-being (*ātma-svabhāva-niyatā*). One who wisely knows the non-dual dharma, wisely knows also the Buddhadharmas. From the comprehension of the non-dual dharma follows the comprehension of the Buddhadharmas and from the comprehension of the self the comprehension of everything that belongs to the triple world. "The comprehension of self," that is the beyond of all dharmas. And what is the beyond of all dharmas? One who does not apprehend this shore, nor minds the other shore beyond, or settles down in it; by the comprehension of that is he called "one who has gone beyond". But again he is not so as one speaks of him. In this way

[1]So Ch. and Tib., but not the Sanskrit Ms.
[2]So Ch., Tib.

should they follow their Bodhisattva-stage—that is the perfection of wisdom of the Bodhisattvas. Therein not even the least thing is to be gone to or to be arrived at. For no coming or going are here conceived.

CHAPTER II: ĀNANDA

Ānanda: Those who are conceited, and who course in a sign, will tremble at this exposition.

Śāradvatīputra: There is, Ānanda, no route in this for those who are conceited, and it is not within their range. But they will not tremble thereat. And why? Those have trembled who are in the hands of a bad teacher, and for them there is no route in it, and it is not within their range. But those again, Ven. Ānanda, who have practised in order to forsake conceit, who have exerted themselves in order to forsake conceit, they will tremble thereat. And why? With the help of a wise understanding of conceit they strive for a state without conceitedness, and they strive to forsake pride. But those who do not apprehend pride, nor review it, nor put their minds to it, nor settle down in it, they will not tremble anywhere, nor will they get frightened anywhere.

But it is not for the sake of conceited people that this demonstration of Dharma takes place. There is no room (20a) here for the conceited, or for those who still struggle to forsake conceit. Conceit implies a claim to superiority. The conceited impute superiority to some things over others, and they do not see things as equal. Even those who see all things as equal remain uncertain about this Dharma. Only those who do not apprehend anything as equal[1] or unequal,[2] do not put their minds to anything as equal or unequal, and who therefore do not settle down in anything as equal or unequal—only those will never be afraid of anything.

There is no route here for all the foolish common people, and it lies outside their sphere. There is no route here either for those who belong to the vehicle of the Disciples, or for those who, belonging to the vehicle of the Pratyekabuddhas, course in deep dharmas,[3] in these stainless dharmas there is no route either for those who, though they belong to the vehicle of the Bodhisattvas, nevertheless course in a sign, have not been taken hold of by a good teacher and are in the hands of a bad teacher. (20a) They lie outside their sphere.

[1]*samam*

[2]*viṣamam*

[3]i.e. they understand conditioned co-production more thoroughly than the Disciples.

We must, however, make an exception for those who belong to the vehicle of the Disciples, but have seen the Truth,[1] are supported by a good teacher, are resolved on deep dharmas, course in agreement with them, plunge and enter into them. But no stupefaction or hesitation is felt towards these dharmas by those Bodhisattvas who have left all signs behind, who course in the signless, make no distinctions, have just absolutely gone forth into deep dharmas, apprehend neither thought nor enlightenment, do not differentiate any dharma whatever and do not review one. And why? They are established in agreement with all dharmas and do not disagree with them. Whenever they are asked about dharmas, they reply and explain (their secret intent)[2] in agreement with just the facts.

The Lord: So it is, Ānanda, as Śāradvatīputra explains. The conceited can find no ground to stand on in this demonstration of Dharma. For it is outside their sphere to enter into this enlightenment of a Buddha. In agreement with reality is this enlightenment of a Buddha. (21a) For the thought of beings of inferior resolve does not stride in sublime dharmas, in Buddhadharmas. For those who are of inferior resolve, and conceited, abide in a condition which is contrary to the enlightenment of a Buddha. They march along under the sway of conceit (and they cannot understand the deep dharma).[3] Pure is this assembly—they have done their duties under the Jinas of the past, they have planted wholesome roots, they have honoured many Buddhas, they are resolved on deep dharmas and have coursed in them. It is thus that the Tathagata confidently and forcibly demonstrates Dharma in this assembly, although he does not demonstrate any dharma which can be preserved.[4] Of substantial excellence[5] is this assembly; it is without grit, gravel or dust; many hundreds of thousands of Buddhas have honoured it; it is established in the (core and) substance.[6] "Grit and gravel" means the foolish common people, and for them there is no room in these dharmas. "Dust" means the conceited people. Free from conceit is this assembly, exceedingly lifted up[7] by its great wholesome roots.

When, Ānanda, the Nāga king of Anavatapta becomes joyful, (21b) full of joy and zest, then[8] he enjoys the five sense-pleasures in

[1]*dṛṣṭasatyam*
[2]*saṃdhayanti*
[3]Ch. adds.
[4]?, *anurakṣya*, *rjes-su bsruṅ-ba*
[5]*sāra*
[6]*sāra*
[7]*abhyudgata*
[8]This "then" is rather puzzling. One would have expected it after "joyous in it".

his own realm and is exceedingly joyous in it, and (in his exuberance) he lets loose a big rain, of the most excellent water. His sons also then become joyful. Possessed of and endowed with the five sense-pleasures they sport about, each one in his own realm, and also let loose a big rain. Just so, Ānanda, when the Tathagata lets loose the great rain of the Dharma, then his finest sons, the Bodhisattvas, the great beings, go to their respective Buddha-fields in this world system, and also let loose, stimulated by this upsurge of Dharma, a great rain of Dharma before the eyes of these Tathagatas, and pour down a great shower of Dharma. The Nāga-king Sāgara, when he feels joyful, releases great rain clouds in his own realm, and the other Nāgas, who reside in that realm, welcome those rain clouds, become contented and feel happiness because of them. His sons also are strong enough to bear[1] these clouds, (22a) and feel elated by them. Other Nāgas, however, are not equal to these rain clouds, would feel no happiness about them and would derive no contentment (from them). Just so, Ānanda, those who dearly love the Dharma-jewel of the Tathagata, and who are his finest sons, Bodhisattvas, great beings who have achieved their wholesome roots, whose resolution is sublime, who have come forth from the principle[2] of deep dharmas, they are cable of enduring this rain of the great principle of dharmas (let loose by) the Tathagata and, when they have heard it, they are elated, full of zest, jubilant, and feel happiness. For these reasons the Tathagata roars the great lion's roar in this pure assembly and lets loose the great rain of Dharma.

A universal monarch might summon his many sons, all of good birth and pure race, and share out his vast store of treasures equally with them all. He would give equally to all, and no one would he pass over. The sons will then feel a surpassing affection for the universal monarch, and a serene trust in him. (22b) They all feel that to him they are equally important. Just so the Tathagata, the king of Dharma, the master of Dharma, the Self-existent, assembles these his sons, shares out to them the treasures of Dharma, and not one of them he passes over. Their affection, trust and respect for Me grow steadily, and, as they all prevent an interruption of the lineage of the Buddhas, they are all equally important to Me. But to other beings this treasure of Dharma means nothing—to those who are of inferior resolve and conceited, who course in false views, who take the data of experience for signs of realities,[3] who assume a basis

[1]*sahante*
[2]*naya*
[3]*nimittacarita*

somewhere, who are hit by the pride which thinks "I am", who are overcome by greed, hate and delusion, and who have strayed on to a wrong road. Beings of inferior resolve, unlike the sons of a universal monarch, can, of course, find no pleasure in his wealth. What could beggarly beings do with such sublime treasures—with the Wheel, Elephant, Horse, Wishing Jewel, (perfect) Wife, Minister or General—or what use are to them sublime garments of gold, gems, pearls, (23a) vaidurya, conch shells, camphor, coral, worked gold or silver? Even if they could get them they would not be glad, would not know what to do with them, and would either sell them cheaply or lose them through carelessness. For they are not conversant with precious things, and do not recognize them when they meet them. Even so the sons of the Tathagata, the Bodhisattvas who have seen the truth and who are great beings, certainly have an interest in this store of precious dharmas. This precious Dharma, associated as it is with the unascertainable emptiness, and with the dharmas of a Buddha, pleases them well and seems good to them, and their business lies with it. What could beggarly beings do with this store of precious dharmas, since they are but blind fools, destitute of learning, or confused by their learning? Even if they have got it, they are bound to lose it again, or thoughtlessly part with it. For no outcast, refuse worker, juggler or anyone else who lives like a beggar can derive enjoyment from sublimely precious things, and will either sell them cheaply, or lose them. (23b) The heretics of other sects correspond to those "beggarly beings"—and that includes also the Disciples. All the foolish common people are "beggarly beings", all those who have sunk into the mud of false views, who lean on a basis, who are inclined to dullness,[1] who treat the data of experience as signs of realities, who have strayed on to a wrong path. Certainly they cannot enjoy this precious Dharma. When they have got it, they are bound to lose it again, or part with it thoughtlessly. But the sons of the Buddha, who course in the range of the Buddhas, and who exist to ensure that the lineage of the Tathagatas should not be interrupted—when they gain this precious Dharma, they know how to enjoy and use it, they do not lose it again, they perceive its great value.

A jackal does not enjoy the lion's roar. But the lion's whelps, the offspring of the great lion, they enjoy his roar. Even so, like jackals, all the foolish common people, full of wrong views, are incapable of enjoying the great lion's roar of the Tathagata, no more than they

[1]Ch., Ti: attached to their bondage.

can enjoy or use the wealth[1] of the great lion, the fully enlightened Buddha. But those who are the whelps of the fully enlightened Buddha, the offspring of the Buddha, the great lion, (24a) sprung from the cognition of the Self-Existent—they enjoy the roar of the great lion, of the fully enlightened Buddha, and will do so for ever.

Śāradvatīputra: It is wonderful, O Lord, how pure an assembly has congregated here for the Tathagata, it is exceedingly wonderful how pure is this assembly of the Tathagata, which is an assembly of the Self-existent, an assembly which cannot be crushed, an adamantine assembly, an assembly which is immovable, unshakeable, imperturbable.

The Lord: You proclaim the virtues of this assembly?

Śāradvatīputra: I could not possibly proclaim the virtues of this assembly. And why? Like Sumeru is this assembly, endowed with infinite virtues.[2]

The Lord: So it is, Śāradvatīputra. Endowed with infinite virtues is this assembly. Even the fully enlightened Buddhas themselves cannot get to the end of these virtues, how much less other beings¡ But this assembly has not been brought together by the Tathagata, nor has the Tathagata had any zeal with regard to it—but simply by its own wholesome roots has this assembly congregated here, when it heard My name. Nor has anyone in this assembly been set to work by the Tathagata, or been bidden (to come), but simply by their own wholesome roots have they been impelled (to come). That they have come to this assembly, that is in the nature of things.[3] For it is a law that, where there is such a demonstration of Dharma, there an assembly of great beings of this kind takes place. Such an assembly also comes together for those other Buddhas and Lords, who reveal this Bodhisattva-Pitaka which cuts off all uncertainties. That just such an assembly-circle is bound to be effected where there is this demonstration of Dharma, that is in the nature of things.

CHAPTER III: SUCHNESS

The Lord: "Perfection of Wisdom, Perfection of Wisdom," Suvikrāntavikrāmin, what is the Bodhisattva's Perfection of Wisdom?[4] The actual transcendental understanding of all dharmas,[5]

[1] Ti: Dharma, for *dhana.*

[2] or: qualities.

[3] *dharmataiṣā*

[4] *prajñā-pāram-itā.* Lit.: wisdom which has gone beyond. Also: transcendental wisdom.

[5] *gaṅ chos thams-cad-kyi tshu-rol rtogs-pa ste. ā-pāram-itā.*

that cannot be expounded. But to the extent that an understanding takes place in you, to that extent (25a) I will expound the Perfection of Wisdom by way of conventional expressions.

Not are form, or the other skandhas, the perfection of wisdom; nor are they other than it. And why? For what is the Beyond of the skandhas, not that are the skandhas. And as the Beyond of the skandhas, so are the skandhas. And as the Beyond of the skandhas, so that of all dharmas. What is the Beyond of all dharmas, not that are all dharmas; and as the Beyond of all dharmas, so are all dharmas.

The words "what is the (25b) Beyond of the skandhas, not that are the skandhas" expound the disjoining of[1] the skandhas, whereas the words "as the Beyond of the skandhas, so are the skandhas" are an exposition of the own-being of the skandhas. In this way one has expounded the skandhas as they actually are, their essential original nature, their non-apprehension. The words "what is the Beyond of all dharmas, not that are all dharmas" expound the disjoining of[3] all dharmas, whereas the words "as the Beyond of all dharmas so are all dharmas" are an exposition of the own-being of all dharmas. In this way one has expounded all dharmas as they actually are, their essential original nature, (26a) their non-apprehension. And as the reality of all dharmas such as they actually are, as their essential original nature, as their non-apprehension, so is the Perfection of Wisdom.

For the Perfection of Wisdom is not supported by the skandhas, it does not stand inside the skandhas or outside them, nor does it stand about somewhere between the two (i.e. inside and outside) at a remote distance. It is not conjoined with the skandhas, nor disjoined from them; for it is not conjoined with any dharma, nor disjoined from it. But the Suchness of the skandhas, their non-falseness, unaltered Suchness, Suchness such as it actually is, that is the Perfection of Wisdom. (26b)

"Form,"[2] that is without form. And why? Because no form exists in form; and this fact of (its) non-existence (in itself), that is the wisdom which has gone beyond. For form is without the own-being of form; and this being without own-being, that is the wisdom which has gone beyond. For the non-own-being of form that is form; and this absence of own-being, that is the wisdom which has gone beyond. For form is not the range of form; and because it is not its

[1]from

[2]In the following the text first makes a statement about form, and then repeats it for the other skandhas. The reader can supply the repetitions for himself.

range, form does not perceive or see form—this non-knowledge, this not seeing of form, that is the wisdom which has gone beyond. (27a) Nor does form cognize[1] the own-being of form; it is this comprehension of the absence of own-being that is called the wisdom which has gone beyond. For form is not conjoined with form, nor disjoined from it; this absence of conjoining and disjoining, that is the perfection of wisdom which has gone beyond.

They do not increase or decrease, *and this absence of increase and decrease, that is the wisdom which has gone beyond*[2]; they are not defiled or purified; (27b) they are not subject to[3] purity or non-purity; they do not transmigrate or not transmigrate[4]; they are not conjoined nor disjoined; they do not decease nor are they reborn; (28a) they are not born nor do they die; they do not wander about in birth-and-death, nor are they subject to doing so; they do not get extinct and are not subject to extinction; they are not subject to origination or stopping, (28b) nor to production or passing away; they are not liable to reversal nor not liable to reversal; they are not permanent or impermanent, (29a) not ease or ill, not salubrious or insalubrious, not self or not-self; not subject to greed or dispassion, to hate or non-hate, (29b) to delusion or freedom from delusion; they have no doer and no doing,[5] no ariser and no raiser, no knower and no one who makes known, no feeler and no feeling, no cognizer and no one who sees; no annihilation or eternity concerns them, (30b) they have no end and are not endless; they are not bound up with false views, nor have they forsaken that which is bound up with false views; they are not craving or its forsaking; they are not wholesome or unwholesome. (31a)

For of them no going or coming[6] is conceived,[7] no stability or instability, not this shore or the shore beyond,[8] no morality or

[1]So Ti and Ms. against Hikata and Ch who read "abandon".

[2]The following passage has been greatly abbreviated. *They* stands for form and the other skandhas. The second part, put into italics, should be supplied for each item, i.e. and this absence of defilement and purification, that is the wisdom which has gone beyond, etc., etc.

[3]*-dharmin*

[4]*mi 'pho-ba; avakrāmati*, "depart".

[5]*kārayitā, byed-du 'jug-pa*

[6]So Ti. Hikata: not going.

[7]This section is also greatly abbreviated. The original reads: "For, *Suvikrānt-avikrāmin, of form* no going or coming is conceived; *even so of feeling, perception, impulses and consciousness no going or coming is conceived. Wherein one does not conceive the going or coming of form–feeling–perception–impulse–consciousness, that is the wisdom which has gone beyond.* With the help of this example the reader can easily supply the omitted portions.

[8]*āram. pāram*

immorality, (31b) no affection or aversion; they do not give or receive; for them there is no patience and no non-patience, no vigour and no sloth, no concentration and no distracted mentality, no (32a) wisdom or stupidity; no perverted views and no unperverted views; no applications of mindfulness and no non-applications of mindfulness; no right efforts and no non-right-efforts; no roads to psychic power and no boundless states; (32b) no faculties, no powers, limbs of enlightenment or path; no (sacred) knowledge or emancipation; no trances, emancipations, concentrations, attainments, superknowledges, and also no non-superknowledges; no emptiness, signlessness or wishlessness; (33a) they are not conditioned or unconditioned, not attachment or non-attachment, not cognition or non-cognition; no minding, vapouring, or discoursing; (33b) no perception or non-perception; not appeased and not unappeased; not the Blessed Rest nor its absence.

For the wisdom which has gone beyond is not an exposition which implies the real creation[1] of the *five skandhas*; but it is the Suchness of the exposition which implies the real creation of the *five skandhas, its non-falseness, unaltered Suchness, Suchness such as it really is* (=etc.). And the same holds good if we replace the *five skandhas* by: the elements, sense-fields, conditioned co-production; (34a) the perverted views and the hindrances; the thirty-six modes of craving; the sixty-two false views. For the wisdom which has gone beyond is not an exposition of the trances, emancipations, concentrations and meditational attainments; but it is the Suchness, etc., of the exposition of the trances, emancipations, concentrations and meditational attainments; (34b) and likewise for the five superknowledges. For the wisdom which has gone beyond is not an exposition which includes the real creation of *all worldly dharmas, be they wholesome or unwholesome, that are included in the conditioned*; but it is the Suchness, etc., of that exposition; and likewise for: the applications of mindfulness, the right efforts, roads to psychic power, faculties, powers, limbs of enlightenment, and path. (35a) For the wisdom which has gone beyond is not an exposition *of the four holy truths*, but it is the Suchness, etc., of the exposition of the four holy truths; and so for: an exposition of the purity of morality, concentration, wisdom, liberation and vision and cognition of liberation; an exposition of the supramundane dharmas, which do not lean on anything, are without outflows and

[1]*abhinirvṛtti-paryāpanna-nirdeśa*. This is very awkward. An explanation of that which is included in the five skandhas as really created?

are included in the Unconditioned; an exposition of the Dharma which is emptiness, the Signless, the Wishless, Non-production or the Uneffected; (35b) an exposition of (sacred) knowledge, liberation, dispassion, stopping and Nirvana.

And why? Because the wisdom which has gone beyond is not included in form, or the other skandhas; in earth, water, fire, air or space; in the world of sense-desire, the world of form or the formless world; in dharmas which are conditioned or unconditioned, worldly or supramundane, with or without outflows, wholesome or unwholesome; in the world of beings or in the world of non-beings. Nor is the wisdom which has gone beyond (36a) distinct[1] from these dharmas.

For the wisdom which has gone beyond is not included in any dharma whatsoever, nor unincluded in it; but it is the Suchness, etc., of dharmas, both included and unincluded.

"Suchness," Suvikrāntavikrāmin, of what is that a synonym? For these dharmas are not such as they have been apprehended by the foolish common people, nor are they otherwise; but as these dharmas have been seen by the Tathagatas, by their Disciples and by the Bodhisattvas, just so are all these dharmas, (that is their) Suchness, non-falseness, unaltered Suchness, Suchness such as it really is—it is in that sense that one speaks of "Suchness". This is the exposition of the wisdom which has gone beyond for the Bodhisattvas, the great beings.

For certainly this perfection of wisdom has not been set up for the decrease or increase of any dharma, for its conjunction or disjunction, its depletion or repletion, its removal or accumulation, its arrival or (36b) departure, its production or stopping, defilement or purification, for its worldly activity or withdrawal from it, for its origination or disappearance, for marking it as with or without marks, for its sameness or unequality, for conventional or ultimate truth, ease or ill, permanence or impermanence, salubriousness or unsalubriousness, selfness or not-selfness, truthfulness or fraudulence, activity or non-activity, effectiveness or non-effectiveness,[2] possibility or impossibility, own-beingness or non-own-beingness, decease or rebirth, birth or no-birth, real creation or no real creation, for rebirth or the complete cutting off of rebirths, for concord or discord, for causing greed or dispassion, hate or freedom from hate, delusion or freedom from delusion, perverted views or unperverted views,

[1]*vinirmukta*, set free. *rnam-par grol-ba*. Derge as Hikata, but Narthang says, on the contrary, that it *is* set free from these things. That is equally true, but probably not meant here.

[2]*kāraṇatvena vā-akāraṇatvena vā*. om.Ti and Ch.

objective supports or no objective supports, extinction or non-extinction, (37a) cognition or non-cognition, inferiority or superiority, service or disservice, for going or not going, beingness or non-beingness, affection or aversion, light or darkness, sloth or vigorous energy, emptiness or non-emptiness, sign-ness or signlessness, wishfulness or wishlessness, effectiveness or ineffectiveness,[1] disappearance or non-disappearance, (sacred) knowledge[2] or liberation, calm or non-calm, creation or no real creation, wise (attention) or unwise (attention), comprehension or non-comprehension, going-forth and no going-forth, discipline or no discipline, morality or immorality, distractedness or no distractedness, wisdom or stupidity, consciousness or no consciousness, stability or instability, companionship or (37b) no-companionship, becoming or unbecoming, attainment or non-attainment, reunion or non-reunion, realization or non-realization, penetration or non-penetration.

CHAPTER IV: SIMILES

Just as a man when he sees a dream may expound an exposition which in its own-being is a *dream*, and yet no exposition which is in its own-being a dream does exist. And why? The dream just does not exist, how much less the exposition which is in its essence a dream; just so the own-being of the perfection of wisdom is expounded, and yet no own-being of the perfection of wisdom does exist; just as the dream does not entail the definition of any dharma whatever, just so the perfection of wisdom does not entail the definition of any dharma whatsoever.

The same formula with: (38a) *magical illusion*; *reflected image*; (38b) *mirage*.

Just as, Suvikrāntavikrāmin, a man who stands within the range of an *echo*, hears the sound of the echo, but does not perceive it; but when he himself pronounces it, then he hears the sound repeated; just so the words expounding the perfection of wisdom reach the hearing, but it is not the exposition of any dharma which reaches the hearing; it is only (39a) that the words addressed to one are noticed and reach the ear.

Just as, Suvikrāntavikrāmin, a man who sees a *mass of foam* may expound the own-being of the mass of foam, and yet no own-being of the mass of foam can be apprehended, either inwardly or outwardly, how much less will there be an apprehension or own-being of that exposition; just so, the perfection of wisdom is expounded, and

[1] *abhisaṃskārāya vā-anabhisaṃskārāya vā*. Formativeness or non-formativeness.
[2] Ch. has "ignorance", which gives a better sense, against Sanskrit and Tib.

yet no own-being of the perfection of wisdom can be apprehended; just as a mass of foam does not imply the own-being or real creation of any dharma whatever, just so the perfection of wisdom does not imply the own-being or real creation of any dharma whatever.

Just as, Suvikrāntavikrāmin, a man who sees a *bubble* may expound the own-being of the bubble, and yet no own-being of the bubble does exist, how much less will there be an exposition of the own-being of the bubble; just so the perfection of wisdom is expounded, and yet no own-being of the perfection of wisdom does exist; just as the bubble has not been set up by the possibility of the real creation of any dharma whatever, (39b) just so has the perfection of wisdom not been set up by the possibility of the real creation of any dharma whatsoever.

Just as a man may search for the core of a *plantain*, and cannot apprehend it, and nevertheless its leaves do their work; just so there exists no core of the perfection of wisdom, and yet the exposition of the perfection of wisdom does its work.

Just as, Suvikrāntavikrāmin, a man may speak of *space* by way of definite definition, but of space no definite definition exists; just so one uses the conventional expression "perfection of wisdom", but no dharma at all is conventionally expressed by way of definition; just as space is conventionally expressed, but it is not conventionally expressed by way of defining or accomplishing any dharma whatsoever, just so is the perfection of wisdom conventionally expressed, but not by way of defining or accomplishing any dharma whatsoever.

Just as one speaks conventionally of *shadow* and *sunshine*, (40a) although those two have not been set up for the accomplishment of any dharma whatever, and yet the illumination is discerned; just so the Perfection of Wisdom is expressed by way of conventional words, although this does not imply the definition of any dharma whatever, and yet it illuminates all dharmas.

Just as a well-purified *precious jewel* may set up a great illumination, and yet that illumination cannot be seen inwardly or outwardly, just so the Perfection of Wisdom has been set up for the work of illuminating, and yet that illumination cannot be seen either inwardly or outwardly.

Just as the flames of a *burning oil-lamp* do not remain for even a moment, and yet they make an illumination, and through that illumination sight-objects come to be seen; just so the Perfection of Wisdom does not abide in any dharma whatsoever, and yet it illuminates dharmas, and through that illumination all dharmas come to be seen by holy men as they really are.

Thereupon the Ven. (40b) *Śāradvatīputra* said to the Lord: It is wonderful, O Lord, how the Perfection of Wisdom has been explained, and yet at the same time also the lack of total reality of the Perfection of Wisdom has been pointed out.

The Lord: So it is, Śāradvatīputra, so it is. Not totally real is the perfection of wisdom; and that because of the lack of total reality of form, etc., to: consciousness; of ignorance, etc., to: ageing, sickness, death, sorrow, lamentation, pain, sadness and despair; of the elements, sense-fields, (41a) of the impermanent, ill, not-self, quiet calm, of perverted views, hindrances, wandering about in false views, heaping up and accumulation; of ease, ill, not-ill and not-ease; of rise, fall and alteration; of origination, disappearance, of self, being, living soul, creature, man, person, human being, young man, doer, doing, ariser, feeler, one who feels, knower, intimator; of truth, fraud, the conditioned, the unconditioned, of going and not going; of the visible and the invisible, of the inward and the outward; of the elements of earth, water, fire, wind, sense-desire, form, the formless, space, consciousness and dharma; of karma and karma-result, cause and condition, annihilation and eternity, past, future and present, of beginning, end and middle, of giving and meanness, of morality and immorality, of patience and ill-will, of vigour and sloth, of trance and (41b) distraction, of wisdom and stupidity; of thought, mind and consciousness; of decease and rebirth, defilement and purification, of the applications of mindfulness, right efforts, etc., to: the superknowledges, of emptiness, the signless and wishless, of the wholesome, unwholesome, with outflows, without outflows, worldly, supramundane, the faulty, the faultless, conditioned, unconditioned, determined, indetermined, white, black, neither white nor black, included and unincluded, inferior, superior and middling, greed, hate and delusion, what is seen, heard, learnt and discerned, vain conceit, stability, applied and sustained thought, objective support, deceitfulness, envy and meanness, association, the mark of duality, non-production, not being brought about, calming-down, insight, knowledge, liberation, extinction, dispassion, stopping, the rejection of all substrata, conventional truth, ultimate truth, the level of the Disciples, the level of the Pratyekabuddhas, the cognition of the all-knowing, the unattached cognition, the cognition of the Self-Existent, the cognition which equals the unequalled, the vow of the Bodhisattva, the achievements of the Disciples and Pratyekabuddhas, the cognition of the Dharma which equals the unequalled and which is included in the measureless, the vision and cognition of all dharmas to which all dharmas are invisible as they actually are; (42a) of being cooled, calmed, appeased; of the maturing of beings; of the achievement of the marks, the purification of the Buddha-field, of the powers of a Buddha, his grounds of self-confidence, the eighteen special Buddha-dharmas; of Nirvana; etc. to: of all wholesome and unwholesome dharmas. All this should be done in detail.

Just as *space* is immaterial, invisible, non-existence, not totally real, just so is this perfection of wisdom immaterial, invisible, non-existence, not totally real.

Just as a *rainbow* appears in a great variety of hues, and yet the full reality of these hues does not exist, and is not apprehended; just so has the perfection of wisdom been set up by various explanations, and yet with regard to it no own-being of an explanation (42b) is apprehended.

Just as in space no one has ever seen the full reality of (an object) five fingers broad, just so no one has ever seen the own-being of the full reality of the perfection of wisdom.

Śāradvatīputra: This perfection of wisdom is hard to see!

The Lord: Because it does not admit of being seen by anyone.

Śāradvatīputra: Hard to understand, O Lord, is the perfection of wisdom!

The Lord: Because in it no fully real dharma[1] is apprehended which it has fully known.

Sāradvatīputra: Indefinable, O Lord, is this perfection of wisdom!

The Lord: Because it has not been set up by the definition of any dharma.

Śāradvatīputra: Without own-being is this perfection of wisdom!

The Lord: Because of the absence of own-being in form, etc., to: consciousness; in the elements, sense-fields, conditioned co-production; in the perverted views, hindrances, (43a) what is subject to false views; wanderings in craving; in self, etc., to: one who feels; in the worlds of sense-desire, form and formlessness; morality, immorality, etc., to: wisdom and stupidity; the dharmas which act as wings to enlightenment; the holy truths, calming-down, insight, the superknowledges, trances, emancipations, concentrations and attainments; the knowledges and liberations; extinction, dispassion and stopping; the cognition of non-production and the cognition of stopping; in Nirvana; in (43b) the level of Disciples, Pratyekabuddhas and Buddhas; in the vision and cognition of absolute truth,

[1]So Ti.

and of conventional truth[1]; in the unattached cognition and the cognition of the all-knowing.

Śāradvatīputra: This perfection of wisdom has not been set up for the accomplishment of any dharma, nor for its stopping.

The Lord: Because it has not been set up for the production of any dharma, or its accomplishment, stopping, or selflessness.

Śāradvatīputra: This perfection of wisdom has not been set up by way of making any dharma into an objective support.

The Lord: Because all dharmas are without objective support; for just those dharmas do not exist which could act as an objective support.

Śāradvatīputra: This perfection of wisdom has not been set up for the decrease or increase of any dharma. (44a)

The Lord: Because it does not review any dharma which decreases or increases.

Śāradvatīputra: This perfection of wisdom has not been set up for the transcending of any dharma.

The Lord: Because it does not apprehend any dharma which it should transcend.

Śāradvatīputra: This perfection of wisdom has not been set up for the diminution or accumulation of any dharma.

The Lord: Because it does not review any dharma that would be subject to diminution or accumulation.

Śāradvatīputra: This perfection of wisdom has not been set up for association with any dharma, nor for dissociation from one.

The Lord: Because it does not apprehend any dharma with which it could associate or from which it could dissociate.

Śāradvatīputra: This perfection of wisdom has not been set up for the guidance or non-guidance of any dharma.

The Lord: Because it does not (44b) apprehend any dharma which should be guided or not guided.

Śāradvatīputra: This perfection of wisdom has not been set up for rendering service to any dharma, or for doing harm to one.

The Lord: Because it does not apprehend any dharma to which it might render service or which it might harm.

Śāradvatīputra: This perfection of wisdom has not been set up for making any dharma possible or impossible.

The Lord: Because it does not apprehend any dharma which would be possible or impossible.

Śāradvatīputra: This perfection of wisdom has not been set up for conjunction with any dharma, nor for disjunction from one.

[1]The construction is not clear.

The Lord: Because it does not apprehend any dharma which might be conjoined or disjoined.

Śāradvatīputra: This perfection of wisdom has not been set up for intimacy or non-intimacy with any dharma.

The Lord: Because it does not apprehend any dharma which could be intimate or not intimate.

Śāradvatīputra: (45a) This perfection of wisdom has not been set up for the worldly activity of any dharma, nor for its withdrawal from worldly activity.

The Lord: Because it does not apprehend any dharma which would have worldly activity or withdrawal from it.

Śāradvatīputra: This perfection of wisdom has not been set up for the activity or effectiveness of any dharma.

The Lord: Because it does not apprehend any dharma which could be active or effective.

Śāradvatīputra: This perfection of wisdom has not been set up for the sameness or unevenness[3] of any dharma.

The Lord: Because it does not apprehend any dharma which could be even or uneven.

Śāradvatīputra: This perfection of wisdom has not been set up for the attraction of any dharma, or its non-attraction.

The Lord: Because it does not apprehend any dharma which should be attracted or repelled.

Śāradvatīputra: This perfection of wisdom has not been set up for any function whatever. (45b)

The Lord: Because it does not apprehend any dharma which could exert any function.

Śāradvatīputra: Deep, O Lord, is this perfection of wisdom!

The Lord: Because of the depth of form, etc.; of ignorance, etc.; of the perverted views; the five hindrances; the false views; the self; beings; discursiveness; non-discursiveness; morality and immorality; patience; (46a) etc., to: the sameness of the three periods of time, past, future and present; the four grounds of self-confidence, the roads to psychic power, the superknowledges; the cognition of the non-attachment as to past, future and present; the Buddhadharmas; the cognitions of extinction, non-production, stopping, ineffectiveness, and dispassion; the hindrances.

Just as, Śāradvatīputra, the *ocean* is deep, vast and immeasurable, just so is the perfection of wisdom. "Deep", that is the true accumulation of immeasurable precious dharmas, and one cannot get to the

[1] *viṣamatāya*

bottom of it; "deep," of that the route cannot be obtained; "deep," (46b) the limit of its virtues cannot be reached. Just as the sea, the great ocean, contains the collection of all jewels, is filled with immeasurable jewels, is quite full of the great jewels, just so the perfection of wisdom is the collection of all dharma-jewels, the collection of the great dharma-jewels, the collection of immeasurable dharma-jewels.

Śāradvatīputra: This perfection of wisdom has not been set up for the definition of any dharma.

The Lord: Because it has not been set up for the apprehension of any dharma which it could define.

Śāradvatīputra: This perfection of wisdom has not been set up for the cognition[1] or non-cognition of any dharma.

The Lord: Because it does not apprehend any dharma of which there might be a cognition[2] or non-cognition.

Śāradvatīputra: This perfection of wisdom has not been set up for the preservation or protection of any dharma.

The Lord: Because it does not apprehend any dharma which it might preserve or protect.

Śāradvatīputra: This perfection of wisdom (47a) has not been set up for the assembling of any dharma, or the taking hold of one.

The Lord: Because it does not apprehend any dharma which it might assemble or take hold of.

Śāradvatīputra: This perfection of wisdom has not been set up for the support of any dharma.

The Lord: Because it does not review any dharma which could furnish a support.

Śāradvatīputra: This perfection of wisdom has not been set up as a settling place for any dharma, or as a foundation for one.

The Lord: Because it does not apprehend any dharma which could provide a settling place or foundation.

Śāradvatīputra: This perfection of wisdom has not been set up for settling down in any dharma.

The Lord: Because it does not apprehend any dharma in which it could settle down.

Śāradvatīputra: This perfection of wisdom has not been set up as an inclination for[3] any dharma.

The Lord: Because (47b) it does not apprehend or review any dharma towards which it would be inclined.

[1] *'tshal-ba*
[2] *śes-pa*
[3] *adhyavasānena*

Śāradvatīputra: This perfection of wisdom has not been set up for intimacy with any dharma, or non-intimacy with one.

The Lord: Because it does not apprehend any dharma with which it might dwell together.[1]

Śāradvatīputra: This perfection of wisdom has not been set up for the composition or decomposition of any dharma.

The Lord: Because it does not apprehend any dharma which should be composed or decomposed.

Śāradvatīputra: This perfection of wisdom has not been set up for the sake of an attitude of greed or dispassion towards any dharma.

The Lord: Because it does not apprehend any dharma with regard to which one could be impassioned or dispassioned.

Śāradvatīputra: This perfection of wisdom has not been set up for the sake of an attitude of hate or no-hate towards any dharma.

The Lord: Because it does not apprehend any dharma which would be with or without hate. (48a)

Śāradvatīputra: This perfection of wisdom has not been set up for the sake of an attitude of delusion or one that is without delusion.

The Lord: Because it does not apprehend any dharma which would be deluded or undeluded.

Śāradvatīputra: This perfection of wisdom has not been set up as a cognizer or knower of any dharma.

The Lord: Because it does not apprehend or review any dharma which it would cognize, or of which it would be the knower.

Śāradvatīputra: This perfection of wisdom has not been set up for the original nature of any dharma, or its non-original nature.

The Lord: Because it does not review the original nature or the non-original-nature of any dharma.

Śāradvatīputra: This perfection of wisdom has not been set up for the cleansing or purification of any dharma.

The Lord: Because it does not review any dharma which it might cleanse or purify.

Śāradvatīputra: (48b) Perfectly pure in its original nature is this perfection of wisdom!

The Lord: Because of the perfect purity of form, etc.; of ignorance, etc.; of the perverted views, hindrances and that which is subject to false views; of greed, hate and delusion; of self, being, etc., of annihilation and eternity; (49a) of ends and the endless; of the perfection of giving, etc., of the faculties, powers, etc.; of friendliness, etc.; of the applications of mindfulness and the right efforts; of the absence of perverted views; of ill, origination, stopping, path;

[1]cohabit

of the superknowledges; of the path; the level of the Disciples, of the Pratyekabuddhas, of the Buddhas; of Buddha, Dharma and Samgha; of the dharmas of the Disciples (49b), the dharmas of the Pratyekabuddhas, the vision of past, future and present, the unattached vision and cognition, the eighteen special Buddha-dharmas, the world of sense-desire, the world of form, the formless world, the element of earth, etc.; the world of beings, the realm of Dharma, the element of ether.

Śāriputra: It is wonderful, O Lord, how perfectly pure in its original nature is the perfection of wisdom!

The Lord: From the perfect purity of the ether is the perfection of wisdom perfectly pure.

Śāriputra: The perfection of wisdom is immaterial and indefinable.

The Lord: Because it has not been set up for the (50a) accomplishment of[1] form on the part of[1] any dharma, nor for the definition of any dharma.

Śāradvatīputra: Unobstructed is this perfection of wisdom.

The Lord: Because it does not review any dharma by which it could be obstructed.

Śāradvatīputra: Unmade is this perfection of wisdom.

The Lord: Because no doer can be apprehended.

Śāradvatīputra: Unmeetable is this perfection of wisdom.

The Lord: Because it does not review any dharma which it could meet.

Śāradvatīputra: Inconceivable is this perfection of wisdom.

The Lord: Because it does not apprehend any dharma by which it could be conceived.

Śāradvatīputra: Unshared is this perfection of wisdom.

The Lord: Because it does not review any dharma with which it could be shared.

Śāradvatīputra: Markless is this perfection of wisdom.

The Lord: Because no mark can be apprehended.

Śāradvatīputra: Non-apparent is this perfection of wisdom.

The Lord: Because its apparition cannot be apprehended.

Śāradvatīputra: An infinite perfection is the perfection of wisdom.

(50b) *The Lord:* Because of the infinitude of form, etc.; of the perverted views; the hindrances; ignorance, etc.; of what is subject to false views, of greed, hate and delusion, of annihilation and eternity, of the past beginning, of the future end, of giving, morality, etc., of the applications of mindfulness, right efforts, roads to psychic power, etc.; of the absence of perverted views; of

[1-1] I do not understand the significance of *rūpa/gzugs* here.

trances, etc.; (51a) of the objective supports; of (sacred) knowledge and the vision and cognition of emancipation; of the level of the Disciples, etc., of the dharmas of the Disciples, Pratyekabuddhas and Buddhas; of self and (living) beings; of the world of sense-desire, etc.; of the superknowledges, hindrances, vision and cognition of past, future and present, of non-attachment, of the ether, of the realm of Dharma. Of this perfection of wisdom no beginning, middle or end can be apprehended, nor has it been apprehended by anyone; it is an infinite, an unlimited perfection, this perfection of wisdom.

Just as of *space* no end can be apprehended, just so with the perfection of wisdom. (51b) From the infinitude of the earth element should the perfection of wisdom be seen, etc. to: the element of consciousness. As without end, middle and limit should the perfection of wisdom be understood. For the perfection of wisdom is not anywhere located or placed. From the boundlessness of form should the perfection of wisdom be known as boundless; etc., as in previous lists. (52b) Because no bounds can be apprehended is the perfection of wisdom called "boundless"; because no end can be apprehended is it called "endless"; "endless" that is another word for "boundless". From the not grasping at a self should the endlessness of all dharmas be known. From the endlessness of space should the endlessness and boundlessness of all dharmas be known.

Śāradvatīputra: Of what kind, O Lord, are the Bodhisattvas who have their range in these dharmas?

The Lord: They are Bodhisattvas who do not apprehend dharma, much less no-dharma; who do not apprehend the path, much less the no-path; who do not apprehend or mind morality, much less immorality; who are unincluded in all the triple world, unincluded in the deceases and rebirths in all destinies and becomings; not bent on their bodies or lives, much less on outward objects; who have achieved the end of the stream of Samsara, have crossed the flood of the great becoming, have escaped from the great battle; (53a) it is of these Bodhisattvas, great beings that this is the range and route in these dharmas. These true men are those who comprehend that all ranges are no-ranges; they are not bent on all ranges, they are the great lions; these true men have not violated all ranges, they are unstained by all ranges, not submerged by them; they have quite transcended all ranges, they who are the great caravan leaders. These[1] have their range and route in these dharmas. Not do I see in this assembly even one single Bodhisattva who has not his range in these dharmas and who is not resolutely intent on

[1]*de-dag-gi* for *yeṣām*

them; or who hesitates about these dharmas or is in doubt about them. Free from hesitation is this assembly with regard to these dharmas, free from doubt, unperplexed; these Bodhisattvas have no perplexity about these dharmas, these true men have been established for the uprooting of the perplexity of all beings. For they are free from uncertainty about dharmas of this kind, and they have quite transcended all uncertainty.

And those also who at a future (53b) time, in a future period, will hear this demonstration of Dharma, they will be free from uncertainty with regard to all dharmas, and they will have progressed so as to cut off the uncertainties of all beings, and free from uncertainty they will demonstrate Dharma. I do not speak of the resolute faith towards these dharmas on the part of beings who have but tiny wholesome roots. There is no room for them in these dharmas, nor is this their wealth. Nor will those beings be endowed with tiny wholesome roots who will come to hear of this demonstration of Dharma, how much less so those who will take it up, bear it in mind, preach and study it. Certainly they are predicted by the Buddhas, the Lords to the Buddhadharmas. Just so will they roar the lion's roar as I just now roar the lion's roar, the fearless roar, the roar of the Superman, the roar of the Self-Existent. Those who, once they have engendered faith for these dharmas, generate an urge for the supreme enlightenment, they also will have this demonstration of Dharma.[1] And why? Because hard to find are those beings who, when they have heard these dharmas, (54a) will find zest, generate joy, and resolutely believe. Even harder to find are those beings who, having heard the deep dharmas, raise their thought to the supreme enlightenment, generate an urge towards it; they are endowed with great wholesome roots. I say that those beings have not set out for a long sojourn in Samsara who come to hear of this explanation of the perfection of wisdom, who, having heard it, will recite it, firmly believe in it, generate a sublime zest and gladness for it, and who will generate an urge for these dharmas, first repeatedly to hear them, and then, what is more, to explain them, to repeat them, to demonstrate them to others. I predict to supreme enlightenment those who have not quite definitely set out in the vehicle of the Disciples and Pratyekabuddhas, who are not yet quite fixed on it.

I do not see any room in this supreme dharma[2] for beings who are endowed with inferior dharmas. Sublime is this Buddha-enlightenment, but the ordinary run of beings are intent on what is inferior,

[1]*chos bstan-pa*, for *vyākaraṇam*
[2]*chos-kyi mchog 'di-la* = *agrato dharmeṣv.*

endowed with inferior dharmas, and, since they have not done what is lovely,[1] they are unskilled in (54b) these deep and stainless dharmas. But as to those sublime beings who are intent on sublime dharmas, have set out in the great vehicle, have done their work well, have well put on the great armour, have well considered their welfare, have set out on the great road—which is not uneven, but straight, untangled, even, free from stumps and thorns, free from holes and cliffs, clean, free from filth, not crooked, not tricky[2]—who have set out for the weal of the world, for its happiness, out of compassion for the world, for the weal and happiness of a great number of people, both gods and men, and who are bringers of light, true fords for beings, greatly compassionate, mindful of the weal of others, desirous of their welfare, happiness and safety, set up for the bestowal of happiness on all beings—of beings of this kind, who are Bodhisattvas, great beings, this is the great wealth. It is these great beings who search for this treasure of Dharma, and to them it seems to constitute the supreme wealth. And why? For those beings who have done no meritorious deeds, have not done (55a) what is lovely, are intent on what is inferior and deficient in faith, they do not generate any resolute belief in this sublime wealth. And this I have taught with a hidden intent: "Beings agree according to their dispositions[3]—those intent on the inferior with those intent on the inferior, those intent on the sublime with those intent on the sublime."

Śāradvatīputra: What is the sphere of the perfection of wisdom?

The Lord: Infinite is the range and sphere of the perfection of wisdom. Just as the element of *air* has an infinite range and sphere, so has the perfection of wisdom. Just as the range and sphere of the element of air is infinite like the element of space, so is the range and sphere of the perfection of wisdom like that of the element of space. Just as the element of *space* has an infinite range and sphere, so the perfection of wisdom. Just as the element of space and the element of air do not appear anywhere, (55b) and are not set up by the mark of any produced dharma; just so the perfection of wisdom does not appear in any dharma, and has not been set up by the mark of any produced dharma. Just as the element of space and the element of air, because not to be seized and without total reality, do not derive their names from the sign of colour[4]; just so the perfection of wisdom,

[1] *akṛtakalyāṇa, dge-bar ma byas śiṅ.* Add to MDPL.
[2] Ti Narthang 62a differs greatly.
[3] Or "character", *dhātuśaḥ*, lit. through their element. MS V ii 137, 16: *dhātutaḥ sattvāḥ saṃsyandanti iti.*
[4] *'varṇa-nimitta, kha-dog-gi mtshan-ma'i.*

because not to be seized and without total reality, does not derive or get its name from any sign of colour. Just as the element of space and the element of air cannot be approached by the vision of the total reality of any dharma; just so the perfection of wisdom.

Śāradvatīputra: What is the mark of this perfection of wisdom?

The Lord: Without mark is this perfection of wisdom. Just as the element of space and the element of air cannot be approached by the mark of the total reality of any dharma, just so the perfection of wisdom. In this way[1] the perfection of wisdom is without mark, and thus does not exist. Just as the element of space is not attached anywhere, so also the perfection of wisdom. That is why one speaks of the mark of non-attachment. For non-attachment has not any mark. But that is a conventional expression when one says that "marked with non-attachment is the perfection of wisdom". For that must be explained as a no-mark,[2] because non-attachment has neither mark nor sign. "Non-attachment," that is the comprehension of attachment, the non-apprehension of attachment, attachment as it really is, the comprehension of the non-perversion[2] of attachment. For no attachment is found in attachment, (56b) and that is why one speaks of attachment as it really is as the non-apprehension of attachment. "Non-attachment" is this perfection of wisdom, which is an explanation and cognition of the mark of non-attachment. For all dharmas have non-attachment for their mark. Whatever mark a dharma may have that is, however, no mark.[3] For no dharma has been set up by[4] the production of any mark; that wherein no mark exists, that is called "markless"; and what is markless, that has no attachment. If there were a mark of dharmas, then all dharmas would have attachment. But because no mark exists of all dharmas, therefore they have no attachment. Therefore one says that "all dharmas have non-attachment for their mark". But it is not so as one says. Because the mark of non-attachment cannot be expressed in words. And why? Because of the non-beingness of the mark of non-attachment, its isolatedness, its non-apprehension. For any dharma which is marked by non-attachment has not been set up by any definition,[5] much less by a non-definition.[6] But it is for the sake of beings that this exposition[7]

[1] *'di ltar*, for *hi.*
[2] So Ti
[3] Or: a no-mark
[4] Or: for, *phyir*
[5] *nidarśana, mthoṅ-ba*
[6] *na saṅgadarśanena; mi mthoṅ-bar yaṅ ma yin mod kyi*
[7] *nidarśana, bstan-pa*

of the mark of non-attachment has been made. What is the mark of defilement, that is a no-mark. (57a) For defilement has not been set up by a mark, but by the perverted views. But what is perverted view, that is without mark. What is without mark that is even by way of worldly convention without mark; so it is certainly without mark. And also what is purification, that has no mark. And why? Even defilement is markless, how much more so purification! What is the comprehension of defilement, that is it as it really is. But therein there is no defilement. It is because they have perverted views that beings are defiled, and what is perversion that is not real, and in the unreal there is no total reality or mark. This comprehension, that is called "purification". Even defilement is markless, how much more so purification! Defilement and purification, both these dharmas are markless and without total reality. But the marklessness of all dharmas and their lack of total reality, that is called "non-attachment". "All dharmas are marked with non-attachment," for in all dharmas no attachment exists. (57b) All foolish common people therefore get attached to non-attachment. This is the exposition of the sphere of the cognition of the mark of non-attachment of all dharmas; and that is the sphere of the perfection of wisdom. The sphere of the perfection of wisdom is thus the cognition of the mark of non-attachment, therefore the sphere of the perfection of wisdom is called infinite. What is non-attachment, that has an infinite range and sphere. "Sphere," that is a synonym of no-sphere; for the perfection of wisdom is not developed by the mark of the exposition of the sphere. "Range," that is the no-range of all dharmas, their state as they really are, their state such as they are. Because they are not[1] are all dharmas a no-range. To comprehend dharmas thus, that is called the "range and sphere". But it is not so as one speaks of it. This comprehension of all dharmas implies no attachment anywhere. This is called the "mark of non-attachment". Therefore one says that "the perfection of wisdom is marked with non-attachment".

Not many adherents are found for such dharmas. (58a) This indication, revelation and analysis of dharmas is the exposition of the range of the cognition of the Tathagata. For there can be no other adherents of these dharmas except Disciples who have seen the Truth, or irreversible Bodhisattvas, great beings, or persons who have achieved right views and cannot be turned back. But even those who have achieved right views may, when they course in these

[1]*med-pa'i phyir*, for: *aviṣayatvāt*

dharmas, feel uncertainty about them. Without uncertainty, however, is the Bodhisattva who is an eye-witness and who has acquired the patient acceptance of these dharmas.[1] There is no ground in these dharmas for the foolish common people. This exposition of the perfection of wisdom will not fall into the hands of beings who are intent on what is inferior. Endowed with perfectly pure wholesome roots will be those beings into whose hands this exposition of the perfection of wisdom will fall, and they will have honoured many Buddhas. These beings will have planted wholesome roots, they will have lovely intentions, they have done their duties under the Buddhas and Lords, for the sake of enlightenment they have planted the seed of Buddhahood, they have mounted on the Buddha-vehicle, they have stood near the Buddhas and Lords, they have wisely questioned them—they into whose (58b) hands this exposition of the perfection of wisdom will fall. Near to the acquisition of patience will be those into whose hands this exposition of the perfection of wisdom will fall, or they will have already acquired the patience. And those who are predicted, they will soon know the supreme enlightenment, except (if they wish to postpone it) by the force of their original Vow. Those who are not yet predicted will soon face to face acquire their prediction. And they also should be considered as predicted, for beings with immature wholesome roots cannot come to hear of this Sūtrānta, and much less can they acquire it, or copy it, or bear it in mind, or explain it, or study it, or reveal it to others in detail. That is quite impossible that those beings have immature wholesome roots who will hear this Sūtrānta, copy it, preach and study it. But splendid will be the wholesome roots of those beings into whose hands this discourse on dharma will fall. Moreover, Śāradvatīputra, I announce to you, (59a) I make known to you, that son or daughter of good family, whether they belong to the vehicle of the Bodhisattvas or to that of the Disciples, should, when they have acquired these dharmas, not become careless, or lazy, or sleep too much, or be unaware of what they do, or unmindful, or distracted in their thought, or greedy for material things, or tremulous, or garrulous, or frantic, or arrogant, or with their faculties uncontrolled. May they not go back on their promising past![2] But the Bodhisattva should, when he has gained these dharmas, continuously cultivate vigilance, vigour, will-power, desire-to-do, he should not have any sloth, control his faculties, and not talk nonsense; he should make efforts to set up mindfulness

[1]So Ti, + *chos 'di-la.*

[2]Lit. on the wholesome roots which they have done.

and to learn much; putting forth his vigour he should exert himself to fulfil all these virtues.

This is not the fruit of hearing such dharmas that the Bodhisattva or the person who belongs to the vehicle of the Disciples, after having heard them, should become careless, rest on his laurels, lose his desire-to-do, (59b) display laxness, or become full of ill-will—that would not be the fruit of the hearing. He would not really have heard these dharmas. To have heard is a synonym for true progress, and not of failure to progress. For one who fails to progress has not really heard this dharma. May you, Śāradvitīputra, become skilled in hearing the meaning, may you be established in the progress! Those who fail to progress have not (even) the adaptable patience. One speaks of progress in this dharma when one correctly progresses in these dharmas as they have been explained. A person who has achieved patience and who is established in progress no more goes to the states of woe, and quickly he gains full knowledge of these dharmas; one who has but a tiny wholesome root should not feel too confident; even one who is perseverant should not feel any confidence until he becomes accomplished in these dharmas. One who has become accomplished in these dharmas, has trained in them, and has patiently accepted them, he would no more perform any karma conducive to going to the states of woe, he would no longer have any sloth, or anything that lowers him, nor would he have any fear of turning back; (60a) nor would he be lax in any way. And why? He has fully comprehended both defilement and purification; he has seen as it really is that "all dharmas have arisen from perverted views and are unreal". Thus rightly seeing he becomes one who has achieved patience, heroic, of few words, established in the purity of morality, one who has achieved restraint in all his actions. Even the gods aspire to be like those beings, how much more so do men! To the gods even they seem enviable, how much more so to men! Even the gods wish to approach them, how much more so do men![2] To the gods even they seem worthy of respect, how much more so to men! The gods even wish to protect them, how much more so do men! Just so[3] do nagas, yakshas, rakshasas, garudas and gandharvas wish to protect them, and they are zealous on behalf of their shelter, defence and protection.

[1]*saphalam; thos-pa's 'bras-bu*

[2]Ti Skr. om.

[3]Read *evaṃ* for *deva; de bshin-du*

CHAPTER V: SUBHUTI

Thereupon the Ven. Śāradvatīputra said to the Ven. Subhuti: Why, Ven. Subhuti, do you spend your time in silence, is it not clear to you concerning the perfection of wisdom that the Teacher himself is here present, (60b) and that this assembly is a fit vessel for the demonstration of the deep Dharma; pure, Ven. Subhuti, is this assembly and it desires to hear the deep Dharma.

Thereupon the Ven. *Subhuti* replied to the Ven. Śāriputra: Not do I, Venerable Sir, review that dharma concerning which anything could become clear to me; not do I, Ven. Śāriputra, review the perfection of wisdom, nor the Bodhisattva, nor the flash of insight, nor that which would become clear, or that by which it would become clear, or that through which it would become clear. When thus, Ven. Śāriputra, I do not see the perfection of wisdom, or the Bodhisattva, the great being, or that which would become clear, or whereby it would become clear, or through what it would become clear, or him to whom it would become clear—how can I then explain anything, or on the basis of what can I make what clear? This perfection of wisdom in fact lies outside all conventional discourse, it is unutterable, unpronounceable, it cannot be talked about. For it is not possible to utter this perfection of wisdom, to express it in conventional words, or to talk about it; an answer of this kind, that is the perfection of wisdom. (61a) For the perfection of wisdom is not past, future, or present; for it cannot be pointed out by a past mark, a future mark, or a present mark; markless and inexpressible is this perfection of wisdom. Not do I see that mark of the perfection of wisdom by which one could point it out. For that which is the past, future or present mark of form, that is not the perfection of wisdom; and so for the other skandhas. But the Suchness of the past, future and present mark of form, the non-falseness, the unaltered Suchness, the Suchness such as it is, that is the perfection of wisdom. And so for the other skandhas. (61b) But the Suchness, non-falseness, unaltered Suchness, Suchness such as it is, of the past, future and present mark of form, feeling, perception, impulses and consciousness, that cannot possibly be made known, nor can it possibly be uttered, or talked about, or answered by any action of speech. He who enters into the explanation of the perfection of wisdom in this matter, he recognizes the perfection of wisdom. For the perfection of wisdom has not been set up by the mark of the explanation of any dharma whatever, not by the mark of the explanation of form, or the other skandhas, or the formative forces, or of conditioned co-production; not by the mark of name-and-form, or of self, or of a being, or of the Dharma-element, of conjunction, of disjunction, of cause, of condition, of ill, of ease, of definite distinction, (62a) of not definite distinction, of production, of passing away, of defilement, of purification, of original nature, of convention, of ultimate reality, of truth, of fraud, of passing on, or of descent. And why? For the perfection of wisdom is free from all marks, and no one can see that "this is the perfection of wisdom, or here is the perfection of wisdom, or through that is the perfection of wisdom, or he has the perfection of wisdom".

Not do I see that dharma through which the perfection of wisdom could be explained. For the perfection of wisdom does not envisage the explanation of any dharma whatever. For it does not envisage the explanation of form, nor of the other skandhas, nor of eye-ear-nose-tongue-body-minds, nor of the elements or sense-fields, (62b) or conditioned co-production, or of knowledge and emancipation. It is because this is a wisdom which is supramundane and which leads to penetration[1] that the perfection of wisdom does not lend itself to explanation, for how can there be an explanation in words of a dharma which does not lend itself to explanation! But those who wisely know the dharmic method[2] of dharmas, they wisely know the explanation of the perfection of wisdom.

For the perfection of wisdom has not been set up for the exhibition of any dharma, or its definition. For it has not been set up for the exhibition or definition of form, or the other skandhas; nor of name and form, of defilement or purification, nor of conditioned co-production; (63a) nor of the perverted views, or of the world of beings or the element of self; of the elements of earth, water, fire, or air; of the world of sense-desire, of form, of formlessness; of generosity and meanness; morality and immorality; of patience and ill-will, vigour and sloth, trance and distraction, wisdom and stupidity; of the applications of mindfulness, right efforts, roads to psychic power, Unlimited, faculties, powers, limbs of enlightenment, trances, emancipations, concentrations, attainments, superknowledges; of the truths and the fruits of the path; of the levels of the Disciples, Pratyekabuddhas and Bodhisattvas; of the dharmas of Disciples, Pratyekabuddhas, Bodhisattvas, or Buddhas. (63b) It has not been set up by the cognition of any dharma or its non-cognition, by its definition or non-definition; not by the definition or non-definition of the cognition of non-production, the cognition of

[1] *nirvedhagāmini*
[2] *naya;* also principle

extinction, the cognition of stopping or of Nirvana. Just as any dharma which has not been set up for either exhibition or non-definition can obviously not possibly be explained in conventional terms. But he who understands this explanation in this manner, i.e. that the perfection of wisdom has not been set up by the exhibition of any dharma or by its non-definition, he cognizes the perfection of wisdom, he wisely knows the explanation of the perfection of wisdom. For the perfection of wisdom has not been set up by the junction of any dharma or by its disjunction. And why? Because it does not conjoin form, or disjoin it; and so for (64a) the other skandhas, etc. (64b) etc., to: it does not conjoin or disjoin the cognition of non-attachment or non-production, nor the cognition of extinction, or Nirvana. An explanation of a dharma is obviously impossible when it has not been set up by conjunction or disjunction with any other dharma. Considering this sequence of thought, Ven. Śāriputra, I therefore say that I do not see that dharma which could become clear to me as a dharma, or that by which it could become clear, or through which it could become clear, or wherein anything could become clear to me concerning anything.

CHAPTER VI: PRACTICE

Thereupon *The Lord* said to the Bodhisattva Suvikrāntavikrāmin, the great being: Here a Bodhisattva, a great being who courses in[1] Perfect Wisdom certainly courses in no dharma whatever. And why? Because all dharmas have arisen from the perverted views, and are unreal, non-existent, wrong and false. As long as he courses in any dharma whatever, (65a) he courses in perverted views; and when he courses in perverted views he does not course in what is real. A Bodhisattva is obviously not brought forth[2] by the practice of either perverted views or what is unreal; when he courses in perverted views and in what is unreal, he does not course in Perfect Wisdom; and since perverted views indicate unreality and no real practice is possible in what is unreal, a Bodhisattva does not course therein. "Perverted views" are false; foolish common people have seized upon them; these dharmas are not, however, as they have seized upon them; and that is why perverted views are called "unreal". A Bodhisattva, a great being of course does not course in either

[1] *carati*, also: practises. As in the chapter heading, *caryā*. Also later "coursing" may as well be rendered as "practice", and my translation alternates between the two alternative equivalents.

[2] *prabhāvito*

perverted views or what is unreal. For a Bodhisattva speaks of what is real and courses in what is not pervertedly viewed; but in what is real and without perverted view[1] there can be no coursing; that is why a Bodhisattva's coursing is called a non-coursing. For the practice of a Bodhisattva has completely cut off all practising, and one cannot point to it and say that this is the practice of a Bodhisattva, or by this is the practice of a Bodhisattva, or here is the practice of a Bodhisattva, or from this is the practice of a Bodhisattva. It is thus that the practice of a Bodhisattva cannot be discerned.[2] (65b) For Bodhisattvas course in the course of a Bodhisattva by turning away from all practices—be they practices of the common people, Disciples or Pratyekabuddhas. And as for the dharmas of a Buddha, in them also the Bodhisattvas do not course, nor do they settle down in any convictions about them, i.e. to the effect that "these are the Buddhadharmas, or here are the Buddhadharmas, or by that are the Buddhadharmas, or he has the Buddhadharmas"—in all this Bodhisattvas do not course. For all this is a coursing in false discrimination, but a Bodhisattva does not course in either discrimination or non-discrimination, because his coursing has forsaken all discrimination. "Thought-construction,"[3] that is the false discrimination[4] of all dharmas; for it is not possible to mentally construct all dharmas, since they are all indiscriminate[5]; therefore, when someone mentally constructs a dharma, he makes a false discrimination. For dharma itself is neither thought-construction nor no-thought-construction.[6] "Thought-construction," that is one extreme; no-thought-construction—that is a second extreme; Bodhisattvas (66a) however, do not course in extremes[7]—nor in the endless[8] either. When one does not course in either the end[7] or the endless, then one does not review the middle[9] either. In fact, if he were to review the middle, or to course in it, then he would just course in an extreme[7], and so one cannot course in the middle or exhibit it. "The middle," that is a term for the holy eightfold path;

[1]So Ti.

[2]*prabhāvita*

[3]*kalpa, rtog-pa*

[4]*vikalpanā, rnam-par rtog-pa*

[5]*rnam-par mi rtog-pa yin-pas.* Hikata: *akalpitā*

[6]*vikalpo,* here=*mi rtog-pa*!

[7]*anta,* end

[8]*ananta*

[9]*madhyam.* One cannot see anything in the middle between them. This refers, of course, to the "middle way".

but the holy eightfold path has not been set up as a basis for the apprehension of any dharma, nor for its reviewing.

But at the time when the Bodhisattva in his meditation does not either develop[1] or annihilate[2] any dharma, then one speaks of his "having finished with the path"[3]; neither developing nor annihilating all dharmas, he completely transcends any kind of development and reaches the sameness of dharma(s). In consequence a perception of the Path will no longer occur to him—how much less will he see the Path! "One who has finished with the Path," that is a synonym of a monk who is an Arhat whose outflows are extinct. And why? Because that path has been annihilated (*vibhāvito*=brought to an end), neither developed (*bhāvito*) nor annihilated (*vibhāvito*), therefore is it called "annihilated" (*vibhāvita*). Even annihilation (*vibhāvanā*) is not in it, that is why it is called "annihilated" (*vibhāvita*); gone away[4] is his development (*bhāvanā*) (66b), therefore one speaks of "un-development" (*vi-bhāvanā*). If again there were any development or annihilation, and if it were apprehended, then there would be no annihilation of that. "Annihilation" (*vibhāvanā*) that is annihilation because all development (*bhāvanā*) has gone away from[4] it and also all existence (*bhāvo*, *dṅos-po*) has departed from[4] it; that is why it is called "annihilation". But it is not such as one speaks of it. And why? For that annihilation cannot be expressed by words, since it is a mere departure.[5] In what sense is it a departure? Because the perverted views do not rise up, nor that which is unreal; for a perverted view cannot give rise to a perverted view, and that perverted view has in fact not really arisen; in fact in this situation nothing arises at all. Even if there were here any arising, one could not speak of it; but since it has arisen as something unreal, therefore is it called a "perverted view"; for a Bodhisattva has understood all dharmas as (they are), unperverted. And why? Because he has cognized perverted views as unreal, and so in perverted views no perverted views do actually exist. If someone has cognized that perverted views are unreal, and do not actually exist in perverted views, then he has fully understood all dharmas as (they are), unperverted. (67a) And where there is an understanding of non-perversion, there is no longer any perverted view; and where there is no perverted view, there is also no coursing. For all coursings have

[1]*bhāvayati*
[2]*vi-bhāvayati*, undevelop. The following section often defies translation.
[3]*pratiprasrabdha-mārga*
[4]*vigata*
[5]*vigama*

arisen from coursing, and because of the discrimination of coursing there is perverted view; but a Bodhisattva makes no discrimination with regard to the coursing, therefore is he called "one who is established in the absence of perverted views". And he who is unperverted, he no longer courses—therefore the coursing of a Bodhisattva is called a no-coursing. A "no-coursing"—when he does not course in any dharma, nor course apart from[1] one, nor shows up[2] the mark of coursing—that is called "the coursing of the Bodhisattva". One who courses thus, he courses in the perfection of wisdom.

For when the Bodhisattva courses in form as an objective basis, then he does not course in the perfection of wisdom; and so for the other skandhas. And why? For he has cognized all objective bases as isolated; and what is (in) isolation, therein there is no coursing; therefore is the coursing of a Bodhisattva called a no-coursing. For when the Bodhisattva courses in the eye as an objective basis, then he does not course in the perfection of wisdom; and so for the ear, etc., to: (67b) mind. And why? Because he has cognized all objective bases as unreal; and when he has done so, then he does not course anywhere; therefore is the coursing of a Bodhisattva called a no-coursing. For when the Bodhisattva courses in form, sounds, smells, tastes, touchables and mind-objects as an objective basis, then he does not course in the perfection of wisdom. And why? Because he has cognized all objective bases as having arisen from perverted views; and what is perverted view, that he has comprehended as unreal; in consequence he does not course in any objective basis; therefore is the coursing of a Bodhisattva called a no-coursing. For when the Bodhisattva courses in name-and-form as an objective basis, then he does not course in the perfection of wisdom. And why? Because he has understood all objective bases as having no objective basis (support); in consequence he does not course in any objective basis; therefore is the coursing of a Bodhisattva called a no-coursing. For Bodhisattvas, great beings who course in self and (living) beings as an objective basis, they do not course in the perfection of wisdom. And why? Because they have comprehended that the notion of a (living) being (68a) or of a self is unreal, and in consequence they do not course in any coursing whatever, and are therefore without coursing; therefore is the coursing of a Bodhisattva called a no-coursing. For Bodhisattvas who course in the notion of a living soul,

[1] *vi-carati*
[2] *sandarśayati;* Tib. *spyod-pa'o.*

a person, etc.,[1] do not course in the perfection of wisdom. And why? Because they have annihilated all notions,[2] and thus no longer course in any notion whatever; therefore is the coursing of a Bodhisattva called a no-coursing. For Bodhisattvas who course in the perverted views, or in the false views,[3] or in the hindrances, they do not course in the perfection of wisdom, nor do those who course in the objective supports of the perverted views, the false views and the hindrances. And why? Because they have fully comprehended the objective supports of these perverted views, false views and hindrances; but this full comprehension is a no-coursing; therefore is the coursing of a Bodhisattva (68b) called a no-coursing. For the Bodhisattvas who course in the objective support of conditioned co-production do not course in the perfection of wisdom. And why? Because they have fully comprehended conditioned co-production and its objective support; but the full comprehension of conditioned co-production and of its objective support involves not any coursing; therefore is the coursing of a Bodhisattva called a no-coursing. Also Bodhisattvas who course in the objective support of the world of sense-desire do not course in the perfection of wisdom, nor do those who course in the objective support of the world of form and the formless world. And why? Because they have annihilated[4] the objective supports of the triple world, and of that annihilation there is no coursing; therefore is the coursing of a Bodhisattva called a no-coursing. Nor do Bodhisattvas who course in the objective supports of giving or meanness, morality or immorality, course in the perfection of wisdom. And why? Because they have fully comprehended (69a) the objective supports of giving or meanness, morality or immorality, and in that comprehension of their objective supports there is no coursing; therefore is the coursing of a Bodhisattva called a no-coursing. Nor do Bodhisattvas who course in the objective supports of patience or ill-will, vigour or laziness, trance or distraction, wisdom or stupidity course in the perfection of wisdom. And why? Because they have fully comprehended all their objective supports, and in that comprehension of their objective supports there is no coursing; therefore is the coursing of a Bodhisattva called a no-coursing. Nor do Bodhisattvas who course in the objective supports of the non-perversions, the right efforts, the applications of mindfulness,

[1]The text gives 12 further synonyms.

[2]*saṃjñā*, also "perceptions".

[3]*dṛṣṭigata*, "what is subject to false views", = *the* 62 false views; *dṛṣṭi* alone = any false view.

[4]*vibhāvita*, undone

and the boundless states course in the perfection of wisdom. And why? Because they have cognized all objective supports as void; and of that comprehension of the voidness of the objective supports there is no coursing; therefore is the coursing of a Bodhisattva called a no-coursing. Nor do Bodhisattvas who course in the objective supports of the faculties, powers, limbs of enlightenment, trances, concentrations and meditational attainments course in the perfection of wisdom. And why? Because they have annihilated (in their meditations) the objective supports of the faculties, etc., and of that annihilation there is not any (69b) coursing; therefore is the coursing of a Bodhisattva called a no-coursing. Nor do Bodhisattvas who course in the objective supports of ill, origination, stopping and path course in the perfection of wisdom. And why? Because they have annihilated the objective supports of ill, origination, stopping and path, and in that annihilation there is no development nor any further coursing; therefore is the coursing of a Bodhisattva called a no-coursing. Nor do Bodhisattvas who course in the objective supports of (sacred) knowledge and emancipation course in the perfection of wisdom. And why? Because they have annihilated the objective supports of sacred knowledge and emancipation, and in that annihilation there is no coursing; therefore is the coursing of a Bodhisattva called a no-coursing. Nor do Bodhisattvas who course in the objective supports of non-production, of extinction, of the Uneffected, course in the perfection of wisdom. And why? Because they have annihilated these objective supports, and in that annihilation there is no further coursing; therefore is the coursing of a Bodhisattva called a no-coursing. Nor do Bodhisattvas who course in the objective supports of earth, water, fire, air and space (70a) course in the perfection of wisdom. And why? Because they have annihilated their objective supports, and in that annihilation there is no coursing, therefore is the coursing of a Bodhisattva called a no-coursing. Nor do Bodhisattvas who course in the objective supports of the levels[1] and dharmas of the Disciples and Pratyekabuddhas course in the perfection of wisdom. And why? Because they have annihilated their objective supports, and in that annihilation there is no coursing; therefore is the coursing of a Bodhisattva called a no-coursing. Nor do Bodhisattvas who course in the objective support of Nirvana course in the perfection of wisdom. And why? Because they have comprehended the objective support of Nirvana, and in that comprehension there is no coursing; therefore is the

[1]*bhūmi*

Bodhisattva's coursing called a no-coursing. (70b) Nor do Bodhisattvas course in the perfection of wisdom when they course in the objective support of the perfect purity of the marks (on the body of a Buddha), or of the perfect purity of the Buddha-field, or of the accomplishment of the Disciples, or of the accomplishment of the Bodhisattvas. And why? Because they have annihilated[1] their objective supports; and in that annihilation there is no coursing; therefore is the coursing of a Bodhisattva called a no-coursing. When they course thus, the Bodhisattvas do course in the perfection of wisdom. This is of the Bodhisattva the coursing in the perfection of wisdom that, when he courses in perfect wisdom, he courses in the comprehension of all objective supports and in their annihilation (by way of meditation).

When he courses thus, the Bodhisattva does not even course in the perfect purity of the objective support of the skandhas. And why? Because he has comprehended that the objective support of the skandhas is perfectly pure in its original nature. (71a) That kind of coursing is the Bodhisattva's coursing in the perfection of wisdom. (The formula is then applied to:) the sense-organs, the sense-objects; name-and-form; self and living beings; (71b) the view of a living soul, etc., to: one who feels; the perverted views and the false views; the hindrances; conditioned co-production; (72a) the triple world; giving and meanness, etc., to: wisdom and stupidity; past, future and present; (72b) non-attachment; the superknowledges; all-knowledge. A Bodhisattva courses in the perfection of wisdom when he courses thus, i.e. when he does not course in the purity of any objective support. And why? Because all objective supports are by their original nature perfectly pure. This is for the Bodhisattva, the great being, who courses in perfect wisdom, the perfect purity of the original nature of all objective supports.

When he courses thus, the Bodhisattva does not review that "this is form", "by that is form", "of that is form", "through that is form". Thus not reviewing form, he throws up no form, (73a) nor throws it down, does not produce or stop form, does not course in form or apart from it, does not course in the objective support of form or apart from it. When he courses thus, the Bodhisattva courses in the perfection of wisdom. And so with the other skandhas.

Moreover, when he courses thus the Bodhisattva does not course in the idea that "form is past", "form is future", or "form is present"; nor that "form is the self" or "belongs to the self"; (73b)

[1] = got rid of in their meditation.

or that "form is ill", or that "form is mine and no one else's". And so for the other skandhas. When he courses thus, the Bodhisattva courses in the perfection of wisdom.

Moreover, the Bodhisattva who courses in the perfection of wisdom does not course in the origination of form, nor in its stopping; nor in the idea that form is deep or shallow, empty or not empty, sign or signless, wish or wishless, or that form has been put together or has not been put together. And so (74a) for the other skandhas. And why? All these are imaginings, vapourings, futile discoursings, forms of craving: "It is I who course", that is a vapouring; "it is here that I course", that is a futile discoursing; "it is through this that I course", that is a form of craving; "it is in this that I course", that is an imagining. Since the Bodhisattvas have cognized all this as so many imaginings, vapourings, futile discoursings and forms of craving, they do, in order to uproot all kinds of non-knowledge, not mind any dharma; not minding it, they do not course[1] or settle anywhere; without a settling place, unconjoined and undisjoined, they do not rise up[2] anywhere. This is of the Bodhisattva, who courses in the perfection of wisdom, the uprooting of all vain conceits.

Moreover, the Bodhisattva who thus courses in the perfection of wisdom does not course in the idea that form is permanent or impermanent, empty or not-empty, (74b) like a mock show, a dream, a reflected image or an echo. And so for the other skandhas. And why? These are all conjectures, deliberations, futile considerations. When he has cognized that, a Bodhisattva courses in the perfection of wisdom for the sake of uprooting all coursings and of fully comprehending them. This is the explanation of all the coursings of a Bodhisattva.

Suvikrāntavikrāmin: Unthinkable, O Lord, is this coursing of a Bodhisattva in the perfection of wisdom! (75a)

The Lord: So it is, Suvikrāntavikrāmin. It is unthinkable through the unthinkability of: the skandhas, of name-and-form, conditioned co-production, karma and karma-result, the core, the perverted views, the false views, the triple world, the self, a living being, giving, etc., (75b) greed, hate and delusion, the applications of mindfulness, etc., to: meditational attainments, the places of rebirth, ill, origination, etc., sacred knowledge and emancipation, the cognition of extinction, etc., the level of the Disciples, etc., the dharmas of the Disciples, etc., (76a) the superknowledges, the

[1]Ti: exert themselves, *sbyor ro.*

[2]*ldaṅ-ba; utthāpayanti, samutthāpayanti*

cognition of past, future and present, the unattached cognition, Nirvana and the Buddhadharmas. And why? Because the Bodhisattva's coursing in the perfection of wisdom is not thought-generated[1]; therefore is it called "unthinkable".

To speak of "the production of (the) thought (of enlightenment)", that is perverted view. To speak of "thought, born of thought", that is the abolition of mental activity.[2] For the original nature of thought is neither produced nor born; a thought is born only in association with perverted views. Thereby the thought has been uncovered,[3] as well as the perverted view by which it is produced. But the foolish common people do not cognize that thought as uncovered, or that wherein it is produced, or that whereby it is produced. Not cognizing the isolatedness of both thought (76b) and its covering (by objective supports),[4] they settle down in the conviction that "I am thought, mine is thought, that has thought, from that is thought"; having settled down in thought, they settle down in such ideas as "wholesome" or "unwholesome", "ease" or "ill", "annihilation"[5] or "eternity", "false views", "hindrances", "giving", etc., "the world of sense desire", etc., "conditioned co-production, name-and-form, greed", etc., "envy" and "meanness", "the pride that says 'I am' ", "ill", "origination", "stopping", "path", "the applications of mindfulness", etc., to: "meditational attainments", "the cognition of non-production", etc., (77a) "The level of the Disciples", etc., "the dharmas of the Disciples", etc., "the path", "the superknowledges", "Nirvana", "the Buddha-cognition", "the marks", "the Buddha-field", "the accomplishment of Disciples, Pratyekabuddhas and Bodhisattvas".

When a Bodhisattva reviews inclinations of this kind on the part of beings as born of the perversion of thought, then he does not raise his thought to any perversion. And why? Because the perfection of wisdom has left behind all thought. In the transparent lucidity of the original nature of thought, in the perfect purity of its original nature, no genesis of a thought takes place. Where there is an objective support, there the foolish common people produce a thought. The Bodhisattva, however, wisely considers the objective support, as well as the genesis of thought, and asks himself wherefrom the thought is

[1]*citta-janika, sems-kyis bskyed-pa*

[2]To speak of "thought" implies that one reaches an understanding of mental activity.

[3]*sgrib-pa med-pa; vivṛtam*

[4]Ti: *ārambaṇa;* Ms: *āvaraṇa*

[5]*uccheda!*

produced. Bearing in mind that "this thought is translucent in its original nature", he thinks to himself, "this thought is being produced conditioned by an objective support". (77b) Once he has comprehended (the function of) the objective support, he does not produce a thought or stop it. And so that thought of his becomes translucent, undefiled, beautiful, perfectly pure. Established in non-production that thought does not produce or stop any dharma. This is of the Bodhisattva, who courses in the perfection of wisdom, the comprehension of the non-production[1] of thought. A Bodhisattva who courses thus courses in the perfection of wisdom. When he thus courses it does not occur to him, "It is I who course in the perfection of wisdom, I course in this perfection of wisdom, by this[2] I course in the perfection of wisdom, through this[3] I course in the perfection of wisdom". If again he perceives, "this is the perfection of wisdom, by that is the perfection of wisdom, his is the perfection of wisdom (through that is the perfection of wisdom)",[4] then he does not course in this perfection of wisdom. Even this perfection of wisdom, however, he does not review and apprehend, but when he does not course in "I course in the perfection of wisdom", then he does course in the perfection of wisdom.

Suvikrāntavikrāmin: Utmost, O Lord, is this coursing of a Bodhisattva, i.e. (78a) his coursing in the perfection of wisdom. It is translucent, unsurpassable, most lofty. It cannot be conquered[5] by Mara and his hosts, nor can it be assailed successfully by any others who course in signs or in the basis, who have the false view of a self, a being, a living soul or a person, of becoming or unbecoming, of annihilation or eternity, of individuality, of the skandhas, elements or sense-fields, of the Buddha, Dharma, Samgha or Nirvana, who perceive their attainments,[6] who are conceited, who are addicted to greed, hate or delusion, who are addicted to the perverted views, or who have set out on the wrong path. This coursing of the Bodhisattva, i.e. his coursing in the perfection of wisdom, rises loftily high above all the worlds.

The Lord: (78b) So it is, Suvikrāntavikrāmin, so it is. This coursing of a Bodhisattva cannot be conquered by Mara, or the deities of Mara's host, or Mara's assembly, or even by those who have the

[1]Tib. 'production'.
[2]*anena, 'dis*
[3]*asmād, 'di-nas*
[4]So only Tib. 89a.
[5]*anavakrānta.* Correct MDPL.
[6]*prāptasaṃprajña*, thob-par 'du-śes-pa. Add to MDPL.

view of Nirvana, or who settle down in Nirvana, and it cannot be successfully assailed by all the foolish common people. This coursing of the Bodhisattvas, that is not the coursing of the foolish common people, nor is it the coursing of those belonging to the vehicle of the Disciples, be they still in training or adepts, or of those who belong to the vehicle of the Pratyekabuddhas. If this were a coursing for those who belong to the vehicle of the Disciples and Pratyekabuddhas, then they would not have the idea that they belong to the vehicle of the Disciples and Pratyekabuddhas; but they would be Bodhisattvas, or Tathagatas who have attained the four grounds of self-confidence. Since therefore this is not a coursing for those belonging to the vehicle of the Disciples and Pratyekabuddhas, therefore they are not reckoned as "Bodhisattvas", nor are they Tathagatas who have attained the four grounds of self-confidence. This coursing in the perfection of wisdom is an activity (79a) which takes place on the level of supreme self-confidence. When they course thus, the Bodhisattvas will, even though they have not yet known full enlightenment, quickly reach the state where they have the four grounds of self-confidence, through the force of their original Vow and through the sustaining power of the Buddhas and Lords. For those who belong to the level of the Disciples and Pratyekabuddhas do not have the four grounds of self-confidence, nor does the Tathagata sustain them (in their efforts to win them). To reach the four grounds of self-confidence by the force of the original Vow, that is (possible only on) the stage of a Bodhisattva. And why? The Bodhisattvas who course in the perfection of wisdom reach the four analytical knowledges. Which four? i.e. the analytical knowledge of the meaning, of dharma, of languages, and of ready speech. Endowed with these four analytical knowledges they acquire, even before they have known full enlightenment, the grounds of self-confidence by the force of their original Vow. And the Tathagatas who know them as endowed with wholesome roots, and who know that they have reached the stage of the perfection of wisdom, sustain (79b) them in (their efforts to win) the grounds of self-confidence. Therefore then the Bodhisattva, who wants to reach the four analytical knowledges, and to quickly become one skilled in the four grounds of self-confidence should train and course in the perfection of wisdom.

Moreover the Bodhisattva who courses in the perfection of wisdom penetrates to the cause of all dharmas, their origination, disappearance and stopping, and there is no dharma which he does not join to the perfection of wisdom. He wisely knows the cause, origination, stopping, path and mark of all dharmas, and in consequence he neither develops nor undevelops form; and so for: the other skandhas; name-and-form; defilement and purification; perverted views, what is subject to false views, hindrances; greed, hate and delusion; the world of sense-desire, etc.; the element of beings, or of self; (80a) the view of annihilation or of eternity; giving, etc., to: stupidity; the applications of mindfulness, etc., to: the meditational attainments; conditioned co-production; ill, etc.; the cognition of non-production, etc.; the level of the foolish common people, of Disciples, Pratyekabuddhas and Bodhisattvas; the dharmas of the foolish common people, of Disciples and Pratyekabuddhas; calming-down and insight; Nirvana; (80b) the vision and cognition of the past, future and present; attachment, non-attachment, the Buddha-cognition, the grounds of self-confidence of a Buddha. And why? For all these are not to be developed, i.e. form, etc., to: the cognition of the fully enlightened Buddha. And why? Because no existent has full and total reality; unreal are all these, just conventional expressions, and in them there is no (81a) own-being. With non-existence for their own-being are all dharmas,[1] unreal, impossible.[1] And why? What is perverted view, that is unreal, and all dharmas have arisen from perverted views. What is perverted view, that is non-existence. Devoid of existence are all dharmas, their existence cannot be apprehended, because they have no own-being. "Non-existence," that is (ultimately[2]) unreal, that cannot be[3]; therefore is it called "non-existence". A revelation of what is not[4] is this "non-existence" (*abhāva*); and in what is non-existence (*abhāva*), there can be no development (*bhāvanā*) or undevelopment (*vibhāvanā*). In consequence of their perverted views do beings develop and undevelop, although there is nothing that could be developed (*bhāvya*; *dṅos-po*). And why? Because all dharmas have non-existence for own-being (*abhāvasvabhāva*), they are without existence (*bhāvāpagata*), and because there is (here) no entity (*vastv-asattvāt*) there is nothing in them that could be developed (*bhāvya*; *bsgom-par bya-ba*). When a Bodhisattva who courses in perfect wisdom dwells in these dharmas as one who discerns the (One) Dharma (in them), (and so) does not develop or undevelop any (particular) dharma, then one speaks of "the development of the perfection of wisdom". When he thus

[1]*abhūtā asaṃbhūtā*
[2]*yaṅ-dag-pa ma yin shiṅ; abhūta*
[3]*asaṃbhūta*
[4]*asatparidipana, med-pa yoṅs-su bstan-pa*. Add MDPI.

courses, thus dwells, the Bodhisattva's, the great being's development (81b) of the perfection of wisdom becomes perfect.

Moreover, the Bodhisattva, the great being who courses in the perfection of wisdom, does not produce a thought caused by the conjunction with form,[1] and the other skandhas; nor a thought associated with rigidity; or with ill-will, or meanness, or (moral) defilement, or laziness, or distraction, or stupidity, or sensuous desire; or a thought which is associated with settling down in form as an objective support, or with covetousness, or slander, or wrong views, or settling down in possessions, or in the desire for sovereignty, or for rebirth in good families or among the gods, (82a) or the desire for the world of sense desire, the world of form or the formless world; he does not produce a thought on the level of the Disciples or Pratyekabuddhas, or a thought associated with the desire to course[2] in the coursing of a Bodhisattva; he does not even produce a thought associated with the view of Nirvana. Endowed with this purity of thought he radiates friendliness over beings, as well as compassion, sympathetic joy and impartiality; but he has undone his perceptions of a being and does not stand in the perception of a being; and so he does not settle down in these four Brahma-dwellings, and he becomes wise and endowed with skill in means. When he is endowed with these dharmas and courses in the perfection of wisdom, his development of perfect wisdom will quickly become perfect. When he thus develops the perfection of wisdom, he does not approach form or grasp it; and that applies also to the other skandhas, etc., like the previous lists. (83a) And why? Because all dharmas are unapproachable and ungraspable, and cannot be approached by anyone. For no dharma can be grasped, nor has anyone ever grasped it. And why? Because there is nothing that either should or could be grasped. And why? Because all dharmas are unsubstantial, since they are like an illusion; they are void because no substantiality can be apprehended (in them); they are equal to a reflected image, because they cannot be seized upon; they are worthless, as having no own-being; they are like a mass of foam, because easily crushed; they are like a bubble, because on arising they soon break up and are dispersed; they are like a mirage, since they have arisen from perverted views; they are like the core of the plantain tree, because they have no core; they are like the moon reflected in water, because they cannot be seized upon; they are like the hues of the rainbow, because they result from imagining what is not; they are inactive, because they

[1] *rūpa-samprayoga-nimittam; gzugs daṅ phrad-pa'i rgyur*

[2] So Tib: *spyod-pa-la* for *abhiniveśa.*

cannot raise up anything; they are like an empty fist (83b), because they can be seen to have the mark[1] of being void of own-being. Therein the Bodhisattva who thus reviews all dharmas does not approach or grasp any dharma, does not take his stand on one, feels no inclination for one. This is of the Bodhisattva who courses in the perfection of wisdom the faithful acceptance of all dharmas, though he does not take his stand on them and feels no inclination or desire for them. When he courses thus, the Bodhisattva's perfection of wisdom will become perfect.

Moreover, when he trains thus the Bodhisattva does not train in the skandhas, nor in their transcending. He does not train in their genesis, nor in their stopping; not in their disciplining nor in their non-disciplining; not in their passing-on nor in their descent[2]; not in their stability nor in their non-stability. (84a)

When he trains thus, a Bodhisattva does not train in the permanence or impermanence of the skandhas, nor in their ease or ill, nor in their selfhood or non-selfhood. When he trains thus, a Bodhisattva does not course in the objective support of the past, present or future skandhas. But he investigates the past with the modes of the empty, of the calm, of not-self. "What is past, that is empty, calm, not-self," thus he courses.[3] And so for future (84b) and present. "The past is empty and calm by being the self, by belonging to self, by being permanent, stable, eternal and not liable to reversal"—therein he does not course. And so with the future and the present. When he courses thus, the Bodhisattva's development of the perfection of wisdom becomes perfect. Mara the Evil One gains no entry to the Bodhisattva; but he understands all deeds of Mara, and is not captivated by them.

Moreover, when he courses thus the Bodhisattva does not make the skandhas into objects; nor (85a) the perverted views and what is subject to false views; nor the settling down in a self or in a being; nor annihilation or eternity; nor the end or the endless; nor sight-objects, etc., to: mind-objects; nor the world of sense-desire, etc., or conditioned co-production, or the physical elements of earth, etc., to: space; or truth and fraud, conjunction and disjunction; nor greed, hate and delusion, or the forsaking of greed, hate and delusion; or giving, etc., to: stupidity; or the applications of mindfulness, etc., to: the meditational attainments; or friendliness, etc.; or the cognitions of non-production, etc.; or the levels and dharmas

[1]-*lakṣaṇatayā*, *rtog-pas*

[2]*saṃkrāntaye*, *avakrāntaye*

[3]So Skr. Ch, Ti: does not course.

of the foolish common people, the Disciples and the Pratyekabuddhas; (85b) or ill, etc.; or the vision and cognition of the superknowledges; or emancipation, or the vision and cognition of emancipation; or Nirvana; or (the vision and cognition of[1]) past, future and present; or the cognition of non-attachment, or the Buddha-cognition, or a Buddha's powers and grounds of self-confidence, or the perfect purity of the Buddha-field, or the perfect purity of the marks, or the accomplishments of the Disciples, or of the Pratyekabuddhas, or of the Bodhisattvas. And why? Because all dharmas are without objective support, and there exists with regard to all dharmas not any seizing whereby they could become an object. The existence of an object implies an inclination (for it), a settling down (in it), a grasping (at it), and that in its turn implies pain and sadness and the possibility of the darts of sorrow, lamentation and despair. Objects imply bondage; objects imply absence of the Path, imply all kinds of pain and sadness; they imply (86a) vain conceits, vapourings and discoursings; disputes, quarrels and contentions; ignorance, darkness and delusion; fears and terrors; the snares of Mara and the dangers of being ruined by him; they imply oppression by ill and (a vain) search for happiness. Surveying these dangers, the Bodhisattva does not objectify any dharma, and in consequence he does not seize on any dharma, does not take his stand on either the seizure or the acquisition of all dharmas and he does not mind even the void resulting from this absence of an objective support. When he courses thus, the Bodhisattva, the great being does not settle down in any dharma, welcomes none and has no firm inclination towards any dharma. This is of the Bodhisattva, the great being who courses in the perfection of wisdom, the absence of an objective support in all dharmas. When the Bodhisattva courses thus, his development of the perfection of wisdom becomes perfect. Mara the Evil One can cause him no obstacles, nor can the deities belonging to Mara, or his assembly, or those who are under his influence; they can find no opening (86b) by which to harm him, and even if they have taken possession of him they cannot overpower him; but constantly he recognizes (and thereby nullifies) all the deeds of Mara, and does not come under their sway; but he eclipses all the realms of Mara, he is ready to refute all the heretics, he overcomes all heretics, sectarians and wanderers, and cannot be crushed by all the false teachers.

When he courses thus, the Bodhisattva does not stand in the

[1]Only Ch, Ti.

construction of the skandhas, nor in their discrimination.[1] He does not construct or discriminate the skandhas, or any of the other items of previous lists (87a, b), etc., to: he does not construct or discriminate the accomplishments of a Bodhisattva. And why? Where there is construction, there is discrimination; but wherein there is no construction, there is also no discrimination. For (the ideas of) all the foolish common people have arisen from thought-construction, their perceptions (88a) have arisen from discrimination, and they (constantly) construct and discriminate. "Thought-construction" is one extreme, "discrimination"[2] is the second extreme. Wherein there is no thought-construction and no discrimination, therein there is no extreme and no middle. "Middle," that is an extreme for him who constructs. As long as there is thought-construction, so long is there discrimination, and thus discrimination is not completely cut off. But discrimination is cut off completely where there is neither thought-construction nor discrimination.[2] "The complete cutting off of thought-construction" does not mean the cutting off of anything. And why? Because thought-constructions and discriminations are extremes and have arisen from perverted views; their appeasing is the non-perversion and that implies no cutting off (of anything that is)'. "Complete cutting off" is used as a synonym of the complete cutting off of ill; but there is no such thing. There could be a complete cutting off of ill if ill were totally real. But that "complete cutting off of ill" is in fact nothing but a vision of the absence of (the) total reality (of ill), in other words it is the full comprehension of ill. When one neither constructs nor discriminates ill, then this is the appeasing of ill, (88b) its non-production, its non-manifestation. When he sees thus, the Bodhisattva does not construct or discriminate any dharma. This is of the Bodhisattva who courses in the perfection of wisdom the full comprehension of all constructions[3] and discriminations. When he courses thus, the development of a Bodhisattva's perfection of wisdom becomes perfect. Mara the Evil One cannot set up any obstacles for him, nor can his assembly; he understands the deeds of Mara which have arisen, he does not come under their sway, he vanquishes Mara the Evil One, eclipses him, greatly reduces his following, and in that way he becomes one who is free from all fear and terror and who cannot be assailed by the Maras; all possibility of his going to the states of woe is ruled out, and the bad paths (of rebirth) are closed for him; he becomes

[1] *vikalpanāyām; mi rtog-pa-la* (=in non-construction).
[2] Here "non-construction" would clearly be better.
[3] Ch and Ti only.

one who has crossed all the floods, who is free from the darkness of delusion, whose eyes are opened,[1] one who is a true light for all beings, who lives so that the lineage of the Buddhas should not be interrupted; he has acquired the path in the sameness of the path, is compassionate towards all beings, and his eye for dharmas (89a) has been made pure; he has achieved vigour and is not lazy, has acquired the power of patience and his thoughts harbour no ill-will, he meditates and that without leaning on anything, has acquired wisdom and is endowed with sharp wisdom; he is free from remorse and has left the hindrances behind; he has dissociated himself from the snares of Mara, has cut his bonds, by separating himself from the net of all the cravings; he is established in mindfulness because his nature is unbewildered, pure in his morality as one who has attained the perfection of moral purity, established in the foremost virtues because all his faults are suppressed, has attained impregnation with the power of wisdom because he is unshakeable, is not put out of joint by all the false teachings (inspired by) Mara; he is unfailing because he has attained the purity of all dharmas, self-confident when demonstrating all dharmas, unembarrassed in his approach to his audiences; not niggardly, but one who gives freely of the gift of Dharma; his path is perfectly purified through the sameness of the path, his meditational development is undone by the full comprehension of the bad paths; he is filled with the fragrance of the propensities (acquired in previous lives), because his nature is pure; he is well cleansed and pure, because his wisdom is pure; he is deeply (89b) wise, because he is like the ocean; he is hard to fathom because he is fearless; he is measureless, because the ocean of Dharma is without measure. When he courses thus, the Bodhisattva becomes endowed with these and other virtues, and one cannot possibly reach their limit.

Moreover, Suvikrāntavikrāmin, the Bodhisattva who thus courses in the perfection of wisdom is not deficient in his faculties, nor is he deficient in his body, food, retinue, birth, family or country; he is not reborn among the people of border-countries, does not choose inauspicious rebirths, is not thrown into close contact with impure beings and impure activities, does not lose his own mind and is not deprived of his wisdom; those dharmas which he hears from others, he unites them with[2] the sameness of all dharmas; he lives to ensure the non-interruption of the lineage of the Buddhas, which is the lineage of all-knowledge; he has gained light

[1]Lit. "one who has gained the eye", *pratilabdhacakṣur*

[2]*saṃsyandayati*

in all Buddhadharmas and courses exceedingly near to all-knowledge. (90a) If Mara the Evil One approaches him for the purpose of harming him, he pulverizes that host of Mara, puts it out of countenance, cuts through all the snares of Mara and can easily defy all Mara's hordes. Thereupon the Evil Maras run away, frightened and trembling, and think to themselves; "this man has passed beyond my realm, he no longer courses in it, no longer stands in it, no longer moves into it", and "other beings also he will free from my realm and save them!" Thereupon Mara the Evil One sorrows, cries out aloud, and laments: "This Bodhisattva will greatly reduce my following!" And weakness takes hold of him, and he becomes pained, sad and regretful. At the time when the Bodhisattva courses in the perfection of wisdom, develops it and makes efforts about it, all the realms of Mara are eclipsed and lose their lustre, the Evil Maras become pained (90b), sad and afflicted with the dart of sorrow, pierced with the dart of great sorrow, and think to themselves: "This man will surely lead beings away from our realm, save them from it, free them from it, pull them out of it; he will cut through the snares by which Mara holds beings captive, will lift up beings who have got stuck in the mud of the sense-pleasures, will free them from the net of false views, will rescue them from the reach of the hindrances, will establish them in the true path and will rescue them from the jungle of false views". When they consider this sequence of events, those Maras become pained, sad, pierced with the dart of sorrow. Just as a man who had lost a great mass of wealth would be pained, oppressed by painful feelings, and endowed with great pain and sadness; just so Mara the Evil One becomes pained, sad, regretful, pierced with the dart of sorrow, and he does not feel happy on his own seat, at the time when (91a) the Bodhisattva courses in the perfection of wisdom, develops it and makes efforts about it. Moreover, those Evil Maras having one by one come together in one place, reflect to themselves, "what shall we do now, what then can we do now?" They are pierced with the dart of doubt, and in that frame of mind they approach the Bodhisattva who courses in the perfection of wisdom, searching how to enter him. Nevertheless the Bodhisattva's hairs do not stand on end, his body undergoes no alteration and his mind no agitation; free from hair-raising fear he understands fully that "this is Mara, the Evil One", and, once he has understood that, he can exercise his (spiritual) sustaining power which weakens Mara the Evil One, cows his mind and frightens him, and so he cannot gain entry to this man. He admits to himself that indeed he cannot gain entry to him, nor can his assembly, nor any others who may try to do so. Thereupon those Maras, trembling, having lost their fortitude, go off to their respective abodes and stay there full of painful and sad reflections, for (91b) even for the time of a finger-snap they cannot delude the thought of the Bodhisattva who courses in the perfection of wisdom, how much less cause him any obstacles! This is the impregnation with the power of wisdom with which the Bodhisattva[1] becomes endowed when he courses in the perfection of wisdom. If all the beings in all the great trichiliocosms were to become Maras and if they all, together with vast masses of followers, were to approach that Bodhisattva who courses in the perfection of wisdom, with the intention to harm him, then all these Evil Maras have no power to cause him an obstacle. And why? Because the Bodhisattva has become endowed with this impregnation with the power of wisdom, has become endowed with the scymitar of wisdom, with the sword of wisdom, and thereby with a wisdom which is unthinkable, measureless, equalling the unequalled. That is why Mara the Evil One is incapable of overcoming this man. For the sword of wisdom is a great sword, and its scymitar is a great scymitar. (92a) In wisdom there is no route or range for the Evil Maras, and they find there no ground to stand on. Even those seers who are outsiders,[2] who have gained the four trances, as well as the four formless attainments, who, having transcended the world of sense-desire, which is the range of Mara, are reborn in the world of Brahma and in the four heavens of the formless gods—even for those there is no route or range in this kind of wisdom which comes natural to Bodhisattvas, how much less in the wisdom of him who courses in the perfection of wisdom; what need is there to speak of the Evil Maras, since the world of form and the formless world lie outside their range. The Bodhisattva will at that time be someone who has attained the impregnation with the power, with the great power, i.e. with the power of the perfection of wisdom. Those again who are endowed with the power of the perfection of wisdom, and with the sharp sword of wisdom, they cannot be assailed or conquered by the Evil Maras—and they manufacture no support, but remain unsupported. And why? For support means shaking, shaking means vapouring, and vapouring means discoursing. And all those who have supports, shakings, vapourings and discoursings, they come under the sway of Mara the Evil One, and they are not freed from his realm. Even those beings who are reborn near the summit of existence, if they are

[1]So Ch, Ti only.
[2]*bāhyā*—as distinct from *anyatīrthikā*, previously as "heretics".

supported, fastened to supports, intent on supports, even they will once again come within Mara's range, are not freed from his snares and are still caught in them, as for instance Udraka Rāmaputra and Arāḍa Kālāma and any others who in the formless worlds are supported, tied to supports and reside in supports. Bodhisattvas, on the other hand, who course in the perfection of wisdom, develop it and make efforts in it, (93a) do not manufacture any support whatever and become unsupported everywhere. But at the time when the Bodhisattva gives himself up to his endeavours about the development of the perfection of wisdom, at that time he is not supported by form, nor by the other items enumerated in previous lists (93b), nor by the cognition of the all-knowing, the accomplishment of the marks, of the Buddhafield, of the array of the Disciples and of the array of the Bodhisattvas. Unsupported by all dharmas he does not shake or quiver, and he has undome all supports (94a); unsupported he does not even settle down in the Path. And he also does not put his mind to the non-support, and does not think, "this support is not apprehended, the support here is not apprehended, his support is not apprehended, the support through that is not apprehended". Not putting his mind to all supports, not apprehending them, not settling down in them, he does not approach any support, points out none, delights in none, feels no inclination for one; unstained by all supports, unattached to them, he reaches purity from the support of all dharmas. This is of the Bodhisattva who courses in the perfection of wisdom, the vision and cognition of the purity from the support of all dharmas, and through that the Evil Maras can gain no entry to him and they cannot conquer him, but he overcomes them all.

CHAPTER VII: ADVANTAGES

Moreover, Suvikrāntavikrāmin, from the very beginning, as soon as he has raised his thought to the supreme enlightenment, the Bodhisattva is one who has fully attained to the equipment with many wholesome roots; (94b) he has honoured many Buddhas and questioned them, has done his duties under the Buddhas and Lords and has achieved a firm resolution; he delights in the distribution of gifts, attaches weight to the purity of his morality, has achieved gentleness and patience, is energetic and attaches weight to the purity of his vigour, attaches weight to the purity of his trances, is wise and attaches weight to the purity of his wisdom. With his thought raised to the supreme enlightenment and practised in the perfection of wisdom, he stands up to the Evil Maras through the force of his wisdom and cognition. As a result of his sustaining thought to the effect that "the Evil Maras may not gain entry into me and not do me any harm!" the Maras do not in fact gain entry (to him), nor do they set up obstacles for him, nor does it occur to them to seek to gain entry into this Bodhisattva and do him harm. If, however, they should think of impeding him, they at once feel themselves threatened by some terrible ruin, a great fear (95a) is set up in them, and they become perturbed by the thought, "may we not in every way cease to be!" In consequence they again withdraw the idea of harming (the Bodhisattva) and it vanishes away. It is in this way that the Evil Maras, intent on impeding the Bodhisattva, gain no entry into him.

Moreover, the Bodhisattva, the great being, when the perfection of wisdom is being taught and demonstrated, produces in himself zest, earnest intentions, respect and esteem as well as the notion that he is in the presence of the Teacher; when a sermon associated with the six perfections is being taught, no hesitation, perplexity or doubt arise in him; when he has heard deep dharmas, no hesitation, bondage or doubt arise in him; he has never heaped up any karma conducive to the ruin of Dharma, nor has he ever produced a thought conducive to the ruin of Dharma; and he instigates many other beings (95b) to the perfection of wisdom and they become thrilled by all the six perfections and filled with enthusiasm for them. Because of the purity of his thoughts and resolutions in the past, because of his absence of all defilements in his past resolutions, the Evil Maras can set up no obstacles for him and can gain no entry into him, whereas he looks through all the deeds of Mara, whether produced or still to be produced, is not captivated by them and does not come under their sway. It is in this way that the Evil Maras cannot harm the Bodhisattva.

Moreover the Bodhisattva, who courses in the perfection of wisdom, does not course in the sign of the connection with form nor in the sign of the disconnection from it; he does not course in the sign of the connection with feelings–perceptions–impulses–consciousness, nor in the sign of the disconnection from them; he does not course in the sign of the connection with the marks of the skandhas nor in the sign of the disconnection from their marks. And so for: the sign of the purity of the skandhas, the no-sign of their purity, (96a) the sign of the purity of the objective supports of the skandhas, the no-sign, etc.; the association with the purity of the possibility of the skandhas, the dissociation from the purity of their possibility; the association with the purity of the own-being of the objective support of the skandhas, the dissociation from the purity of the own-being of their objective support; in the purity of the essential original nature of the skandhas; the association with the purity of the essential original nature of the objective support of the skandhas, the dissociation from, etc.; (96b) the purity of the past, future and present skandhas; the purity of the past, future and present objective supports of the skandhas; the association with the purity of the past, future and present skandhas, the dissociation from, etc.; the association with the purity of the past, future and present objective supports of the skandhas, the dissociation from, etc. When he courses thus he is not associated with the skandhas nor dissociated from them, and so for: (97a) name and form, perverted views and false views, the world of sense-desire, of form, of formlessness; greed, hate and delusion; the notions of self, being, soul, person, existence and non-existence; annihilation or eternity; the elements or sense-fields; the (physical) elements of earth, water, fire, wind, ether and consciousness; conditioned co-production; the five sense-qualities; defilement and purification; generosity and meanness, morality and immortality, patience and ill-will, vigour and sloth, trance and distraction, wisdom and stupidity; unperverted views, right efforts, applications of mindfulness, bases of psychic power, (97b) the faculties, powers, limbs of enlightenment, concentrations, attainments; ill, origination, stopping, paths; calming down or insight, the secret lores and the emancipations; the vision and cognition of emancipation, the superknowledges, the levels of common people, Disciples or Pratyekabuddhas, the dharmas of the common people, Disciples or Pratyekabuddhas, the cognition of non-production, the cognition or extinction or the cognition of the Unconditioned, Samsara or Nirvana, the cognition of a Buddha, his powers or grounds of self-confidence, the accomplishment of the marks, the arrays of the Buddha-fields, the accomplishments of Disciples, Pratyekabuddhas or Bodhisattvas. And why? (98a) Because all dharmas are neither associated nor dissociated. And why? Because they have not been set up through association or through dissociation. "Association," that bears the track of eternity, "dissociation," that is annihilation. For of all dharmas there is not any recognition by which they could be associated or dissociated. Because no dharma at all has been set up for either association or for dissociation. If there were between dharmas any state of association or dissociation, then one would with regard to dharmas have got hold of a doer or a doing, an ariser or an arising, a raiser or a raising, a feeler or a feeling, a knower or a knowing, an associator or a dissociator, and the Tathagata would have taught us that this is the case. But because no dharma at all has been set up for association or dissociation, therefore with regard to dharmas no doer (98b) or doing are apprehended, no ariser and no arising, no raiser and no raising, no feeler and no feeling, no knower and no knowing, no associator and no dissociator. And the Tathagata teaches without positing any basis, since all dharmas have arisen from perverted views. But a perverted view is not associated with or dissociated from anything. And why? For perverted views imply no apprehension of an objectively existing entity, and even its possibility cannot be apprehended. And why? For a perverted view is unreal, false, fraudulent in its nature, and vain. No dharma is therein apprehended which could be called "perverted view". "Perverted views" are peoples' unfounded disquisitions, teasings, imaginings of what is unreal, vain conceits, vapourings and futile discoursings. Just as a little child, when teased with an empty fist, forms the notion that there is something real in it, just so the foolish common people are teased by an objectless perverted view and in their delusion think to themselves that this is real. Forming with regard to something unreal (99a) the notion that it is real they are seized by the perverted views, and it is hard to free them from them. It is thus that all foolish common people err about, neither associated nor dissociated, and yet tied by bonds. They vainly imagine "association", apprehend it, see it as if it were an established fact, settle down in the conviction that there is such a thing. And where there is association there is also dissociation. But on the other hand, he who does not apprehend association, does not vainly imagine it, does not settle down in the conviction that there is such a thing, and who also does not vainly imagine dissociation, he is absolutely free. If he would vainly imagine dissociation, or apprehend it, or settle down in the conviction that there is such a thing, then he would be just associated, and not dissociated. The Bodhisattva who considers this reasoning does not get associated with any dharma, nor dissociated from it; nor does he set himself up for association with any dharma whatsoever, or dissociation from it. This is of the Bodhisattva, the great being, who courses in the perfection of wisdom, the full comprehension of association or dissociation. When he courses thus the Bodhisattva quickly arrives at the Beyond of all dharmas.

Moreover, the Bodhisattva who courses in the perfection of wisdom (99b) does not course in the non-attachment to the skandhas, nor in the purity of such non-attachment, nor in the objective support of such non-attachment, nor in association with it or dissociation from it; or in association with the purity of such non-attachment or in dissociation from it; or in the association with the purity of the objective support of the skandhas or in the dissociation from them. And why? The Bodhisattva has comprehended all these as wavering signs, as vacillating doings, or rather undoings, (100a) and he no longer courses, or courses apart (*vicarati*).

Moreover the Bodhisattva who courses in the perfection of wisdom does not course in attachment to past, future and present skandhas, nor in non-attachment to them; he does not course in the purity of the past, future and present skandhas, nor in their impurity; nor in the purity of the objective supports of the non-attachment to past, future and present skandhas, nor in their impurity. And why? Because the Bodhisattva who courses in the perfection of wisdom does not review his coursing. A Bodhisattva who courses in the perfection of wisdom (100b) has in fact entered into this comprehension of all courses as no-courses. When he courses thus he quickly arrives at the fulfilment of the dharmas which constitute the state of all-knowledge.

Moreover the Bodhisattva who courses in the perfection of wisdom does not course in the idea that the skandhas are uncovered or that they are not uncovered; nor in the idea that the skandhas are calm or not calm, that in their essential original nature they are uncovered or not uncovered, that in their essential original nature they are calm or not calm, or that past, future or present skandhas by their essential original nature are isolated or not isolated, calm or not calm. (101a) When he courses thus the Bodhisattva quickly arrives at the fulfilment of the dharmas which constitute the state of all-knowledge.

Moreover the Bodhisattva who courses in the perfection of wisdom does not mind the skandhas, or their purity, or the purity of their objective supports. Moreover he does not settle down in the skandhas, or in their purity, or in the purity of their objective supports. When he courses thus the Bodhisattva quickly arrives at the fulfilment of the dharmas which constitute the state of all-knowledge.

When he courses thus he (101b) is near to the ten powers of a Tathagata, his four grounds of self-confidence, the eighteen special dharmas of a Buddha, the great friendliness, the great compassion, the great sympathetic joy and the great impartiality. He is near to the thirty-two marks of a superman, to the golden hue of his skin, to the endless splendour of a Tathagata, to His Elephant-look, His state of having His head gazed upon (i.e. revered[1]), to His vision of past, future and present non-attachment, to a Tathagata's miraculous display of instruction and admonition, to his prediction to the vision and cognition of past, future and present non-attachment. When he courses thus, the Bodhisattva quickly arrives at the fulfilment of all Buddhadharmas, as well as the perfect purity of the Buddha-field, and he quickly obtains the accomplishment of the array of the Disciples and Bodhisattvas. When he courses thus he is not firmly grounded in (102a) the skandhas; nor in name and form, in false views, hindrances or perverted views, in the worlds of sense-desire, form or formlessness, in the element of self or of beings, in the notions of person or soul, in the (physical) elements of earth, water, fire, air, ether or consciousness, in the elements or sense-fields, in defilement or purification, in conditioned co-production; in renunciation or meanness, morality or immorality, patience or ill-will, vigour or sloth, trance or distraction, wisdom or stupidity; in the applications of mindfulness, right efforts, roads to psychic power, faculties, powers and limbs of enlightenment; the trances, emancipations, concentrations, or attainments; ill, origination, stopping, or paths; the cognitions of non-production, of the unconditioned, and of extinction; calming-down or insight; the superknowledges; the secret lores and the emancipations; the levels of Disciples, Pratyekabuddhas or fully enlightened Buddhas; the dharmas of the common people, of Disciples or Pratyekabuddhas; (Samsara or[2]) Nirvana, the cognitions of a Buddha, his powers and (102b) his grounds of self-confidence, the cognition of non-attachment, visions and cognitions of past, future or present, the accomplishment of the Buddha-field, of the Disciples-array and of the Bodhisattva-array. And why? Because all dharmas are unsupported, since there exists no support for them. And why? Because all dharmas are without a settling place, and that is why they are not firmly grounded. If there were a support for dharmas, if there were a settling place or immobile ground,[3] the Tathagata would have pointed out the support of dharmas, saying "this is the support of dharmas, this is their settling place, this is their (place of) accumulation".[4] But because all dharmas are unsupported, without a settling place, without (a place of) accumulation, therefore no dharma has an immobile ground (beneath it). And the

[1]So Edgerton for *avalokitamūrdhitā* (Gv). Ms and Hikata: *anavalokitamūrdhatāyāḥ*.

[2]Only Chi.

[3]*kūṭastha*, or: if they overtower all change.

[4]*sañcaya*. Perhaps just "accumu lation" is better.

Tathagata therefore does not point out a support for dharmas, or a settling place or (a place of) accumulation. For dharmas are not totally real, and no own-being whatsoever abides anywhere, because of the impossibility of dharmas and their lack of total reality. (103a) For that reason are all dharmas called unsupported, and that by way of having no standing place, of having no (lasting) abode. There is no firm position for all dharmas. Just as there is for the four great rivers which gush forth from Lake Anavatapta no (lasting) abode except in the great ocean, just so all dharmas have no firm position until they are annulled in the Unconditioned. In "the Unconditioned" there is no standing place, no no-standing-place, no (permanent) abode[1]—no such reckoning is possible there, no such enumeration as "standing place", "no-standing-place", or "conditioned existence". Like the act of gazing at the proceeding of beings is that done—no-standing-place, or standing place, or firm foundation.[2] In the Unconditioned there are no longer such enumerations; therefore one says that "all dharmas are unsupported". This is on the part of the Bodhisattva who courses in perfect wisdom the devotion to the (fact or insight that) all dharmas are unfounded. When he courses thus the Bodhisattva quickly fulfils the dharmas of all-knowledge, (103b) and comes near to the supreme enlightenment, he quickly approaches the terrace of enlightenment, acquires the cognition of the all-knowing, arrives at the fulfilment of past, future and present cognitions and goes to the Beyond of the quivering thoughts and doings of all beings.

Therefore then the Bodhisattva, the great being who wants to work the weal of all beings, to give them gifts, to refresh them with the gift of Dharma, to break the egg-shell of their ignorance, to bring them the great cognition, the Buddha-cognition, to become full of pity towards all beings and to become solicitous for them, who wants to supply them abundantly with Dharma, food, morality, with gentleness and patience, with vigour, the trances, wisdom and emancipation, with rebirth in the heavens, (104a) the secret lores and the emancipations, the vision and cognition of emancipation, Nirvana, the Buddhadharmas and the accomplishments of all virtuous qualities, who wants to turn the wheel of Dharma, which has never before been turned by Śramaṇa or Brahmin or god or Māra or Brahmā or anyone else in any world, who wants to teach Dharma in accordance with Dharma, who wants to be predicted to

[1] *adhiṣṭhāna;* Tib. *rgyun mi 'chad-pa*, "uninterrupted existence".

[2] ? *yathāsatvapravṛttisaṃdarśanam etat kṛtam asthānaṃ vā sthānaṃ vā prasthānaṃ vā. Saṃdarśana* can also mean "revealing", "teaching"—Edgerton 556.

the level of a Buddha, a Disciple or a Pratyekabuddha, who wants to impel all beings to benefit from the wholesome roots (generated by) his past Vow: he should train in this perfection of wisdom, should work on it, make efforts in it, he should give himself up to the development of the perfection of wisdom. I see no dharma which can bring a Bodhisattva as quickly to the fulfilment of all dharmas, as the persistent application to this perfection of wisdom as it has been explained, as the progressing in it, (104b) and as the refusal to relinquish this dwelling, i.e. the dwelling in perfect wisdom.

And whichever Bodhisattvas course in this perfection of wisdom, they should be quite sure that they are near the supreme enlightenment. And those who have come to hear of this perfection of wisdom, and who firmly believe in it, take delight in it, and produce a true perception—of them also I say that their wholesome roots nourish the supreme enlightenment; and of that one can be quite sure. For these sons or daughters of good family have heaped up a huge equipment with wisdom, and other wholesome roots they will acquire as well. And as to those Bodhisattvas who get hold of this explanation of the section (or: chapter) on perfection of wisdom and skill in means—although there are among them some who have not been predicted face to face by the Buddhas and Lords, nevertheless one should know that they are near their prediction and before long will obtain it face to face.

Just as one can be quite sure that those beings who behave in conformity with the ten wholesome paths of action are near to rebirth in Uttarakuru, just so one should know that any Bodhisattva, into whose hands this perfection of wisdom has fallen, is near to the supreme enlightenment.

Just as one can be quite sure that beings will quickly become rich and achieve a high social status if they bestow gifts and give freely, win over beings with gifts, with kind words, with actions for the benefit of others and by the consistency between their words and deeds, and if they guard their morality and become people who have slain all pride. Or just as one should know that before long beings will bring about a World-rulership if they observe generosity, have become accomplished in morality and patience, are established in vigour and the trances, and endowed with wisdom, if they produce friendliness towards beings and instigate them to morality, and thus heap up karma conducive to sovereignty. Just so one should know that any Bodhisattva, into whose hands this perfection of wisdom has come, (105b) will quickly approach the terrace of enlightenment.

Just as one should know that if the jewel of the Wheel appears to a

Warrior King who is seated on the day of the full moon, on the fifteenth day of the month, in front of his council, he will become a universal monarch and the seven treasures will soon after appear to him. Just so one should know that a Bodhisattva, into whose hands this book on the perfection of wisdom has come, will soon after be endowed with the objective bases of all-knowledge.

Just as one should know that beings will quickly be reborn in the company of the deities of the Four Great Kings and there exercise overlordship, if they are endowed with superior wholesome roots, with beautiful conduct and with sublime faith, if they are definitely established in their aversion to being reborn with a human personality, and if they become accomplished in morality, do their duties by a great number of people and aspire for rebirth among the gods. And as for those who are endowed with still purer wholesome roots, whose wholesome roots are in fact so superior (106a) that they first give away gifts and only thereafter enjoy things for themselves, that first they do their duties by other beings and only thereafter look after themselves, who feel no greed for what is not Dharma and what is not rightful, and who aspire for sovereignty and overlordship among the gods: one should know that before long they will, immovably and firmly, exercise sovereignty and overlordship over the gods of the Thirty-three and will become Śakras, chiefs of gods. Just so, when this perfection of wisdom presents itself to a Bodhisattva, then one should be quite certain that soon he will reach control, sovereignty and overlordship over all dharmas.

Just as one should know that those beings who become recipients of the four stations of Brahma shall quickly be reborn in the world of Brahma. Just so, when this exposition of the perfection of wisdom presents itself to a Bodhisattva, then one should know that he shall soon turn the wheel of Dharma.

When the months of the rainy season come round, the rain clouds (106b) soak this great earth with moisture, the rain goes on and on and the deity pours down water from above. Many thereupon regain their energies, the surface of this great earth is refreshed, thoroughly irrigated and soaked with moisture, and the water which is conveyed from above refreshes also the low-lying pieces of ground. In consequence this great earth, irrigated from above by the rain-clouds, in its turn irrigates the herbs, shrubs, plants and trees, with the result that many branches and leaves and much foliage sprout forth, and there are many flowers and fruits. This great earth emits a fragrant scent and becomes adorned with fountains, lakes and ponds which bear many flowers and fruits. Men and ghosts become contented when they enjoy those flowers and fruits and enjoy that scent. Just so, when a Bodhisattva comes face to face with this perfection of wisdom and makes efforts about it, then one should know that before long he will be irrigated by the (107a) cognition of the all-knowing, will clarify and reveal it, and he will moisten beings with his revelation of the supreme jewel of the Dharma.

Just as those beings who are reborn in the realm of the Nāga-king of Lake Anavatapta, emit the four great rivers which replenish the great ocean; just so all those Bodhisattvas, into whose hands this perfection of wisdom has come, and who train in it, rain down great streams of Dharma, and their gift of Dharma refreshes all beings.

All beings who come near Sumeru, the king of mountains, assume one colour only, i.e. that of gold; just so those Bodhisattvas into whose hands this exposition of Perfect Wisdom will fall, will all go to one single goal, the goal of Tathagatahood, the goal of all-knowledge.

Just as the sea, the great ocean, holds together all the water, and constantly all the water comes together in it, (107b) just so, whenever the exposition of the perfection of wisdom has come into the hands of any Bodhisattva, then one can be quite sure that he will soon reach the ocean of all dharmas, the repository of all dharmas, the coming together of all dharmas, and soon he will become imperturbable as a result of the verbal expression of Dharma.

When the disk of the sun arises, all other sources of light are eclipsed; just so the Bodhisattva, who courses in this perfection of wisdom, is set up for the work of spreading the light of the Dharma among all beings; the Bodhisattva who advances to this, he has been set up for the task of spreading the light of the wholesome roots among all beings and he goes to a state where he is worthy of the gifts of all beings; he goes to a state of purity where he is a field of purity for all beings, and becomes for all beings someone to be courted, someone to be worshipped, someone to be praised.

The Bodhisattva who courses in this perfection of wisdom courses in the heights, he courses for the purpose of clearing the path to Nirvana for all beings. And why? (108a) For this training in the perfection of wisdom is the foremost training, the finest, the best, the most excellent, the utmost and the highest. When he trains in it, the Bodhisattva attains the perfection of all trainings, advances in conformity with them, demonstrates them and causes them to be brought about. For when they were coursing in the course of a Bodhisattva the past, future and present Buddhas and Lords have trained in this training, will train in it and do train in it. Well established in this training the Buddhas and Lords have revealed to all beings the utmost perfect purity of the training, will reveal it and do reveal it. And why? For this training in perfect wisdom is a training which has risen above the entire world, the most distinguished training in the entire world. This training in perfect wisdom is that training which is (that which is) self-existent in the entire world. When he trains in the perfection of wisdom, the Bodhisattva is not trained (108b) in any dharma whatsoever—be it worldly or supramundane, conditioned or unconditioned, with or without outflows, faulty or faultless; he does not generate any attachments, he becomes one who dwells unattached to all dharmas. And why? Because all dharmas are unattached, unbound, unfreed; they are not set up by the attachment of any dharma, or its bondage; for the skandhas are unattached, unbound, unfreed. And so are name and form; the perverted views, false views and hindrances; greed, hate and delusion; the six inward and the six outer sense-fields; the worlds of sense-desire, form and formlessness; the element of self, and of being; conditioned co-production; defilement and purification; renunciation and meanness, morality and immorality, patience and ill-will, vigour and sloth, (109a) trance and distraction, wisdom and stupidity; suffering, origination, stopping, paths; the applications of mindfulness, right efforts, roads to psychic power, boundless states, unperverted views; the faculties, powers, limbs of enlightenment, concentrations and attainments; the (physical) elements of earth, water, fire, wind, ether and consciousness; the cognitions of non-production, extinction and the Unconditioned; the secret lores and the emancipations; the non-attachment to the superknowledges; the vision and cognition of emancipation; the dharmas of the common people, of Disciples and Pratyekabuddhas; Nirvana; the cognition of the Buddha, his powers and grounds of self-confidence; the past, future and present vision and cognition of non-attachment is unattached, unbound and unfreed. And why? For of all dharmas the bondage cannot be apprehended, because they are unattached and unbound; their emancipation can therefore not be apprehended; since they are unattached (anyhow) (109b) there can be no liberation (of them); in fact, what is called the vision of all dharmas that is the vision and cognition of non-attachment. "Non-attachment," because of the non-apprehension of attachment; non-attachment from non-attachment-ness, non-attachment from being in its true reality non-attachment, it is called "non-attachment", and nothing can be apprehended in it which could join or bind; and because nothing can be apprehended which could be joined or bound, therefore is it called "non-attachment". "Unbound," because of the non-apprehension of bondage, because of the unreality of bondage, it is called "unbound"; for therein no bondage exists, nor is anything therein apprehended which is the piercing, and because that which is the piercing is not apprehended, therefore is it called "non-piercing". And what is non-attached and non-piercing, how could that be freed; and what is not attached and not bound, that is freed, dissociated, cooled, released; and therein there is no longer any penetration, therefore it is "set free", and its freeing no further exists. This is of the Bodhisattva who courses in the perfection of wisdom the entrance into the vision and cognition of all dharmas as unattached, unbound and unfreed. When he courses thus, the Bodhisattva is near to the supreme (110a) enlightenment, and he acquires soon the cognition of the all-knowing. I affix this seal so as to cut off the doubts of the Bodhisattvas who practise the perfection of wisdom and course in it. I myself sustain this exposition of the seal, and my disciples will not be able to bear this seal of the perfection of wisdom in the last time, in the last period, in the last five hundred years.

Thereupon *the Lord* said to the five hundred Bodhisattvas preceded by Bhadrapāla and Susārthavāha, and to the Bodhisattva Suvikrāntavikrāmin: After the Tathagata has entered into his final Nirvana there will come the last time, the last period, the last five hundred years, the time of the disappearance of the good Dharma, when it collapses and becomes extinct. It is then that you, sons of good family, can bear this storehouse of the precious Dharma of the Tathagata, which he has procured for many hundreds of thousands of kotis of niyutas of aeons, which is controlled by the perfection of wisdom and is its product and foundation—and you can illuminate it in full detail for others.

Thereupon *the Bodhisattvas* said to the Lord: (110b) We can, O Lord, bear this supreme storehouse of the precious Dharma of the Tathagata, which he has procured for many hundreds of thousands of kotis of niyutas of aeons, which is controlled by the perfection of wisdom and is its product and foundation, and we can illuminate it in full detail for others. That time, O Lord, will be one of great fear, devastation and frightfulness; furthermore beings will then be endowed with a karma conducive to the ruin of the good Dharma, covetous with an unlawful covetousness, greedy with an unlawful greed, greedy with a greed for unrighteousness, their minds overcome by envy and covetousness, angry, cruel, harsh, abusive, dishonest, cheats, deceitful, coursing in unrighteousness, given to much strife and many fights, disputes and quarrels, unrestrained, covetous, overcome by covetousness, lazy, of inferior vigour, robbed of their mindfulness, unwise, frantic, garrulous, arrogant, with their evil deeds concealed within their inmost hearts, choking with greed, hate and delusion, hemmed in by the eggshell of ignorance and the blinding darkness of delusion; they will act like people on Mara's side, they will be foes to this deep Dharma-Vinaya and to the precious treasury of the Dharma, and they will have failed to advance to mental morality. (111a) And yet we will nevertheless, O Lord, strive to bear in mind and to preach this Dharma of the Tathagata which is a most precious treasure, which has been procured by wholesome roots (cultivated for) many hundreds of thousands of niyutas of kotis of aeons. We know, of course, that in the last days there will be only very few beings who are desirous of these dharmas and who want to train in them, who are free from dishonesty, straight and free from deceit, who would give up even their lives, and who would not be foes to these dharmas, or reject them or be averse to them. And we, we shall work their weal, encourage them to just these dharmas which we shall show them, fill them with enthusiasm and make them rejoice!

Thereupon the Lord on that occasion sustained this exposition of the perfection of wisdom which is the sustaining power of the Dharma, and he exercised his sustaining power for the purpose of cutting off the snares which Mara the Evil One might cast over this discourse on Dharma. He manifested a smile, and in consequence this great trichiliocosm was lit up by a great radiance: the gods could see the men and the men could see the gods; (111b) and those gods, nagas, yakshas, gandharvas, asuras, garudas, kinnaras and mahoragas who had assembled there, they all scattered heavenly flowers over the Lord, threw down heavenly strips of cloth, made a great din and said in a loud voice:

By a great sustaining power indeed has this been sustained by the Tathagata, so that the evil Maras cannot do anything, for all their snares have been cut off; by this systaining power of Dharma those sons and daughters of good family can moreover expect that the evil Maras will be frightened when they bear in mind this discourse on Dharma, preach it and illuminate it in detail for others. These Bodhisattvas will have escaped from Mara, and they will vanquish the armies of those Evil Ones, they will bear in mind this discourse on Dharma, preach it, and illuminate it in detail for others.

Thereupon *the Lord* said to the Bodhisattva Suvikrāntavikrāmin:

So it is, so it is, as these gods have just said. The evil Maras are hemmed in when the Tathagata teaches this discourse on Dharma. (112a) But when those sons and daughters of good family will take up this discourse on Dharma, bear it in mind, preach it, and illuminate it in full detail for others, then Mara, the Evil One cannot do anything, and they become unassailable by the Evil Maras, they can slay Mara's hostile deeds, they have escaped from the battle, they will take up this discourse on Dharma, bear it in mind, preach it and illuminate it in full detail for others. But this discourse on Dharma will certainly not fall into the hands of defiled beings, or of those who are tied down by Mara's snares. For (it takes place on) the level of the thorough-bred, which is not for those who are not thorough-bred. Just as thorough-bred elephants and horses do not serve upon the commander of a fort, and do not go to see cruel people. But such thorough-bred elephants and horses go to universal monarchs (112b), advance to them for their use, attendance and service, because to universal monarchs they can be of use. Just so these discourses on Dharma will fall into the hands of thorough-bred human beings who can use them. Just as the Nāga-kings Uposhadha, Supratishthita and Airāvaṇa do not come along to please human beings, do not approach to be seen by them, do not even come along to be enjoyed and used by other deities, but come along only for the use of thorough-bred deities. Whenever Śakra, Chief of Gods, comes out having made a display, then the Nāga-kings, having made a similar display, approach so as to be of use to him. Likewise this discourse on Dharma will be enjoyed and used by those who are chiefs among human beings, chiefs among men, who are able to preach, demonstrate and illuminate it. These my discourses on Dharma will for them become a great display, a great radiance, a great lamp of the Dharma, (113a) and in these discourses on Dharma they will experience a great zest for Dharma, will be endowed with great zest and rejoicing, when they bear in mind the one single principle of this discourse on Dharma—what do I say of those who have copied it in its entirety, and then bear it in mind, preach it, worship it and spread it far and wide! That is why such people are chiefs among men, thoroughbreds among human beings. They certainly will have been taken hold of by this discourse on Dharma and there is no route to it for those who are not thoroughbred—this also I say, so that all doubts may be dispelled.

When the Lord had taught this discourse on Dharma, countless Bodhisattvas obtained the patient acceptance of dharmas which fail to be produced, innumerable beings raised their thoughts to the supreme enlightenment, and the Tathagata pointed out that they were definitely destined for enlightenment. Thus spoke the Lord. Enraptured Suvikrāntavikrāmin, the Bodhisattva, the great being, the four assemblies, and the world with its gods, men, nagas, yakshas, gandharvas, (113b) asuras, garudas, kinnaras and mahoragas rejoiced in the Lord's teaching.

THE PERFECTION OF WISDOM IN 700 LINES

Oṃ! Homage to the Perfection of Wisdom, the Lovely, the Holy!

A. THE EXPOSITION OF THE FIELD OF MERIT

Thus have I heard at one time. The Lord dwelt at Śrāvastī, in the park of Anāthapiṇḍada in the Jetavana, together with a large community of monks, with a thousand monks who were Arhats and with a million Bodhisattvas, great beings who were armed with the great armour and who were all irreversible from the utmost, right and perfect enlightenment, headed by Mañjuśrī (192) the Crown Prince, Maitreya, Asangapratibhāna and Anikshiptadhura.

Thereupon Mañjuśrī, the Crown Prince, rose from his peaceful seclusion, left his own dwelling, approached the dwelling of the Tathagata, and stood outside the door, so as to behold the Tathagata, to revere and honour him. The Ven. Śāradvatīputra also left his own dwelling and approached the dwelling of the Tathagata, so as to behold the Lord, to revere and honour Him. And likewise the Ven. Pūrṇa, son of Maitrāyanī, and the Ven. Mahāmaudgalyāyana, the Ven. Mahākāsyapa, the Ven. Mahākātyāyana, the Ven. Makākauṣṭhila and the other great Disciples left each one their own dwelling, approached the dwelling of the Lord, and stood on one side. (193)

Thereupon *the Lord*, having noticed that the assembly of the great Disciples had approached, left his own dwelling, seated himself on one side on the seat spread outside his door, and (although he knew the answer) asked the Ven. Śāradvatīputra: Where did you come from before you came at daybreak to the door of the Tathagata's dwelling?

Śāradvatīputra: In fact, O Lord, Mañjuśrī the Crown Prince was the first to stand at the door of the Tathagata's dwelling. We came afterwards, because we loved to see you.

Thereupon *the Lord* (although he knew the answer) asked Mañjuśrī the Crown Prince: Were you, Mañjuśrī, in fact the first to stand at the door of the Tathagata's dwelling, so as to behold the Tathagata, to revere and honour him? (194)

Mañjuśrī: So it is, O Lord, so it is, O Well-Gone! I was the first to arrive here. I left my own dwelling, approached the dwelling of the Tathagata, and have stood on one side, so as to behold the Lord, to revere and honour Him. Because I will never get tired of seeing the Tathagata, revering and honouring Him. But when I approach the Tathagata so as to behold, revere and honour Him, then I do so for the sake of all beings. If, O Lord, the Tathagata should be seen, revered and honoured, he should be seen, revered and honoured just as I do see, revere and honour Him. Then the Tathagata does in fact become seen, revered and honoured. For the sake of all beings I have come to see the Tathagata. (195)

The Lord: How then, Mañjuśrī, should the Tathagata be seen, revered and honoured?

Mañjuśrī: Through the mode of Suchness (*tathatā*) do I see the Tathagata, through the mode of non-discrimination, in the manner of non-observance. I see Him through the aspect of non-production, through the aspect of non-existence. But Suchness does not attain (enlightenment)—thus do I see the Tathagata. Suchness does not become or cease to become—thus do I see the Tathagata. Suchness does not stand at any point or spot—thus do I see the Tathagata. Suchness is not past, future or present—thus do I see the Tathagata. Suchness is not brought about by duality or non-duality—thus do I see the Tathagata. Suchness is neither defiled nor purified—thus do I see the Tathagata. Suchness is neither produced nor stopped—thus do I see the Tathagata. In this way the Tathagata is seen, revered and honoured. (196)

The Lord: When you see this, Mañjuśrī, what do you see?

Mañjuśrī: When I see this, O Lord, I do not see anything, neither the production of a dharma nor its stopping.

Śāradvatīputra: When, Mañjuśrī, you thus see the Tathagata and honour Him, you are a doer of what is hard to do. Although you have set up the great friendliness towards all beings, yet you apprehend no being and are inclined to no being. Although you have progressed with the final Nirvana of all beings as your aim, yet there proceeds in you no inclination towards any being whatever. And although (197) you have put on the armour for the sake of all beings, you have done so by way of non-observation, etc. to: by way of non-existence.

Mañjuśrī: So it is, Rev. Śāradvatīputra, as you say. This armour has been put on so that all beings may win final Nirvana, and yet I have no apprehension of a being, no inclination towards one. This armour, Rev. Śāradvatīputra, has not been put on with the intention to effect the depletion of the world of beings, or its repletion. If, Rev. Śāradvatīputra, to put an imaginary case, in each single Buddha-field there were Buddhas and Lords countless as the sands of the Ganges, and if each single Tathagata were to abide for aeons countless as the sands of the Ganges, demonstrating Dharma night and day, and if each single Tathagata by each single demonstration of Dharma were to discipline as many beings as have been disciplined by each single demonstration of Dharma on the part of the Buddhas and Lords countless as the sands of the Ganges (198)—even if that were done one could not conceive of a depletion of the world of beings or its repletion. And why? Because of the isolatedness of beings, because of their non-beingness.

Śāradvatīputra: If, Mañjuśrī, because of the isolatedness of beings and because of their non-beingness one cannot conceive of the depletion or repletion of the world of beings, why then do you just now, having fully known enlightenment, demonstrate Dharma?

Mañjuśrī: If, Ven. Śāradvatīputra, there is absolutely no apprehension of a being, who then (199) will fully know (anything)? Or to whom will he demonstrate Dharma? Because absolutely no dharma can be apprehended.

The Lord: If, Mañjuśrī there is absolutely no apprehension of any dharma, how then can you speak meaningfully of a being? If someone were to ask you how many beings there are, what would you tell him?

Mañjuśrī: If he were to ask me that, I would tell him, "just as many as there are Buddhadharmas". If, O Lord, he would then further ask me how great the extent of the world of beings might be, I would tell him that it is as great as the extent of the Buddha's domain.

The Lord: If further again, Mañjuśrī, someone (200) were to ask you wherein the world of beings is included, what would you tell him?

Mañjuśrī: I would tell him that it is included wherein non-production and unthinkability are included.

The Lord: If, further again, Mañjuśrī, someone were to ask you whereon the world of beings is supported, what would you tell him?

Mañjuśrī: I would tell him that that which supports the element (*dhātu*) of non-production, that also supports the world (*dhātu*) of beings.

The Lord: Supported whereon do you then, Mañjuśrī, develop the perfection of wisdom at the time when you do so?

Mañjuśrī: I have no support at all at the time when I develop the perfection of wisdom. (201)

The Lord: When you are unsupported, Mañjuśrī, is that then your development of perfect wisdom?

Mañjuśrī: When one is not supported anywhere, just that, O Lord, is the development of perfect wisdom.

The Lord: At the time when you, Mañjuśrī, develop the perfection of wisdom, which wholesome root of yours does at that time accumulate or decrease?

Mañjuśrī: None, O Lord. No one can develop perfect wisdom as long as the accumulation or decrease of any dharma whatsoever happens to them. That should not be known as a development of perfect wisdom where any accumulation or decrease of any dharma whatsoever is set up. That, O Lord, (202) is a development of perfect wisdom, where one neither forsakes the dharmas of an ordinary person, nor grasps at the dharmas of a Buddha. Because the development of perfect wisdom is not set up by taking as one's basis any dharma which one could forsake or grasp at. That, O Lord, is a development of perfect wisdom when one approaches neither the faults of birth-and-death nor the virtues of Nirvana. For one does not review birth-and-death, how much less its faults! And I do not apprehend Nirvana, how much less can I see its virtues! That, O Lord, is a development of perfect wisdom, where one appropriates no dharma whatsoever, seizes on none and escapes from none. That, O Lord, is a development of perfect wisdom where one apprehends the diminution of no dharma whatsoever, nor its growth. For non-production neither diminishes nor grows. Such a (203) development is a development of perfect wisdom. That, O Lord, is a development of perfect wisdom whereby no dharma is either produced or stopped, whereby no dharma is either depleted or repleted. Moreover, that is a development of perfect wisdom, when one strives after neither unthinkable nor definitely tangible dharmas. That which is striven after does not exist, he who strives does not exist, that wherewith he strives does not exist. Such a development is set up as a development of perfect wisdom. One does not think that these dharmas are superior and that those dharmas are inferior (204), and one also does not apprehend the dharmas which might be superior or inferior. Thus giving himself up to the practice (*yoga*) of the development of perfect wisdom, a son of good family does not apprehend any dharma at all. The development of perfect wisdom, O Lord, does not imagine any dharma as superior or inferior. There is nothing superior or inferior about non-production, or about Suchness, the Reality Limit, or all dharmas. Such a development, O Lord, is a development of perfect wisdom.

The Lord: Are then again, Mañjuśrī, the Buddhadharmas not supreme?

Mañjuśrī: They are supreme (*agrā*), but just because they cannot be seized upon (*a-grāhyatvād*). Has again, O Lord, the Tathagata fully known all dharmas to be empty? (204)

The Lord: So he has, Mañjuśrī.

Mañjuśrī: But one cannot, O Lord, conceive of superiority or inferiority in emptiness?

The Lord: Well said, Mañjuśrī, well said! So it is, Mañjuśrī, as you say! Are then the Buddhadharmas not unsurpassed?

Mañjuśrī: They are unsurpassed (*anuttara*), O Lord. Because in them not even the least (*aṇu*) dharma is found nor apprehended, the Buddhadharmas have not surpassed anything. Moreover, O Lord, the development of perfect wisdom does not lead to the winning of the dharmas of a Buddha, nor to the forsaking of the dharmas of an ordinary person. It neither trains in the dharmas of a Buddha (206) nor upholds them. Such a development, O Lord, is a development of perfect wisdom. And again, O Lord, if one reflects on no dharma, nor discerns one, then that should be seen as a development of perfect wisdom.

The Lord: Do you, Mañjuśrī, reflect on the dharmas of a Buddha?

Mañjuśrī: No indeed, O Lord. If I could see the specific accomplishment of the dharmas of a Buddha, then I would reflect on them. But the development of perfect wisdom is not set up through disciminating any dharma and saying that "these are the dharmas of ordinary people, these are the dharmas of Disciples, these the dharmas of Pratyekabuddhas, these the dharmas of fully enlightened Buddhas". The son of good family who has given himself up to the Yoga of the development of perfect wisdom does just not apprehend that dharma which would allow him to describe these dharmas as dharmas of ordinary people, (207) or as dharmas of those in training, or as dharmas of the adepts, or as dharmas of fully enlightened Buddhas. Because as absolutely non-existent I do not review those dharmas. Such a development, O Lord, is a development of perfect wisdom. It does not occur, O Lord, to a son of good family who has given himself up to the Yoga of the development of perfect wisdom that "this is the world of sense-desire, this is the world of pure form, this is the formless world, etc. to: this is the world of stopping". Because, O Lord, there is not any dharma which reviews the dharma of stopping. As such a development, O Lord, should the development of perfect wisdom be known. And again, O Lord, the development of perfect wisdom neither benefits nor injures any dharma. For perfect wisdom, when developed, is not a donor of the dharmas of a Buddha, nor an eliminator of the dharmas of an ordinary person. Just that, O Lord, is the development of perfect wisdom (208) where there is neither the stopping of the dharmas of an ordinary person nor the acquisition of the dharmas of a Buddha.

The Lord: Well said, well said, Mañjuśrī, you who demonstrate this dharma which is so deep. You have set up this Seal of the Bodhisattvas, the great beings, so that the greatly conceited Disciples should wake up to what is really true, and also those among the followers of the Bodhisattva-vehicle who lean on a basis. Those sons and daughters of good family (209) who, on hearing this deep exposition of perfect wisdom, will not tremble, be frightened or terrified, are not people who have honoured just one single Buddha or have planted wholesome roots under just one single Buddha. When, on hearing this deep exposition of perfect wisdom, they will believe, and will not tremble, be frightened or terrified, then they are sure to have planted wholesome roots under more than a thousand Buddhas.

Matjuśrī: The exposition of the perfection of wisdom becomes clearer and clearer to me.

"May it become quite clear to you, Mañjuśrī"—said *the Lord* to Mañjuśrī.

Mañjuśrī: This development of the perfection of wisdom, O Lord, apprehends neither the stability nor the unstability of any dharma whatever. Because the notion of stability does not apply to all dharmas. (210) Just that should be known as the development of perfect wisdom that it is not set up for the sake of acquiring the support of any dharma whatever. Because all dharmas lack in objective support. Such a development is a development of perfect wisdom. Moreover, O Lord, that should be seen as a development of perfect wisdom wherein one does not come face to face even with the dharmas of the Buddhas, how much less with those of the Pratyekabuddhas, and wherein one does not come face to face with the dharmas of the Disciples, how much less with those of the ordinary people. Moreover, O Lord, that is a development of perfect wisdom where, in the course of this meditational development, one does not even discriminate the unthinkable dharmas of a Buddha as "the unthinkable dharmas of a Buddha". One should see that this development of perfect wisdom serves the non-discrimination of all dharmas on the part of the Bodhisattvas, the great beings. (211) Moreover, O Lord, that is a development of perfect wisdom where, in the course of this meditational development, one sees all dharmas as Buddhadharmas, as unthinkable dharmas, but without doing any reviewing. Those sons and daughters of good family who on hearing this exposition of perfect wisdom will believe, will not tremble, be frightened or terrified, they will be such as have honoured many hundreds of thousands of Buddhas. Moreover, O Lord, such is the development of perfect wisdom that no dharmas can defile or purify it, nor can it review any dharma. Such is the development of the perfection of wisdom. And this also, O Lord, is the development of perfect wisdom that it does not differentiate between ordinary persons, Disciples, Pratyekabuddhas, (212) and fully enlightened Buddhas. Such is the development of perfect wisdom.

The Lord: How many Tathagatas have you honoured, Mañjuśrī?

Mañjuśrī: As many as there are the mental actions which have been stopped in an illusory man.

The Lord: You have, Mañjuśrī, not yet completed the dharmas of a Buddha?

Mañjuśrī: Can one then, O Lord, possibly apprehend a dharma which has not yet completed the dharmas of a Buddha?

The Lord: Who then has got these dharmas of a Buddha? (213)

Mañjuśrī: Even in you, O Lord, these dharmas of a Buddha do not exist and cannot be apprehended, how much less in other people!

The Lord: Have you, Mañjuśrī, attained non-attachment?

Mañjuśrī: Since I have never been attached to anything, why should I any further reach out for non-attachment?

The Lord: Are you then seated on the terrace of enlightenment?

Mañjuśrī: Even the Lord is not seated on the terrace of enlightenment, how again will I be seated on it—when the Reality-limit is taken as a standard?

The Lord: "Reality-limit", Mañjuśrī, of what is that a synonym?

Mañjuśrī: It is a synonym of individuality (*satkāya*). (214)

The Lord: In what hiden sense do you say that?

Mañjuśrī: Non-existent (*asat*), O Lord, is that body (*kāyo*), not a true individual body (*satkāyo*). It neither transmigrates nor does it fail to do so. That is why that body is not a true individual body (*asatkāya*).

Śāradvatīputra: Destined for enlightenment, O Lord, will be those Bodhisattvas (215) who, on hearing this exposition of perfect wisdom, will believe, will not tremble, be frightened or terrified.

Maitreya: Quite near to enlightenment, O Lord, will be those Bodhisattvas, who, on hearing this exposition of perfect wisdom, will believe, will not tremble, be frightened or terrified. And why? Because the supreme enlightenment is nothing but the full understanding of these dharmas.

Mañjuśrī: As veritable Buddhas should one regard those Bodhisattvas who, on hearing this exposition of perfect wisdom, will believe, will not tremble, be frightened or terrified. And why?

Because, in the ultimate sense of the word, "Buddha" is synonymous with non-production.

Nirālambā Bhaginī: Those Bodhisattvas who, on hearing this exposition of perfect wisdom, (216) will believe, will not tremble, be frightened, or terrified, they will not look for support in the dharmas of ordinary people, of Disciples, of Pratyekabuddhas or of fully enlightened Buddhas. And why? Because all dharmas have no objective support, since they do not exist. That is why no objective support can exist for them.

The Lord: So it is, Śāradvatīputra, so it is. Destined for enlightenment will be those sons and daughters of good family who, on hearing this exposition of perfect wisdom, will believe will not tremble, be frightened or terrified. You should know that those sons and daughters of good family are established on the irreversible stage, if, on hearing this exposition of perfect wisdom, they believe, do not tremble, are not frightened or terrified, (217) and if they accept it, placing it on their heads as a mark of respect. They will be most generous givers, perfect in morality, and endowed with the most excellent patience, vigour and trances, with the most excellent and quite unequalled wisdom, and with everything up to that cognition of the all-knowing which is possessed of the best of all modes. (218)

And *the Lord* said again to Mañjuśrī, the Crown Prince: On what grounds do you wish to fully know the utmost, right and perfect enlightenment?

Mañjuśrī: If I had set out for enlightenment, then I would wish to fully know it. But I do not strive after enlightenment, because enlightenment is just the same thing as this Mañjuśrī, the Crown Prince.

The Lord: You expound well, Mañjuśrī, these very deep stations. That is because you have performed your duties under the Jinas of the past, and have coursed for a long time in the holy life which is devoid of a basis. (219)

Mañjuśrī: If I were one who courses in the baseless, that would be equivalent to my having taken hold of a dharma.

The Lord: Do you see this my assembled company of accomplished Disciples?

Mañjuśrī: I do, O Lord.

The Lord: How do you see it?

Mañjuśrī: In such a way that I see no ordinary people, no learners, and no adepts. I do not see, and I also do not not see. But I see in such a way that I see neither many nor few, neither those who are disciplined nor those who are undisciplined. (220)

Śāradvatīputra: If, Mañjuśrī, you see in such a way those who use the vehicle of the Disciples, how then do you see those who use that of the fully enlightened Buddhas?

Mañjuśrī: I do not review a dharma called "Bodhisattva", nor a dharma "set out towards enlightenment", nor a dharma called "he fully knows". It is in this fashion that I see those who use the vehicle of the fully enlightened Buddhas.

Śāradvatīputra: How then, Mañjuśrī, do you see the Tathagata?

Mañjuśrī: Leave the great Nāga out of it, Rev. Śāradvatīputra! Do not busy yourself about the great Nāga! (221)

Śāradvatīputra: "Buddha," Mañjuśrī, of what is that a synonym?

Mañjuśrī: Of what then is the term "self" a synonym?

Śāradvatīputra: It is a synonym of non-production.

Mañjuśrī: So it is, Rev. Śāradvatīputra. The word "self" denotes the same thing which the word "Buddha" denotes. What is here called "the Buddha" is synonymous with "the trackless" (*apada*; also: wordless). Because it cannot easily be intimated by words (*vāk*). It is not easy to define speech (*vāk*), how much more so the Buddha! You want to know, Rev. Śāradvatīputra, how one can describe the Buddha. (222) He is the one who is not in full possession of enlightenment, who has not been produced, who will not be stopped, who is not endowed with any dharma, of whom there is not track, who is undifferentiated, and just equivalent to the trackless. Those who seek for the Tathagata should seek for the self. For "self" and "Buddha" are synonymous. Just as the self does absolutely not exist, and cannot be apprehended, so also the Buddha. As the self cannot be expressed by any dharma, so also the Buddha. One speaks of a Buddha where definitions fail. As it is not easy to understand what the word "self" means, so it is (223) also not easy to understand what the word "Buddha" means.

Śāradvatīputra: Bodhisattvas who are beginners, O Lord, cannot understand what Mañjuśrī, the Crown Prince, has demonstrated!

Mañjuśrī: I do not, Rev. Śāradvatīputra, demonstrate in such a way that even Arhats who have done what had to be done can understand it. In fact I demonstrate in such a way that no one can discern what I have said. Because enlightenment cannot be discerned by anyone; nor can it be fully known, seen, heard, or recalled; it has not been produced or stopped, and it cannot be pointed out or described. In so far as there is any enlightenment, it is neither existence nor non-existence. For there is nothing that should be fully known by enlightenment, nor does enlightenment fully know enlightenment. (224)

Śāradvatīputra: Has the Lord, then, not fully known the realm of Dharma?

Mañjuśrī: No, He has not. For the realm of Dharma is just the Lord. If the realm of Dharma were something that the Lord had fully known, then the realm of Non-production would be something that ought to be stopped. In fact, however, the realm of Dharma as such is enlightenment. Because there are no beings in it. Enlightenment is synonymous with the non-existence of all dharmas. It is thus that this realm of Dharma comes to be called thus. Because as the Buddha's domain all dharmas are undifferentiated. (225) The word "non-differentiation" does not intimate anything, since one cannot instruct anyone about it, either through the conditioned or the unconditioned. It carries no intimation, and that is why it is something which intimates nothing at all. For all dharmas intimate nothing at all. Because they do not manifest themselves in such a way that they could be objects of instruction.

Even[1] those who have engaged in the deadly sins have engaged in the unthinkable, and those who have engaged in the unthinkable have engaged in what is real. Because "real" is a word that implies no distinctions. Those who are endowed with the unthinkable Dharma are not destined for heaven, the states of woe, or Parinirvana. And why? Because neither the unthinkable nor Parinirvana has been set up for coming or going. (226) Even among those who have committed the four root-offences, the offences are quite groundless (lit. rootless). Because in non-production one can look for neither a root or a top. "A monk who has no roots" means a monk who is not established anywhere. That a dispute (*adhikaraṇam*) has arisen means that a surpassing (*adhika*) superimposition has taken place; and coursing in that surpassing superimposition one becomes worthy of the offerings of the world. Because that surpassing superimposition is self-identical. A believing monk is not worthy to enjoy gifts given in faith, whereas a non-believing monk is worthy to do so. (227) A proper monk is not worthy to enjoy those gifts, but an improper monk is worthy to do so. A monk whose clinging to existence is quite unimpaired (*asamupahatanetrīko*) is called "an Arhat whose outflows have dried up".

Śāradvatīputra: In what hidden sense, Mañjuśrī, do you say that?

Mañjuśrī: The sameness (*samatā*) is quite unimpaired, and it is

[1]The following contains some puns based on Vinaya terms which lose their point in English. Nor am I quite sure that I have always properly understood these monastic jokes. It would, however, be undesirable to abbreviate this holy scripture to suit one's own convenience.

the sameness which is the guide (*netrī*). Another synonym for an Arhat whose outflows have dried up is "one who has not risen above fear".

Śāradvatīputra: In what hidden sense, Mañjuśrī, do you say that? (228)

Mañjuśrī: He fears not even the least thing; what then will he rise above?

Śāradvatīputra: What then is a synonym for "the one who patiently accepts what fails to be produced"?

Mañjuśrī: He is so called because through him not even the least dharma has been produced.

Śāradvatīputra: What is a synonym for an "undisciplined monk"?

Mañjuśrī: It is the synonym of an Arhat whose outflows have dried up. (229). For what has been disciplined is the non-discipline, and not the discipline. With this hidden meaning do I say that "the monk who needs no discipline" is a synonym of an Arhat whose outflows have dried up.

Śāradvatīputra: What is a synonym for "someone who courses in the higher thought (*adhicitta*)"?

Mañjuśrī: That term is synonymous with "the ordinary people".

Śāradvatīputra: In what hidden sense, Mañjuśrī, do you say that?

Mañjuśrī: Because he is superior to them (*?adhikaroti*). (230)

Śāradvatīputra: Well said, Mañjuśrī, well said! You speak like an Arhat whose outflows have dried up.

Mañjuśrī: So it is, Rev. Śāradvatīputra, as you say! And yet although I am one whose outflows (*āsrava*) have dried up, I am not an Arhat. Because my longings (*āsā*) for the level of a Disciple or Pratyekabuddha have also dried up.

The Lord: Is it possible that a Bodhisattva, seated on the terrace of enlightenment, might be incapable of fully knowing the utmost, right and perfect enlightenment?

Mañjuśrī: Yes, it is. (231) Because in enlightenment even the least (*aṇu*) dharma does not exist and cannot be apprehended. That is why it is called the utmost (*anuttara*), right and perfect enlightenment. And that enlightenment is unproduced. In it no dharma exists or can be apprehended which could be seated on the terrace of enlightenment, or which could fully know enlightenment, or by which enlightenment could be fully known, or which could rise from the terrace of enlightenment. By this method, O Lord, one can see that the Bodhisattva, when seated on the terrace of enlightement, is incapable of fully knowing the utmost, right and perfect enlightenment.

The Lord: "Enlightenment", of what is that a synonym?

Mañjuśrī: Of the five deadly sins. Because as non-existent those five deadly sins have just the essential original nature of enlightenment, (232) and therefore this enlightenment has the essential original nature of the deadly sins. It fully knows the deadly sins, but it is not a meditational development which provides a direct intuition of all dharmas. For all dharmas are absolutely beyond all direct intuition. No one can fully know them, see, recognize or ascertain them. Such is this enlightenment. The conceited, however, put out that these dharmas can be fully known, etc. to: can be made into an object of direct intuition.

The Lord: In My presence does it occur to you, Mañjuśrī, that the Tathagata is with you?

Mañjuśrī: It does not, O Lord. And why? Because thus is Suchness (*tathatā*) (233), and as the Suchness is so is the Tathagata. For, O Lord, Suchness does not intimate the Tathagata, nor does the Tathagata intimate Suchness. And why? Because in the ultimate sense both Suchness and the Tathagata are non-existent. It does therefore not occur to me that the Tathagata is with me. On the contrary, "Tathagata" is a mere designation. Which is the duality in this Tathagata with reference to which it would occur to me that the Tathagata is with me?

The Lord: Have you any uncertainties about the Tathagata?

Mañjuśrī: None indeed, O Lord! Though I would have such uncertainties if there were any accomplishment, genesis or Parinirvana of a Tathagata. (234)

The Lord: Does it not occur to you that the Tathagata has been produced?

Mañjuśrī: That might occur to me if there were a genesis of the realm of Dharma.

The Lord: Do you not firmly believe that "Buddhas and Lords countless like the sand of the Ganges have gone to Parinirvana"?

Mañjuśrī: Is it not so, O Lord, that the Buddhas and Lords have one single domain, i.e. the unthinkable domain?

The Lord: So it is Mañjuśrī?

Mañjuśrī: Is it not so that the Lord stands there just now?

The Lord: So it is, Mañjuśrī. (235)

Mañjuśrī: These Buddhas and Lords, countless like the sands of the Ganges, have therefore never entered Parinirvana. Because they have one single domain, i.e. the unthinkable domain. Unthinkability, however, is not produced or stopped. When the Lord won full enlightenment, those who will in the future be Tathagatas, Arhats and fully enlightened Buddhas have therefore also known full enlightenment. Because unthinkability is not past, future or present. Therefore, O Lord, those who form the notion that the Tathagata has been produced, or that he will go to Parinirvana, will in consequence still further whirl around in the world and stay in it, and they will thereby prolong their sojourn in the world.

The Lord: You may therefore, Mañjuśrī, announce the fact that this unthinkability of a Tathagata (236) is unthinkable and inconceivable in front of a Tathagata, or of an irreversible Bodhisattva, or of an Arhat whose outflows have dried up. Because, having heard it, they will neither sanction nor reject it. For that which they think about is unthinkable and inconceivable.

Mañjuśrī: When, O Lord, all dharmas are unthinkable and inconceivable, who will be able to do any sanctioning or rejecting?

The Lord: Just as the Tathagata, so also the ordinary people are inconceivable.

Mañjuśrī: Are the ordinary people also in just that way inconceivable?

The Lord: They are. (237) Because all that can be thought is inconceivable.

Mañjuśrī: If, just as the Tathagata, so also the ordinary people are inconceivable, because also their state, like all dharmas, is inconceivable, then those who have set out for Parinirvana must already dwell in it. Because Parinirvana and inconceivability are one and the same thing. In consequence there can be no differentiation in inconceivability. Those, O Lord, who spoke of these dharmas as dharmas of the ordinary people, and of those as the dharmas of holy men, should in fact have said: "Let us, to begin with, honour the good spiritual friend, and thereafter let us cognize, 'these are the dharmas of ordinary people and those are the dharmas of holy men'." (238)

The Lord: Do you, Mañjuśrī, look for a Tathagata who is the foremost of all beings?

Mañjuśrī: I would do so if one being could be more perfect than another.

The Lord: Do you look for a Tathagata who is endowed with unthinkable dharmas?

Mañjuśrī: I would do so if anyone could be endowed with unthinkable dharmas.

The Lord: Do you again look for Disciples who have been disciplined by the Tathagata?

Mañjuśrī: I would do so if anyone could be subjected to the discipline of the unthinkable element. The production of a Buddha has not been set up (239) by the bestowal or by the removal of anything. Because this unthinkable element is established and uncontaminated, and in it one can apprehend no differentiation between Disciples, ordinary people, and so on.

The Lord: Do you then, Mañjuśrī, not look upon the Tathagata as an unsurpassed field of merit?

Mañjuśrī: Because of his non-existence is the Tathagata a field of merit, and for that reason he is also an unsurpassed field of merit. This field of merit is unsurpassed, because it is a field of merit, and not a field of demerit. It is a field of merit in the sense that therein no dharma can reach the fullness of its perfection or wane away. (240) A seed placed into it neither grows nor diminishes.

The Lord: In what hidden sense do you say that, Mañjuśrī?

Mañjuśrī: Because, O Lord, this field is a field of merit in the sense that it is unthinkable.

Thereupon on that occasion, through the Buddha's might, the earth shook in six ways. And the thought of 16,000 monks were freed from the outflows without any further clinging, and 700 nuns, 300 laymen, 40,000 laywomen and 6,000 niyutas of kotis of gods of the sphere of sense-desire produced the dispassionate, unstained eye of Dharma in dharmas.

The *Ven. Ānanda* thereupon rose from his seat, (241) put his robe over one shoulder, placed his right knee on the ground, bent forth his folded hands to the Lord, and said to the Lord: "What, O Lord, is the cause, what the reason, for the manifestation in the world of this great shaking of the earth?"

The Lord: This discourse on Dharma, Ānanda, called "The Exposition of the Field of Merit" has been taught in this very place by the Buddhas and Lords of the past. That is the cause, that is the reason for the manifestation in the world of this great shaking of the earth.

B. The Second Part

Śāradvatīputra: Unthinkably majestic (*śrī*), O Lord, is this Mañjuśrī. And why? For whatsoever may inspire him, all that inspires him as something unthinkable.

The Lord: So it is, Mañjuśrī, as the monk Śāradvatīputra has said: "Whatsoever inspires Mañjuśrī, the Crown Prince, all that inspires him as just something unthinkable".

Mañjuśrī: But, O Lord, it is not really the unthinkable that does inspire. There would have to be something thinkable if the unthinkable were to inspire. But what is not thinkable that is not anything. Each word,[1] O Lord, is unthinkable, but unthinkability is neither a word nor a no-word; nor can a non-word be pointed out.

The Lord: Do you then, Mañjuśrī, enter into the unthinkable concentration?

Mañjuśrī: No indeed, O Lord. I do not enter into the unthinkable concentration. And why? Because, O Lord, just I am (24a) the unthinkable concentration. I would enter into the unthinkable concentration it I were thinkable. "Concentration"—inconceivably unthinkable is that. How then can I enter into an unthinkable concentration? Moreover, O Lord, there occurred to me formerly, when I was a beginner, the idea that "one should enter into the unthinkable concentration". But, O Lord, now I no longer form with regard to that the idea that "I (may) enter into the unthinkable concentration". Just as a teacher of archery has formerly, when he trained himself on the stage of a beginner, had the idea "May I hit the cows' tethering posts!" But when he has become so accomplished that he can split a hair, then the idea no longer arises in him, "how can I hit the cows' tethering posts", because he is well trained in his ability to split a hair. But when he plans to split a hair, then he splits it just without any effort. Just so in the past, O Lord, I had the idea that "I (may) enter into the unthinkable concentration"; once (24b) having entered into this concentration I just dwell in it, and it no longer occurs to me that "one should dwell in this concentration". And why? Whenever I dwell in that concentration, then I always am one who has just a concept of this foremost concentration.[2]

Śāradvatīputra: But Mañjuśrī, the Crown Prince, does not, O Lord, rely on this[3] when he dwells in the unthinkable concentration. Is there again, O Lord, some other concentration which is more peaceful than that unthinkable concentration?

Mañjuśrī: How do you, Śāriputra, know that "this unthinkable concentration is peaceful"? And as to your other question whether "there is some other concentration than this unthinkable concentration?"—if, Reverend Sir, this unthinkable concentration could exist, then one might indeed be able to apprehend some other concentration (25a) more powerful than it.

[1]Sound, *śabdo.*

[2]*samādhi-vara-prajñaptikaḥ.* MDPL—"one who has an intimation" of this concentration.

[3]*yid mi rton na; na viśvasiti;* also: does not depend on this, or trust in it.

Śāriputra: But, Mañjuśrī, this unthinkable concentration does not exist, is not apprehended.

Mañjuśrī: Rev. Śāriputra, it is because this concentration is unthinkable that it does not exist and is not apprehended. Nevertheless, Rev. Śāriputra, not anyone is not a recipient of the unthinkable concentration, but all beings also are recipients of the unthinkable concentration.

The Lord: Well said, well said, Mañjuśrī, who you expound all these suchlike deep stations. For you are one who has performed his duties under the Jinas of the past, who has for long led a holy life in the baseless. Does it then occur to you, Mañjuśrī, that, having stood in the perfection of wisdom, one has spoken thus?

Mañjuśrī: If it occurred to me, O Lord, that "having stood in the perfection of wisdom one has spoken thus", then it would also occur to me that having stood in a basis one has spoken thus, having stood in the notion of a self one has spoken thus, etc., to: having stood in the notion of an existent (25b) one has spoken thus. Therefore (I do) not (think that) "having stood in the perfection of wisdom one has spoken thus!" And why? If I had a standing place in the perfection of wisdom, or a non-standing place, there would be no perfect wisdom. But on the contrary, O Lord, a standing in the self is the standing in perfect wisdom—(a standing which is in fact) a non-standing, a non-arising, an impossibility, a not coming into being. When one stands thus one has an unthinkable standing place, a standing place for (or: of) not any dharma—in that way is that standing place an unthinkable standing place, a standing place in the perfection of wisdom. "Perfect Wisdom," O Lord, that is the same as the non-production of all dharmas. What is called "perfect wisdom" is a term for the unthinkable element. And the unthinkable element is the non-production-element, and that again is the Dharma-element, and that again is the element in which there are no ideas which persist by force of habit,[1] and again that is the unthinkable element. The unthinkable element in its turn (26a) is the element of self, and that is the element of the perfection of wisdom. It is thus that the element of perfect wisdom, and the element of self, are not two nor divided. Therefore this is the unthinkable element. Whereby it is the unthinkable element, thereby it is the non-production element; whereby it is the non-production element, thereby it is the Dharma-element; whereby it is the Dharma-element, thereby it is the element in which there are no ideas which persist by force of habit;

[1] *niḥsamudācāra-dhātu*

whereby it is the element in which there are no ideas which persist by force of habit thereby it is the unthinkable element; whereby it is the unthinkable element, thereby it is the element of self; whereby it is the element of self thereby it is the element of perfect wisdom; whereby it is the element of perfect wisdom, thereby one does not gain full knowledge[1]; one who does not gain full knowledge, he does not exist; what does not exist, that is not destroyed; what is not destroyed, that is unthinkable; it is thus that the element of the Tathagata and the element of self are not two nor divided.

As to what the Lord has said, i.e. "the development of self is the development of perfect wisdom",—why that? "Perfect wisdom", O Lord, of the element of not-self is that a synonym. And why? One who would, O Lord cognize the element of not-self, he would cognize non-attachment; he who would cognize non-attachment, he would not cognize any dharma. And why? Because the unthinkable cognition is the Buddha-cognition, the cognition of not any dharma is the Buddha-cognition. And why? (26b) For there that cognition does not exist in the ultimate sense. And what does not exist in the ultimate sense, how will that turn the wheel of dharma? And when the cognition in the ultimate sense does not exist, then that cognition is non-attachment; and when that cognition is non-attachment, then that cognition is non-existence; and when that cognition is non-existence, then that cognition is unsupported; and when that cognition is unsupported, then that cognition is nowhere established; and when that cognition is nowhere established, then that cognition has not been produced, nor acquired, and it also will not be produced. And why? For that cognition is neither conditioned by the virtuous qualities nor conditioned by the absence of virtuous qualities. And why? For that cognition . . . . ? . . . . Therefore is that cognition unthinkable. And that cognition is Buddha-cognition. But by way of non-observation by this cognition also (not) any dharma has been fully known, or got at. Nor has that cognition come, either at its beginning or end. Nor is that cognition prior to its (non-) production, because of the fact of its non-production. What has not been produced, (27a) that is not destroyed, nor will it be produced. Nor is any other cognition similar to that cognition. Therefore that cognition is unthinkable and incommensurable. And also no beginning, middle or end of that cognition is got at. Nor is that cognition the same as[2] space, nor can one get at anything that

[1]*na samudāgacchati*
[2]*samam*

is equal to[1] that cognition or unequal[2] to it. Therefore that cognition equals the unequalled[3]. Nor is any other cognition got at which resembles this cognition; therefore this cognition does not resemble anything.

The Lord: And does this cognition, Mañjuśrī, stand up to any test (when threatened with disturbance by outside forces)[4]?

Mañjuśrī: Unmade is that cognition, therefore it stands up to any test. Just as it makes no sense to say of a Karshapana coin, before it has been stamped, that it is being tested for whether it consists of base metal or genuine gold, just so, O Lord, this cognition is unmade, not brought about, not generated, nor produced, not stopped, and therefore it stands up to any test.

The Lord: Who will believe (27b) when the exposition of the cognition of the Tathagata is thus expounded?

Mañjuśrī: They will, O Lord, not be doomed to birth-and-death, nor are they, doomed to Parinirvana, set free; they are not shaken by their individuality, and yet their greed, hatred and delusion are not extinct. And why? Because non-extinction does not get extinct, nor go to complete extinction. Not having transcended birth-and-death, they are reckoned among birth-and-death; not lacking in the path they do not produce a notion of the path. It is they who will understand the meaning of this teaching.

The Lord: Well said, well said, Mañjuśrī. Your words are well spoken.

Makākāśyapa: Will there be, in a future period, O Lord, somewhere hearers of this deep Dharma-Vinaya, and of this deep perfect wisdom, who will be more believing, more understanding, and more receptive? (28a)

The Lord: The monks and nuns, the laymen and laywomen in just this assembly will be those who in a later period will be the hearers of this deep Dharma-Vinaya and of this deep perfect wisdom, who will be more believing, more understanding, more receptive. A householder, Kāśyapa, or the son of a householder, who had lost a jewel worth a hundred thousand, would be sad, distressed, and sorry; when he had got it back again he would be happy and joyful, and his mental activities would be freed from his obsession. Just so those monks and nuns, laymen and laywomen, who do not hear that this deep perfect wisdom is unborn, not produced, gone to

[1]*samam*
[2]*viṣamam*
[3]*asamasamam* (Tib)
[4]*akupyam*

Nirvana in its essential original nature, etc. to: is non-existent, will think to themselves: How may we come to hear this deep perfect wisdom, which is unborn, not produced, gone to Nirvana in its essential original nature, etc. to: which is non-existent. And when at a future time they have heard it, they will become enraptured, happy, (28b) glad, and their mental activities are freed from their obsession. And they will say: To-day we have had a vision of the Tathagata, to-day we have honoured the Tathagata. Because we have heard this deep perfect wisdom, up to that it is unborn and unproduced, etc. to: that it is non-existent. The Gods of the Thirty-three become enraptured, and rejoice, when they have seen the flowers of the shade-giving Kovidāra tree open out their blossoms, because surely before long the shade-giving Kovidāra tree will be in full bloom; just so the monks and nuns, the laymen and laywomen, when they have heard this deep perfect wisdom—as unborn, unproduced, etc. to: as non-existent—will be enraptured and rejoice. And one must expect that they who are enraptured and rejoice will, in a future period, through just their rapture and rejoicing, before long reach the blossoming out of everything, i.e. the blossoming out of the Buddhadharmas. And this deep perfect wisdom, etc. to: (29a) which is unborn, non-existent, not produced, will abide and proceed even after the passing away of the Tathagata. In the future period it also should be cognized through the sustaining power of the Buddha, through the might of the Buddha. Therefore then, Kāśyapa, those who hear this deep perfect wisdom, up to: which is unborn, non-existent, not produced, for them this is not the first time that they have asked questions about it. Just as when a jeweller, on seeing a precious jewel, becomes enraptured, one can be sure that it is not for the first time that he has seen that precious jewel and that in the past that jeweller has often seen this jewel; just so those who, when they have heard this deep perfect wisdom as unborn, as non-existent, as not produced, become enraptured and rejoice, become elated, full of joy and zest—this is not the first time that they have heard it. Those who speak thus: Just so great is that light which comes spontaneously from the exposition of Mañjuśrī, the Crown Prince, of the perfection of wisdom as unborn, as non-existent, as not produced, they have in the past often honoured Mañjuśrī, the Crown Prince. (29b) It is as if some man had gone to some village or town or country on some business. Then at a later time someone else would have come to that (place) and he would praise that town, and would praise the loveliness of the gardens, of the countryside, of the parks, of the crowded lakes and ponds, of the flowers and fruits. And when the first man had heard that, he would find contentment. Filled with happiness he would again and again entreat the other one (and say): "just about that only speak to me!" That person can be sure that in the past he has experienced that town, and the loveliness of those gardens, of that countryside, of those lotus ponds, of those parks, of those crowded lakes and ponds, of those flowers and fruits. And why? (30a) Because when he has heard about it, he becomes contented, enraptured, elated, full of joy and zest. Just so with him who honours Mañjuśrī the Crown Prince, has repeatedly approached him, and, having heard (from him the perfection of wisdom as) unborn, non-existent and non-production, feels a sublime zest and rejoicing, produces a sublime zest and rejoicing. And he will say: "just about that only do I want to hear, i.e. just My exposition of the perfection of wisdom as unborn, non-existent, not produced".

Mahākāśyapa: Will those modes, tokens and signs which the Lord has expounded be also those of the believing sons and daughters of good family who will be in a future period?

The Lord: So it is, Kāśyapa, as you say. These modes, tokens and signs which I have just now expounded will be those of the believing sons and daughters of good family who will be in the future. (30b)

Mañjuśrī: How can there be a mode, token or sign of that dharma which is without mode and without token, when the perfection of wisdom is without mode, (token and) sign? The demonstration of dharma is without mode, without token, and without sign. How then can there be an exposition of that which is without mode, token and sign?

The Lord: Just these will be the modes, tokens and signs of those sons and daughters of good family who will firmly believe etc. to: who will study this deep perfect wisdom when it is demonstrated as unborn, as non-existent, as not produced. For in this elucidation of the perfection of wisdom one should see the elucidation of all dharmas, one should see the elucidation of unthinkability. The son or daughter of good family who wants to procure the wholesome roots of those who in the past coursed in the course of a Bodhisattva, (31a) by which they have fully known this perfect enlightenment, should listen to just this perfect wisdom, firmly believe in it, copy it out, bear it in mind, preach it, point it out, repeat it, spread it, study it, attend to it wisely, develop it, etc. to: he should worship and honour it, according to his ability and power, with flowers, incense, perfumes, garlands, unguents, aromatic powders, robes, umbrellas, banners, bells, flags, and ensigns, and with acts of worship involving lamps, offerings and oblations. The son or daughter of good family who wants to pass beyond the level of all Disciples and Pratyekabuddhas should listen to just this perfect wisdom, etc. to: should honour it. And so should one who wants to hear how the entrance into the irreversible stage takes place; (31b) and so should one who wants to firmly believe that all dharmas that there may be are the same in non-production; and so should one who wants to firmly believe in this exposition which says that "all dharmas also have not been fully known by the Tathagata". And why? For no dharma exists or can be got at, which would fully know, or through which one would fully know, or which one would fully know. And so one should listen to just this perfect wisdom, etc. to: should honour it, if one wants to firmly believe in that just this is the meaning[1]; or if one wants to firmly believe that "there is not any dharma that is not enlightenment". Or if one wants to discriminate all dharmas. And why? (32a) In that case the perfection of wisdom, the genetrix of the accomplishment of any dharma, respectively determines and demonstrates[2]. One should listen to just this perfect wisdom, etc. to: should honour it, if one wants to cross over to the conviction that all dharmas are neither defiled nor purified; or if one wants to firmly believe that all dharmas are not past, future, or present. And why? For non-production is neither past, nor future, nor present. And why? Because all dharmas come together in non-production[3]. One should listen to just this perfect wisdom, etc. to: one should honour it, if one wants to reach the absence of uncertainty in all these kinds of dharmas; and so should one who wants to hear how the turning of the wheel of Dharma, with its three revolutions and its twelve aspects, takes place, who wants to progress in it, firmly believe in it, (32b) accomplish it. And so should one who wants to irradiate all beings with friendliness, or who wants to stand in the perception of beings, or who wants to contend with the entire world, and who wants to understand the non-apprehension of the whole world, etc. to: one who wants to understand the non-production of all dharmas should train just in this perfect wisdom, by way of (its) non-observation.

Mañjuśrī: What are the qualities and what are the advantages of a perfect wisdom which has no qualities? How can one speak of the qualities or advantages of a perfect wisdom which is incapable of doing anything, neither raises up nor destroys anything, neither

[1] *arthagatim adhimoktu-kāmena*

[2] The text seems corrupt.

[3] *anutpāda-samavasaraṇā*

accepts nor rejects any dharma, is powerless to act and not at all busy, if its own-being cannot be cognized, if its own-being cannot be seen (33a), if it does not bestow any dharma, and does not obstruct any dharma, if it brings about the non-separateness of all dharmas, does not exalt the single oneness of all dharmas, does not effect the separateness of all dharmas, if it is not made, not something to be done, inexhaustible, if it does not destroy anything; if it is not a donor of the dharmas of the common people, of the dharmas of the Arhats, of the dharmas of the Pratyekabuddhas, of the dharmas of the Bodhisattvas, and not even of the dharmas of the Buddhas, and also does not take them away; if it does not toil in birth-and-death, nor cease toiling in Nirvana, neither bestows nor destroys the dharmas of a Buddha, if it is unthinkable and inconceivable, not something to be done, not something to be undone; if it neither produces nor stops any dharma, neither annihilates them nor makes them eternal; if it neither causes to come nor to go, brings about neither detachment nor non-detachment, neither duality nor non-duality, and if, finally, it is non-existent? (33b)

The Lord: Just so, Mañjuśrī, should one know the qualities of this perfect wisdom, up to its non-existence and its lack of power to act. But nevertheless, a Bodhisattva, a great being, should train in just this perfection of wisdom, in the manner of non-training, if he wants to train in, and to accomplish, that concentration of a Bodhisattva which allows him to see all the Buddhas, the Lords, if he wants to see their Buddha-fields, and to know their names, and if he wants to perform the supreme worship of those Buddhas and Lords, and to firmly believe in and to fathom their demonstration of Dharma.

Mañjuśrī: For what reason is this the perfection of wisdom?

The Lord: It is called "perfect wisdom" because it is neither produced nor stopped. And it is so because it is calmly quiet from the very beginning, because there is no escape, because there is nothing to be done, and, finally, because of its non-existence (*abhāva*). For what is non-existence, (34a) that is the perfection of wisdom. For that reason should one expect a development (*bhāvanā*) of the perfection of wisdom on the part of the Bodhisattvas. And she is the range of the Bodhisattvas, the great beings, the rangeing in all dharmas. And coursing therein a Bodhisattva, a great being, is called one who is "begotten in the range". Thus is that the range, i.e. a no-range, for those who belong to all the vehicles. And why? Because that range is not made; therefore is it called a "no-range".

Mañjuśrī: Coursing wherein will a Bodhisattva, a great being, quickly know full enlightenment?

The Lord: Coursing in the perfection of wisdom will a Bodhisattva, a great being, quickly know full enlightenment. There is a concentration called "One Single Array".[1] When he courses in it a Bodhisattva, a great being will quickly know full enlightenment. (34b)

Mañjuśrī: How should a Bodhisattva, a great being enter on the concentration on "One Single Array"? For what reason is the concentration on "One Single Array" so called?

The Lord: "One single array," of non-production is that a synonym. A son or daughter of good family who wants to enter on the concentration on one single array should first of all ask questions about the perfection of wisdom. After that he will enter on the concentration on one single array. And why? Because non-production is immaterial, undisturbed, unshakeable, unthinkable, beyond all reflection, inconceivable. A son or daughter of good family who wants to enter on the concentration on one single array, must live apart, must become one who is not fond of company; he must sit down with his legs crossed without paying attention to any sign; but he should pay attention to the Tathagata, and to all dharmas, by way of non-observation. And when he pays attention to a Tathagata, (35a) he should grasp his name. And when he has heard that name and apprehended it, he should sit down facing the direction in which that Tathagata is. And when he pays attention just to that Tathagata, through the attention to him all the past, future and present Buddhas and Lords are attended to. And why? One single is this Tathagatahood. Just as one single Tathagata has immeasurable Buddha-qualities and an immeasurable understanding, just so, when one has arrived at the concentration on one single array, from one single non-production immeasurable spheres of discourses on dharma must be expected, which proceed from it, and which have been taught by the Tathagatas, Arhats, fully Enlightened Ones. Just as many as have been kept in mind by Ānanda, so many discourses on dharma should be expected for him. And when he has accomplished this concentration on one single array, he would abide until the end of his life-span demonstrating dharma together with its foundations. And if again it occurs to some (35b) of those who belong to the vehicle of the Bodhisattvas, "which (of the many concentrations) then is this concentration on one single array", one should say to them: It is that which has been proclaimed as of unthinkable qualities. Having taken it upon yourselves in so far as it has been proclaimed as of unthinkable qualities, you should go on with it.

[1]*eka-vyūho samādhi*. Defined in *P*202 as "the reviewing of the duality of no dharma whatsoever".

To the extent that you go on with it, to that extent you shall see the qualities of the concentration; and according to the rule, as it has been expounded, you should sit down. But that concentration cannot be accomplished by those who have a basis in view, who have an entity in view, up to: who have an existent in view. It is as if someone had a priceless precious jewel, unpolished. Someone else would say to him: What is that jewel of yours, or which are its qualities? He would reply: You must know that the qualities of this jewel are measureless. Thereupon that person would give to the other person that jewel so that he might polish it (and say): "First of all polish this jewel, then you will know." (36a) Thereupon the other person, having taken that jewel, would polish it by means of the necessary apparatus. When he would thus polish that jewel, it would reveal its great worth. To the extent that he would polish that jewel, to that extent he would see its qualities. Just so, Mañjuśrī, as again and again that son or daughter of good family enters thus into the concentration and goes into it, so he will see its qualities. Just as for the disk of the sun there is no boundary beyond which it does not radiate rays, just so, Mañjuśrī, when one has resorted to the concentration on the one single array, has entered on it, has acquired it, there is no demonstration of dharma that is not a demonstration of the perfection of wisdom. Just so he would plunge into it: he would not see any dharma, since they are all unborn and unstopped. If in the four corners of the great ocean four men were to take water out of it, all that water which they take out would have one and the same taste, i.e. a salty taste; just so, Mañjuśrī, whatever demonstration of dharma (36b) has been demonstrated by me, all that has one single taste only, i.e. the taste of non-production, of non-existence, of dispassion, of emancipation. And whatever dharma a son of good family who has stood in this concentration, may demonstrate, all that he will demonstrate as of one taste only, i.e. the taste of non-production, of non-existence, of dispassion, of emancipation, of cessation. It is thanks to this concentration that that son of good family would teach, explain, expound, just as he plans, any dharma that I have demonstrated. It is thus that that son or daughter of good family, thanks to this concentration, will demonstrate all his demonstrations as (referring to) just the unborn, to the not produced, to non-existence, by way of non-observation. Furthermore, thanks to this concentration a Bodhisattva, a great being, having quickly fulfilled the dharmas which act as wings to enlightenment, shall quickly know full enlightenment. Furthermore, to the extent that a Bodhisattva, a great being, does not see the production of the element of self, etc., to: the element of dharma (37a) nor their stopping, or their single oneness, or their manifoldness, as he patiently accepts that, the Bodhisattva, the great being, shall quickly know full enlightenment. Or when he does not reflect on full enlightenment, then that patience of that son of good family is also fit for the acquisition of the dharmas of a Bodhisattva, of the dharmas of a Buddha, and he does not strive after enlightenment for the sake of Buddhahood. Of a son of good family who possesses that patience I say that he will quickly know full enlightenment. When he firmly believes, and is not cast down when he thinks that "all dharmas are the dharmas of a Buddha", then I say of him that he is irreversible from full enlightenment. And that son or daughter of good family should be called not lacking in all the dharmas of a Buddha, if, when they have heard this exposition, they feel neither stupefaction nor hesitation.

Mañjuśrī: Led on by which cause is full enlightenment?

The Lord: Not so, Mañjuśrī. (37b) Full enlightenment has no cause, nor is it led on by a cause. And why? Because non-production and non-existence have no cause, and are not led on by a cause. And why? Because all dharmas are unborn. Therefore then, Mañjuśrī, if a son or daughter of good family, when they have heard this exposition, feel no despondency, also then I say of them that they are irreversible from full enlightenment. Therefore then, Mañjuśrī, the monks and nuns, the laymen and laywomen, who, when this deep perfect wisdom is being expounded, are not cast down, etc., to: do not despond, they have gone to Me for refuge, they have left the world for My sake, I am their Teacher. A son or daughter of good family who has not trained in this deep perfect wisdom does not train in the training of a Bodhisattva. Just as any living beings, or seeds, or grasses, shrubs, herbs and trees (38a) that may grow anywhere all depend on the great earth, just so any wholesome dharmas that there may be on the part of Bodhisattvas and great beings, that undergo growth, growing up, and abundance, and that do not go back on full enlightenment—they are all upheld by the perfection of wisdom.

Mañjuśrī: As to this exposition of perfect wisdom by the Lord, will there be of that exposition of the perfection of wisdom here in Jambudvipa, in the villages, towns, or countryside, any recipients, etc., to: any expositors?

The Lord: Those who, when they have heard just this exposition of perfect wisdom just now, produce the vow: "may we hear just this exposition of the perfection of wisdom again after we have passed through this present birth!", they will hear it, etc. to: they will develop it in extenso—through the fact of non-development. I do not call those (endowed with) weak wholesome roots (38b) who will hear this deep perfect wisdom, and who, having heard it, will acquire a sublime zest and rejoicing. If there is somebody who wants to hear from you, Mañjuśrī, this exposition of perfect wisdom, you should say to him: may you not, son of good family, feel despondency, or be devoid of faith when you have barely heard it! And why? For not of any dharma has the accomplishment been expounded, nor its production, destruction, or acquisition—be it the dharmas of the common people, of those in training, of the adepts, of Pratyekabuddhas or of Buddhas.

Mañjuśrī: If some monk or nun, layman or laywoman, would say to me: "What dharmic sermon has to-day come from the Tathagata?"—I would tell them: "A sermon which does not obstruct any dharma". And why? Because where there is no production, there can also be no obstruction. (39a) But it is not easy for any being to understand that sermon. And why? Because no being can here be apprehended. Furthermore I would tell him: "That demonstration of Dharma was called 'non-genesis'." And why? Because all dharmas are the same as non-production. For just as in this sermon the dharmas of the common people are not destroyed by the dharmas of the Arhats, just so no obtainment superior to that of the Arhats is explained here. Furthermore, I would tell him: "In this demonstration of Dharma there is not anyone who has won Parinirvana, who does win Parinirvana, or who will win Parinirvana". And why? Because a being can absolutely not be apprehended. Thus I would speak if I were asked. Furthermore, if one who wants to hear from me this deep perfect wisdom, were to ask: "what conversation (= sermon) have you had with the Lord to-day?", I would tell him: "If you wish to hear this conversation, you must not with your mind draw near the idea 'I will hear', nor must you produce a thought (to the effect) 'I will hear'." (39b) Having produced a wisdom which is like unto the wisdom of an illustory man will you be capable of understanding this demonstration of Dharma. If you wish to hear this demonstration of Dharma, then you must stand like that. Just as (one can(not) see) the footprints of a bird in the sky, just so one can (not) hear this demonstration of Dharma. If you wish to hear this demonstration of Dharma, then you must not make it into either a dual or a non-dual object. And why? For there is here no proclamation of duality or of non-duality. If you wish to hear this demonstration of Dharma, then you must not destroy the notion of self, you must not transcend the false views, you must not look for support in the Buddhadharmas, nor must you shake off the dharmas of the common people. If someone who wants to hear (about perfect wisdom) were to ask me, I would tell him that, instruct him thus, establish him thus. If that enquiring son or daughter of good family would just so stand and be inclined, then I would, when he has been established in this seal of insight, later on and subsequently demonstrate this deep perfection of wisdom (40a) as unborn, as non-existent, as non-production.

The Lord: Well said, Mañjuśrī. Well taught is this speech of yours. And furthermore you might say to that son or daughter of good family that someone who wants to see the Tathagata should develop (*bhāvayitavyā*) just this perfection of wisdom, by way of (its) non-existence (*abhāva*). A son or daughter of good family should train in just this perfection of wisdom—if they want to honour the Tathagata, and that by way of non-observation; if they want to acknowledge that the Tathagata is their teacher, and that by way of not turning towards him[1]; or if they want to accomplish the skill in all concentrations, by way of (their) non-existence. And why? Because (everything) is unconditioned, unproduced and non-existent, up to the cognition of the all-knowing which is endowed with the best of all modes. One should train in just this perfection of wisdom if one wants to conform to (the conviction that) "all dharmas can escape, there is no dharma that cannot escape", (40b) and that by way of (their) non-existence. (In fact) all dharmas cannot escape, and there is no dharma that can escape. And why? Because of the non-production of all dharmas. One should train in just this perfection of wisdom if one wants to understand this, and also the fact that this is by way of (their) non-existence. And so if one wants to remain undismayed by the thought that all beings course towards their enlightenment, that there is no dharma that does not course towards enlightenment, and that this is so by way of the non-existence (of dharmas). And why? All dharmas are the same as enlightenment; and as all dharmas are the same as enlightenment, so is enlightenment; and as enlightenment, so are all beings; and as all beings so is the coursing. Because it does not exist is all coursing a non-coursing. And that is enlightenment; and what is enlightenment that is non-production and it has not come forth. A son or daughter of good family who does not want to become dismayed by all these kinds of dharmas, (41a) should train in just this perfection of wisdom, etc. to: by way of non-existence and non-production. And

[1]In this passage the Sanskrit omits much that is in the Tibetan.

also the Tathagata's supernatural power as well as His playfulness has been made manifest in the perfection of wisdom. And why? Because undefinable is this perfection of wisdom and she does not manifest anything. And I call irreversible those monks and nuns, those laymen and laywomen if they will take up from this perfection of wisdom even one verse of four lines, study it, bear it in mind, preach it, etc. to: illuminate it. What do I say of them who progress to its true meaning![1] Destined for enlightenment should these sons and daughters of good family be called, established in the Buddha's domain if, on hearing this deep perfection of wisdom up to its being unborn, non-existent and unproduced—they do not tremble, are not frightened nor terrified, but continue to firmly believe in it. Destined they will be for all the Buddhadharmas. And to this, Mañjuśrī, I affix My seal, (41b) the seal which the Buddhas have ordained, which the Tathagatas have discerned and to which all the Arhats have given their assent. I affix this seal which is the sameness of (all) the Buddhas; it has been explained as non-attachment to everything including the Buddhadharmas[2]. And sealed with this seal a son or daughter of good family who belongs to the vehicle of the Bodhisattvas cannot possibly go to the places of woe nor can he possibly descend to the level of a Disciple or Pratyekabuddha.

Thereupon at that time *Śakra*, chief of gods and the gods of the Thirty-three worshipped this perfection of wisdom with heavenly sandalwood powder, with heavenly mandarava flowers, with heavenly blue lotuses, white Nymphaea aesculenta and white lotuses, and with heavenly musical instruments. They strewed and scattered (the powder and the flowers) over the Lord and over Mañjuśrī, the Crown Prince, and said:

"This is a wholesome root which assures that those whom you have sealed with this seal will again and again worship this unsurpassed jewel of the Dharma and will hear it again and again."

Śakra, chief of gods, said furthermore: (42a) Let us also, O Lord, make efforts in this deep perfection of wisdom, etc. up to: which is unproduced. Here in Jambudvipa sons and daughters of good family of this kind will with little trouble come to hear of the exposition of the practice of the perfection of wisdom and will go on doing so until they have accomplished all the Buddhadharmas. And those

[1]Lit. Thusness, *tathatvāya*.

[2]I have not understood this. imāṃ mudrāṃ sthāpayāmi samatā ca buddhānām. iyam asaṅgatā paridīpanā yāvat sarvabuddhadharmeṣu nirdiṣṭā. rgya 'di ni mñam-pa ñid-du(!) rtog-pa rnams-la(!) bshag go. 'di ni saṅs-rgyas-kyi chos thams-cad-kyi bar-du yaṅ chags-pa med-pa yoṅs-su bstan-pa'o.

sons and daughters of good family who, when they have heard it, will firmly believe, and who, firmly believing it, will take it up, study it, etc. to: recite it, they should be quite certain that we gods will bring them to mind.

The Lord: So it is, Kauśika. One should be able to see in those sons and daughters of good family the accomplishment of all the Buddhadharmas, and one should expect them to be destined for full enlightenment. (42b)

Mañjuśrī: Sustain, O Lord, sustain, O Sugata, this deep exhibition of the perfection of wisdom for the sake of those sons and daughters of good family!

Thereupon at that time, immediately after this had been said, through the Buddha's might the earth shook in six ways. And immediately after that the Lord smiled. Thereupon the great trichiliocosm was irradiated by a great light, because the Tathagata was miraculously sustaining this exposition of the perfection of wisdom.

Mañjuśrī: These, O Lord, are the symptoms[1] of the Tathagata sustaining this exposition of the perfection of wisdom?

The Lord: So it is, Mañjuśrī. These signs show that this exposition of the perfection of wisdom is being sustained (by Me). Through these symptoms should one know that: Sustained (43a) is this exposition of the perfection of wisdom. And all those should be known as sealed with this seal who do not revile or sanction any dharma. And why? Because without basis would be either the reviling or the sanctioning. Therefore I have affixed this seal for the sake of those who have been sealed with it. Because they will neither demonstrate nor discriminate any dharma. And why? In the ultimate sense all dharmas are unproduced.

Thus spoke the Lord. Enraptured Mañjuśrī the Crown Prince, the great Bodhisattvas and the great Disciples, as well as the whole world with its gods, men, asuras, garuḍas and gandharvas rejoiced at the Lord's teaching.

[1]*nimittāni*, usually "signs". The talk of the "Seal" and the "Magical Sustaining" of the P.P. belong to the Tantric aspects of the teaching.

THE PERFECTION OF WISDOM IN 500 LINES

Homage to all Buddhas and Bodhisattvas!

Thus have I heard at one time. The Lord dwelt at Rājagṛha, on the Vulture-Peak, together with a large congregation of monks and a great number of Bodhisattvas. Thereupon the Lord said to the Venerable Subhūti: Form, Subhūti, is non-existence,[1] it has a poorish kind of existence, it is existence.[2] And so for the other skandhas, for the eye, etc., to: mind-consciousness. In that way the foolish common people have in three ways[3] not wisely cognized that form as it really is,[4] and they do settle down[5] in that form, aspire for[6] it, cover it up.[7] Having settled down in that form, having aspired for it, having covered it up, they do not go forth[8] by the vehicle of the Disciples or that of the Pratyekabuddhas, how much less by the great vehicle. Thus settling down, aspiring and covering up, they experience old age and death for a long time among the beings in hell, among the animals, ghosts, gods and men. (171a) But the wise[9] have wisely cognized that form in these three ways as it really is, do not settle down in it, do not aspire for it, but open it up,[10] and so they go forth even by the great vehicle, how much more so by the vehicle of the Disciples and Pratyekabuddhas. And they do not experience old age and death among the beings in hell, among animals, ghosts, gods and men. As to the production and cessation of form, etc., Subhūti: The production of form, etc., is its non-production. The non-production of form, etc., has the own-being of the non-production of form.[11] The Bodhisattva, the great being who has wisely known that own-being of the non-production of form, etc., as it really is, gains full knowledge[12] of the non-production

[1]dṅos-po med-pa=abhāva, avastuka

[2]dṅos-po ṅan-pa dṅos-po yod-pa

[3]le'u gsum-du, tri-parivarta

[4]yaṅ-dag-pa ji-lta-ba bshin du=yathāvad

[5]mṅon-par shen to, abhiniviśante

[6]mṅon-par bsgrub bo, abhinirharanti

[7]sgrib-par byed-do, āvārayanti

[8]ṅes-par 'byuṅ-bar mi 'gyur, na niryānti

[9]mkhas-pa

[10]mṅon-par sgrub-par mi byed-kyi gsal-bar byed do (uttānīkaronti)

[11]gzugs-kyi skye-ba med-pa gaṅ yin-pa de ni, gzugs-kyi skye-ba med-pa'i raṅ-bshin te

[12]yaṅ-dag-par sgrub bo, samudānayati, samudāgacchati

of form, etc. (172a) Whoever says of form that it is "the self or something belonging to a self",[1] he belongs to[2] the outsiders and foolish common people, and I have called him "one of wrong views".[3] And so do those who say of form that "it comes about caused by past deeds"[4] or "it comes about caused by the work of a creator",[5] or "it has no cause and no condition"; and those who say that "form has the mark of molesting, feeling that of experiencing, perception that of noting, the impulses that of together-making, and consciousness that of being aware"[6]; and those who say that "form is ill and not calm",[7] "the stopping of form is ease and calm"; and likewise those who say that "form is nothing at all",[8] or that "the teaching of the Lord according to which form, etc., is without own-being, is non-production, non-stopping, calm from the very beginning, and has by its own nature reached final Nirvana—all these teachings are not made with a hidden intention, are not (173a) made with an intention,[9] and should be known just according to the letter.[10]

If form exists,[11] then there is taught with regard to form a settling down, and a production. If form exists, then there proceeds[12] with regard to form a defilement and an abiding. If form exists, then with regard to form there is control[13] by purification, and a continuity.[14] If form exists, when the Bodhisattvas have forsaken and fully comprehended it, they have gained mastery of the teaching. If form exists, when this is forsaken and fully comprehended, one gains mastery of the correct teaching.[15] If form exists, when this is forsaken and fully comprehended, one is endowed with the white

[1]bdag gam bdag-gi, ātmam vā ātmīyam vā

[2]phyogs-la gnas-pa, pakṣe sthita

[3]log-par lta'o, mithyādṛṣṭika

[4]sṅon byas-pa'i rgyu-las byuṅ-ba'o (pūrvakarmahetuka)

[5]dbaṅ-phyug-gis sprul-pa'i rgyu-las (īśvara-nirmaṇa-hetuka)

[6]S 1410: rūpaṇa ('jigs-pa; here: gzugs-su yod-pa); anubhava; anudgrahaṇa ('dzin-pa, here: kun-tu śes-pa); abhisaṃskāra; vijānana

[7]sdug-bsṅal-ba ste, rab-tu ma shi-ba'o; duḥkh(it)a, apraśānta

[8]med-pa ñid do

[9]ldem-por (abhisaṃdhi) dgoṅs-pa (abhiprāya) ma yin-pa, dgoṅs-pa ma yin-pa ste

[10]sgra ji-bshin-pa ñid-du, tathāruta eva

[11]gzugs ni yod de

[12]'jug-par 'gyur-ba'o, pravartate

[13]dbaṅ-du gyur-pa, vaśībhūta

[14]byor-ba(pa); Das=nar-nar

[15]yaṅ-dag-par bstan na

dharmas, has gained mastery over all dharmas, and dwells in the great happiness. (174a)

Whichever Bodhisattva, Subhuti, does not in form review merely form, merely ill, he apprehends a self in form. When he apprehends a self in form, then he apprehends the view of self in form. When he apprehends the view of self in form, then he apprehends everything in form. When he apprehends everything in form, then he does not apprehend everything in form. When in form he apprehends everything and does not apprehend everything, then his apprehending is perfected.[1] Dwelling in this apprehending, he does not go forth by the vehicle of the Disciples or Pratyekabuddhas, how much less by the great vehicle. (174b) But when a Bodhisattva reviews in form merely form, merely ill, then he does not apprehend a self in form. When he does not apprehend a self in form, he does not apprehend the view of a self in form. When he does not apprehend the view of a self in form, he does not apprehend everything in form; when he does not apprehend everything in form, then he apprehends everything in form. When, not apprehending everything in form, he does not apprehend anything, then that apprehending of his is perfected. Dwelling in that non-apprehension, he goes forth by the vehicle of the Disciples and Pratyekabuddhas, how much more so by the great vehicle. (175a)

If anyone, Subhuti, does not review form, etc., as a mere unreal imagination,[2] as a mere delusion,[3] he apprehends form in form. When he apprehends form in form, he apprehends the view of form in form. When he apprehends the view of form in form, then he does not apprehend everything in form. When, not apprehending everything in form, he does not apprehend everything, that apprehending of his is perfected. Dwelling in this apprehending he cannot go forth by the vehicle of the Disciples and Pratyekabuddhas, how much less by (175b) the great vehicle. If anyone, Subhuti, does review form, etc., as a mere unreal imagination, as a mere delusion, then he does not apprehend form in form; when he does not apprehend form in form, he does not apprehend the view of form in form; when he does not apprehend the view of form in form, he does not apprehend everything in form. When he does not (176a) apprehend everything in form, then he apprehends everything in form. When, not apprehending everything in form, he does not apprehend everything (anything), that apprehending of his has been perfected. Dwelling in

[1]yoṅs-su grub-pa yin no; parinispadyati?

[2]yaṅ-dag-pa ma yin-pa kun brtags-pa, abhūtaparikalpa

[3]'khrul-pa, bhrāntu

this non-apprehension he will even go forth by the great vehicle, how much more by the vehicle of the Disciples and Pratyekabuddhas. (176b)

When, Subhuti, a Bodhisattva settles down in form, etc., according to the letter,[1] then, forming the idea of conventional expression,[2] he forms the idea of the view of individuality,[3] and likewise that of craving for becoming,[4] and of the search for cessation[5]—and that is a token[6] of his not having comprehended form, etc. When a Bodhisattva does not settle down in form, etc., according to the letter, he does not form the idea of conventional expression, does not form the idea of the view of individuality, and also not that of craving for becoming, or of the search for cessation—and that is a token of his having comprehended form. (177a)

With regard to any conditions of form which he has taken hold of, the Bodhisattva has these three seeds[7] of a truly purified[8] thought, i.e. the seed of a thought of resolute faith,[9] the seed of a thought of disgust,[10] the seed of the thought of unforgetfulness.[11] The Bodhisattva, Subhuti, should with regard to form produce those three thoughts: a thought of not settling down, a thought which is inseparable,[12] a thought of purification.[13] The Bodhisattva, Subhuti, reviews of the thought of form the production, the non-production, the growth,[14] the co-production[15]; when he reviews thus, he quickly wins the supreme enlightenment. (177a) If, Subhuti, the Bodhisattva reviews in form existence,[16] and likewise existence or non-existence, then he should be known as a Bodhisattva who does not know. But when a Bodhisattva reviews in form non-existence,[17] and likewise the non-being of non-existence,[18] then he should be known as a Bodhisattva

[1]yathāruta
[2]tha-sñad kun-tu spyod na, vyavahāram samudācaran
[3]'jig tshogs-la lta-bar, satkāyadṛṣṭim
[4]'byuṅ-ba'i sred-pa, bhavatṛṣṇā
[5]'jig-pa (vyaya, bhaṅga, etc.) yoṅs-su tshol-ba (paryeṣaṇā)
[6]rtags, liṅga
[7]sa-bon, bīja
[8]rnam-par byaṅ-bar 'gyur-ba'i, vyavadānabhūtasya
[9]mos-pa, adhimukti
[10]yid 'byuṅ-ba, nirvid
[11]chud mi g(z?)on-pa, avipranāśa
[12]bral-bar med-pa (aviyoga)
[13]yoṅs-su sbyoṅ-ba, pariśodhana?
[14]cher skye-ba
[15]mñam-du skye-ba
[16]yod-pa ñid
[17]yod-pa ma yin-pa
[18]yod-pa yaṅ ma yin-pa med-pa yaṅ ma yin-par

who knows. (178a) If, Subhuti, a Bodhisattva wishes to concentrate[1] his thought on form, and if, when he resolves on form, his thought shakes with regard to form, is upset, and becomes disturbed,[2] he should be known as a Bodhisattva of inferior resolve.[3] But if, Subhuti, a Bodhisattva wishes to concentrate his thought on form, and when his thought is resolved on form, it is not tied, fastened or attached[4] to form, then he should be known as a Bodhisattva of good resolve.[5] (178b)

The Bodhisattva who has set out[6] so as to fully comprehend that dharmas are without marks, to appease suffering and to become wholly fixed[7] on Nirvana, he should be known as one who has set out. When he has thus set out, the Bodhisattva will quickly win the supreme enlightenment. The Bodhisattva (thus) achieves (what he set out to do),[8] i.e. that he should know marklessness, appease ill and be wholly fixed on Calm. When a Bodhisattva wisely knows form as it really is as disappearance,[9] as all-round illumination,[10] and also the dharmas which dwell in it and enter into it, then he quickly wins the supreme enlightenment. (179a) When he has cognized the dharmas which are disappearance, which are just all-round illumination, and has entered into them and dwells in them, then he attains enlightenment. The Bodhisattva does not apprehend in form the search for form. Not having made form disappear,[11] he will, having penetrated also the Dharmahood of form, quickly win the supreme enlightenment. Having searched without apprehending dharmas,[12] seeing no existence in thought,[13] having well understood the nature of Dharma, the wise attains to enlightenment.

The Bodhisattva, (179b) skilled in the non-existence of form, endowed with the dread of form, never moving away from the Dharma-element of form, quickly wins the supreme enlightenment. Wisely skilled in non-existence, endowed with terror,[14] never moving

[1] mñam-par bshag-par
[2] bskyod, kun-tu bskyod, rnam-par bskyod na
[3] mos-pa ṅan-pa'i, hīnādhimuktika
[4] mi 'dogs kun-tu mi 'dogs rnam-par mi 'dogs
[5] mos-pa bzaṅ-po
[6] shugs na, abhirūḍha?
[7] gcig-tu ṅes-par bya-ba
[8] bsgrub-par byed
[9] snaṅ-ba med-pa, anābhāsa, apratibhāsa; (mi snaṅ-ba, antardhāna, Das)
[10] kun-tu snaṅ-ba, samantāvabhāsa
[11] mi snaṅ-ba byas śiṅ
[12] rab-tu btsal-nas mi dmigs chos
[13] sems-la dṅos-por mi snaṅ-ba
[14] rnam-par 'jig

away from the Dharma-element, he attains all-knowledge. When, Subhuti, the Bodhisattva has wisely known with regard to form as it really is that it is devoid of advantage,[1] that it has no advantage,[2] and that it has a great advantage,[3] he will quickly gain the supreme enlightenment. Because the Bodhisattvas have cognized the absence of advantage, (180a) the lack of advantage, the great advantage, therefore they attain the great enlightenment.

The Bodhisattva, Subhuti, should with regard to form, etc., comprehend five kinds of *greed*, and forsake them, i.e. the greed for the discrimination of form,[4] the greed for imaginations,[5] the greed for information,[6] greed and the great greed. When the Bodhisattva has with regard to form, etc., forsaken these five kinds of greed, he does not apprehend the own-being of form. Not apprehending the own-being of form, he does not apprehend form in form. Not apprehending form in form, he apprehends form in form. When he apprehends form in form, then in fact he does not apprehend form in form. When he does not apprehend the apprehension of that form, then, having transcended form in all ways, he is sure to win the supreme enlightenment.

The Bodhisattva, Subhuti, (181a) should with regard to form, etc., comprehend five kinds of *hate*, and forsake them, i.e. the hate (arising from) the discrimination of form and discoursing on it,[7] the hate from imagining and from discoursing on it, the hate from the information and the discoursing on it, hate and the great hate. The Bodhisattva should, with regard to form, etc., comprehend and forsake five kinds of *delusion*, i.e. the delusion which consists in deludedness,[8] the delusion caused by deludedness,[9] the delusion not caused by deludedness, delusion and the great delusion. When, etc. The Bodhisattva should, with regard to form, etc., comprehend and forsake five kinds of *conceit*, i.e. the conceit from great learning,[10] the conceit from being puffed up,[11] overweening conceit,[12] conceit

[1]don daṅ bral-ba
[2]don med-pa
[3]don chen-por, mahārtham
[4]rnam-par rtog-pa'i 'dod-chags, vikalpa-rāga
[5]rab-tu rtog-pa'i, prarūpaṇā
[6]rnam-par rtogs-pa'i
[7]rnam-par rtog-gi daṅ, rnam-par dpyod-pa'i she-sdaṅ
[8]'khrul-pa'i gti-mug
[9]'khrul-pa'i rgyu'i
[10]maṅ-du thos-pa'i
[11]mṅon-par mtho-ba'i
[12]mṅon-pa'i ṅa-rgyal, abhimāna

and the great conceit. When, etc. (183b) The Bodhisattva should with regard to form comprehend and forsake five kinds of *false views*, i.e. the false view of the perverted own-being,[1] the false view which thinks that something exists, the false view of negation,[2] false view, the great false view. When, etc. (184a) The Bodhisattva should with regard to form comprehend five kinds of *doubt*,[3] i.e. the doubt about dharma, the doubt about one's destiny[4] and its ills, the doubt about Nirvana, the Buddhas and Bodhisattvas, doubt, and the great doubt. (185a)

The Bodhisattva, searching for form, demonstrating the dharmic nature of form, perfectly purifying with regard to form his deeds of body, speech and mind, searches for that form as it is spoken of, as it is demonstrated, as it is uttered, and thus demonstrates Dharma. When he therein perfectly purifies the deeds of his body, speech and mind, he should be known as a Bodhisattva who badly searches for form, as a Bodhisattva whose speech with regard to form does not accord with the good Dharma, (185b) as a Bodhisattva who with regard to form is not perfectly pure in his deeds of body, speech and mind. When, however, the Bodhisattva, searching for form, demonstrating the dharmic nature of form, perfectly purifying with regard to form his deeds of body, speech and mind, does search for that form as not being as it is spoken of, as it is demonstrated, as it is uttered, and thus he demonstrates Dharma. When he therein purifies his deeds of body, speech and mind, he should be known as a Bodhisattva who well searches for form, whose words are expressive of truly real deeds of speech,[5] as a Bodhisattva who is perfectly pure in his deeds of body, speech and mind. (186a)

When, Subhuti, the Bodhisattva wishes to concentrate this thought on form, and becomes resolved on that form,[6] and apprehends in form both the form which should be resolved upon[7] and the form which is the object of resolve,[8] then the Bodhisattva either demonstrates as it really is in the form which is the object of resolve that which should be resolved upon, or he demonstrates as it really is in that which should be resolved upon that which has been resolved upon,

[1]raṅ-bshin phyin-ci log-gi
[2]skur-pa 'debs-pa'i, apavādaka
[3]yid-gñis za-ba
[4]'gro-ba
[5]yaṅ-dag-pa'i ṅag-gi las-kyi
[6]gzugs de-la naṅ-du mos-na
[7]mos-par bya-ba'i gzugs, adhimoktavya-rūpam
[8]mos-pa'i gzugs, adhimukti-rūpam

(186b) and he should be known as a Bodhisattva who demonstrates with regard to form that which is unreal. And why? There is no separation[1] between the marks of the form that should be resolved upon and the form which is the object of resolve. If there were a separation of marks between the form which should be resolved upon and the form which is the object of resolve, then in that which should be resolved upon the beings with various inclinations[3] apprehend as different[2] that which is the same view.[4] With regard to that which, like a dream, etc., cannot be apprehended, there can be no resolve; but the foolish common people see reality[5] in that form; may they not turn[6] on the perfected progress in undiscriminating resolve[7] to the form that should be resolved upon! Thus, Subhuti, with regard to what should be resolved upon the beings with various inclinations do not become different with regard to the same view[8]; apprehending this as a resolve on the unapprehended, as on a dream, etc., also the foolish common people see no reality in it, and they turn on the perfected progress in undiscriminating resolve to the form that should be resolved upon. For that reason should the Bodhisattva see no separation between the marks of the form that should be resolved upon and the form which is the object of resolve, except that the form which should be resolved upon as it really is has been fully attained,[9] and also the form which is resolved upon by a view with a sign.[10] (187a) Thereby another meaning[11] appears.[12] Thus in the Bodhisattva who has vision[13] the perception of the form that should be resolved upon is annihilated.[14] And he thinks to himself: Having cognized[15] that the form which should be resolved

[1]gud

[2]sems-can mos-pa tha-dad-pa rnams

[3]tha-dad-par

[4]daṅ mtshuṅs-par lta-ba

[5]gzugs-la de kho na mthoṅ-bar 'gyur shiṅ

[6]rjes-su 'jug-par mi 'gyur-ba shig na, anuvartayati, imp.

[7]rnam-par mi rtog-pa'i (avikalpanā, nirvikalpa) mos-pa (adhimukti) grub-pa('i) (niṣpanna?) rigs-pa-la (pratipatti)

[8]daṅ mtshuṅs-par lta-ba tha-dad-par ma gyur-pa ciṅ, samam dṛṣṭi nānam na bhavanti

[9]yaṅ-dag-par byuṅ-ba, samudgata

[10]mtshan-ma (nimitta) daṅ bcas-(pa'i) (sa)lta-ba'i (dṛṣṭi)

[11]don gshan

[12]snaṅ ṅo, saṃdṛśyate

[13]mthoṅ-ba, darśana

[14]rnam-par 'jig ste, vināśyati, vibhavati?

[15]rig-nas, viditvā

upon is, and that the form which is resolved upon is not feasible[1] and is not, with regard to form a deluded thought is apprehended; but he annihilates the perception of "form which is an object of resolve", "form which is an object of resolve," he annihilates the perception of all forms; having annihilated with regard to both kinds of form all perceptions, he does not apprehend all forms; not having apprehended all forms, he apprehends forms deludedly; having apprehended forms deludedly, he apprehends with regard to form the cause[2] of deludedness; having apprehended with regard to form the cause of deludedness, he fully attains[3] with regard to form the undeluded dharma[4]; having fully attained with regard to form the undeluded dharma, he fully attains with regard to form the dharmas which are an outpouring of non-delusion[5]; thereby he fully attains with regard to form the deluded, and how much more so the undeluded dharmas. With regard to form relying on[6] the undeluded dharmas and the dharmas which are an outpouring of non-delusion, he develops all the Buddhadharmas, matures beings, purifies the Buddhafield, and quickly wins the supreme enlightenment. When the Bodhisattva demonstrates dharma thus, he is one who demonstrates it correctly. (188a/189a)

The Bodhisattva, Subhuti, should develop with regard to form these five kinds of *friendliness:* (1) the friendliness which adduces[7] the good dharma, (2) the friendliness which brings worldly benefits, (3) the friendliness which brings supramundane benefits, (4) friendliness, (5) the great friendliness. He should with regard to form, etc., develop these five kinds of *compassion:* (1) the compassion with what is disagreeable,[8] (2) the compassion with association (with what one dislikes), (3) the compassion with dissociation (from what one likes), (4) compassion, (5) the great compassion. (189b) He should with regard to form, etc., develop these five kinds of *sympathetic joy:* (1) the sympathetic joy which rejoices at[9] the outflowing of help[10] which leads to faith in the good Dharma; (2) the sympathetic joy

[1] rigs-par 'gyur gyi med na, na yujyate
[2] rgyu; hetu, karaṇa
[3] yaṅ-dag-par bsgrub bo, samudāgacchati (-nayati)
[4] 'khrul-pa med-pa'i chos
[5] 'khrul-pa med-pa'i rgyu mthun-pa'i chos, abhrānti-niṣyanda-dharma
[6] brten-nas, āśritya, āgamya
[7] ñe-bar sgrub-pa'i, upasaṃhāra
[8] mi sdug-pa, aśubha
[9] rjes-su yi raṅ-ba'i, anumodana
[10] brlan-pa (pariṣyanda) daṅ, phan 'dogs-pa (anugraha) daṅ

which rejoices at the outflowing of help which leads to worldly benefits; (3) the sympathetic joy which rejoices at the outflowing of help which leads to supramundane benefits; (4) sympathetic joy; (5) the great sympathetic joy. He should with regard to form, etc., develop these five kinds of *impartiality:* (1) the impartiality which consists in the undefiled deportment[1] with regard to inferior views[2]; (2) the impartiality which consists in undefiled deportment and the avoidance[3] (190a) of all faults; (3) the impartiality which consists in undefiled deportment and the acquisition[4] of all virtues; (4) impartiality; (5) the great impartiality.

The Bodhisattva, Subhuti, who has exerted himself[5] in the *perfection of giving*, should with regard to form, etc., develop these five kinds of giving: (1) the gift of the pledge[6]; (2) the fleshly gift and that which gives[7] fearlessness, (3) the gift of the Dharma,[8] (4) the gift, (5) the great gift. (190b) The Bodhisattva who has exerted himself in the *perfection of morality* should with regard to form, etc., develop these five kinds of morality: (1) the morality which consists in the effort[9] which indicates[10] that one has taken it upon oneself[11] (to observe the precepts), (2) the morality which consists in the effort (to win) the trances, (3) the morality which consists in an effort without outflows, (4) the morality, (5) the great morality. The Bodhisattva who has exerted himself in the *perfection of patience* should with regard to form, etc., develop these five kinds of patience: (1) the patience which endures whatever harm beings may inflict,[12] (2) the patience which endures the pain when one's limbs are cut off,[13] (3) the patience which consists in the meditation on Dharma,[14] (4) the patience, (5) the great patience. (191a) The Bodhisattva who has exerted himself in the *perfection of vigour* should with regard to form, etc., develop these five kinds of vigour: (1) the vigour which

[1] kun-nas ñon moṅs-pa med-pa'i brtul-ba'i, asaṃkleśa-??

[2] lta-ba ṅan-pa, hīnadṛṣṭi

[3] yoṅs-su spaṅ-ba, parivarjana

[4] yoṅs-su bsdu-ba, parigraha?

[5] brtson-pas, prayukta?

[6] dam-bca'-ba, pratijñā

[7] sgrub-pa'i, ?

[8] chos sgrub-pa'i

[9] sdom-pa; saṃyama, saṃvara, saṃlekha

[10] brda'-can-gyi

[11] yaṅ-dag-par blaṅs-pa, samādāna

[12] sems-can gnod-pa byed-pa-la ji mi sñam-pa'i; sattva, ahitāvahita?, —, na iti

[13] sdug-bsṅal (duḥkha) daṅ-du len-pa (aṅgīkar-)

[14] chos-la ṅes-par sems-pa'i. dharme nidhyāna-

consists in always bearing in mind[1] the prediction[2]; (2) the vigour in the avoidance of all faults, (3) the vigour in the accumulation[3] of all virtues, (4) the vigour, (5) the great vigour. The Bodhisattva who has exerted himself in the *perfection of concentration* should with regard to form, etc., develop these five kinds of concentration: (1) the concentration with speech[4] which gives occasion for bliss,[5] (2) the worldly concentration with speech which gives no occasion for bliss and which is pure from the very beginning, (3) the supramundane concentration, (4) the concentration, (5) the great concentration. The Bodhisattva who has exerted himself in the *perfection of wisdom* should with regard to form, etc., develop these five kinds of wisdom: (1) the wisdom which is based on[6] the concentration with words which gives occasion for bliss, (2) the wisdom based on the worldly concentration with speech which gives no occasion for bliss and is pure from the very beginning, (3) the wisdom which is based on the supramundane concentration, (4) the wisdom, (5) the great wisdom. (192a)

The Bodhisattva who is endowed with the *tending of the good friends* should tend, with regard to form, etc., the good friends in five ways: (1) the tending which consists in listening to them,[7] (2) the tending which consists in honouring them,[8] serving them[9] and (following) their method of training[10]; (3) the tending which consists in the earnest desire to please them, (4) the tending, (5) the great tending. When the Bodhisattva thus tends the good friends, he also acquires the means of salvation,[12] he begets much merit, and will soon go forth to the supreme enlightenment.

The Bodhisattva, Subhuti, who has exerted himself in the *worship of the Tathagata* should, with regard to form, etc., worship the Tathagata by five kinds of worship: (1) the worship which emits[13] a

[1]ba-thon (Peking: kha-ton) bya-bar sems-pa'i
[2]luṅ ston-pa, vyākaraṇa; Peking: luṅ nod-pa
[3]yoṅs-su bsdu-ba, parigraha
[4]tshig 'bru-la, vyañjane
[5]ltos-pa'i dge-ba'i
[6]brten-pa, āśrita
[7]mñan-pas
[8]bsñen-bkur bya-ba, paryupāsitavya
[9]yoṅs-su spyod-pa, paricaryā
[10]bslab-pa'i cho-ga daṅ mthun-pas (Peking in Rep: bshin-du), śikṣā-vidhi-sama?
[11]nan-tan-gyi mgu-bar byas-pas, ārādhana
[12]rnam-par thar-pa'i thabs, vimokṣa upāya
[13]ñe-bar bsgrub-pa, upsaṃharati

variety of praises,[1] (2) the worship which brings forth[2] adherence and reverence,[3] (3) the worship which leads to the earnest desire to become without faults,[4] (4) the worship, (5) the great worship. When the Bodhisattva thus has exerted himself in the worship of the Tathagata, he is lauded[5] by the Buddhas and Lords in the countless world-systems in the ten directions, and he is adhered to and revered[6] by the world with its gods, men and Asuras. Innumerable beings he should mature. He purifies the Buddhafield, and quickly he will know the supreme enlightenment.

When a Bodhisattva who is endowed with the perfection of giving develops, with regard to form, etc., the giving with sign, then he does not quickly fulfil the perfection of giving; but when he develops the signless giving, then he quickly does fulfil the perfection of giving. And how does the Bodhisattva with regard to form, etc., develop the giving with sign and the signless giving? If with regard to form, etc., he resolves on[7] giving, and apprehends the giving which should be resolved upon,[8] or the giving which is the object of resolve,[9] the Bodhisattva should be known as one who with regard to form develops the giving with sign. If with regard to form, etc., he resolves on giving, in the sense that form can in its own-being not be apprehended, and so its existence cannot be apprehended and its nature cannot be apprehended; he then does not apprehend the giving which should be resolved upon, but he apprehends the giving which is the object of resolve. Then the Bodhisattva should be known as one who with regard to form develops the signless giving. (194a) And the same applies to morality, etc., to: wisdom.

The Bodhisattva should, with regard to form, etc., fully know the *Emptiness-concentration*. What then is with regard to form, etc., the Emptiness-concentration? When with regard to form, etc., he has apprehended the emptiness of non-existence, and likewise the emptiness of existence, and the emptiness of nature, then that one-pointedness of thought is the Emptiness-concentration. It is thus that by the Bodhisattva the Emptiness-concentration should be fully

[1]bstod-pa,stuti, etc.
[2]ñe-bar bsgrub-pa, upasaṃharati
[3]'thob-pa daṅ, bkur-bsti
[4]nan-tan-gyis ma ñes-par bya-ba'i
[5]bsṅags-pa brjod-pa mdzad do
[6]thob-pa daṅ, bkur-bsti rñed do
[7]mos na, adhimucyate
[8]mos-par bya-ba'i sbyin-pa
[9]mos-pa'i sbyin-pa

known. And the Bodhisattva should also fully know the *signless concentration* with regard to form, etc. And what is with regard to form, etc., the signless concentration? When the Bodhisattva attends in form, etc., to the emptiness of non-existence of form, and so to the emptiness of existence and the emptiness of nature; and when with regard to form, etc., the sign of existence is stopped,[1] the consciousness which follows after the sign of non-existence is left behind,[2] likewise the consciousness which follows after the sign of existence is left behind; with the consciousness which follows after the signs of existence and non-existence are left behind, that one-pointedness of thought, that is with regard to form, etc., the signless concentration. It is thus that the Bodhisattva should fully know the signless concentration. (195a) The Bodhisattva should, with regard to form, etc., also fully know the *wishless concentration*. And what is with regard to form, etc., the wishless concentration? When he has obtained[3] with regard to form, etc., the emptiness concentration and the signless concentration, then with regard to form, etc., the sign of non-existence becomes an apprehension of aversion,[4] and likewise the sign of existence becomes an apprehension of aversion, and the sign of existence and of non-existence becomes an apprehension of aversion; this one-pointedness of thought, that should by the Bodhisattva with regard to form, etc., be fully known as the wishless concentration.

The Bodhisattva should, with regard to form, etc., fully know *impermanence* in its three meanings, i.e. the meaning that it is not,[5] the meaning of destruction,[6] the meaning of being both with and without taints. (196a) The Bodhisattva should fully know with regard to form, etc., *ill* in its three meanings, i.e. the meaning of settling down, the meaning that it has the three kinds of marks, the meaning of being in bondage.[7] The Bodhisattva should also with regard to form, etc., fully know *Not-self* in its three meanings, i.e. the meaning of the not-selfness of non-existence, likewise the meaning of the not-selfness of existence, and the meaning of the not-selfness of nature. Moreover, the Bodhisattva should with regard to form, etc., fully know the *Quiet Calm of Nirvana* in its three meanings, i.e. the

[1] 'gags te
[2] dṅos-po med-pa'i mtshan-ma'i rjes-su 'braṅ-ba'i rnam-par śes-pa daṅ yaṅ bral
[3] rñed-pas, labdhvā
[4] mi mthun-pa'i dmigs-pa, pratikūla upalabdhi
[5] med-pa'i don
[6] rnam-par 'jig-pa, vināśa
[7] 'brel-ba

meaning of the complete calm of non-existence, the meaning of the calm of existence, the meaning of the pure calm which it has by its own nature.

When the Lord had spoken thus, the Venerable Subhuti was delighted and rejoiced at the words of the Lord; and so did the monks and nuns, the laymen and laywomen, and the whole world with its gods, men, Asuras and Gandharvas.

THE DIAMOND SUTRA

Homage to the Perfection of Wisdom,
the Lovely, the Holy!

1. Introduction

1*a*. *The Convocation of the Assembly*

1. Thus have I heard at one time. The Lord dwelt at Śrāvastī, in the Jeta Grove, in the garden of Anāthapindada, together with a large gathering of monks, consisting of 1,250 monks, and with many Bodhisattvas, great beings. Early in the morning the Lord dressed, put on his cloak, took his bowl, and entered the great city of Śrāvastī to collect alms. When he had eaten and returned from his round, the Lord put away his bowl and cloak, washed his feet, and sat down on the seat arranged for him, crossing his legs, holding his body upright, and mindfully fixing his attention in front of him. Then many monks approached to where the Lord was, saluted his feet with their heads, thrice walked round him to the right, and sat down on one side.

1*b*. *Subhuti makes a request*

2. At that time the Venerable Subhuti came to that assembly, and sat down. Then he rose from his seat, put his upper robe over one shoulder, placed his right knee on the ground, bent forth his folded hands towards the Lord, and said to the Lord: "It is wonderful, O Lord, it is exceedingly wonderful, O Well-Gone, how much the Bodhisattvas, the great beings, have been helped with the greatest help by the Tathagata, the Arhat, the Fully Enlightened One. It is wonderful, O Lord, how much the Bodhisattvas, the great beings, have been favoured with the highest favour by the Tathagata, the Arhat, the Fully Enlightened One. How then, O Lord, should a son or daughter of good family, who have set out in the Bodhisattva-vehicle, stand, how progress, how control their thoughts?"

After these words the Lord said to the Venerable Subhuti: "Well said, well said, Subhuti! So it is, Subhuti, so it is, as you say! The Tathagata, Subhuti, has helped the Bodhisattvas, the great beings with the greatest help, and he has favoured them with the highest favour. Therefore, Subhuti, listen well, and attentively! I will teach you how those who have set out in the Bodhisattva-vehicle should stand, how progress, how control their thoughts." "So be it, O Lord," replied the Venerable Subhuti, and listened to the Lord.

2. The Bodhisattva's Career

2a. The Vow of a Bodhisattva

3. The Lord said: Here, Subhuti, someone who has set out in the vehicle of a Bodhisattva should produce a thought in this manner: "As many beings as there are in the universe of beings, comprehended under the term 'beings'—egg-born, born from a womb, moisture-born, or miraculously born; with or without form; with perception, without perception, and with neither perception nor non-perception—as far as any conceivable form of beings is conceived: all these I must lead to Nirvana, into that Realm of Nirvana which leaves nothing behind. And yet, although innumerable beings have thus been led to Nirvana, no being at all has been led to Nirvana." And why? If in a Bodhisattva the notion of a "being" should take place, he could not be called a "Bodhi-being". "And why? He is not to be called a Bodhi-being, in whom the notion of a self or of a being should take place, or the notion of a living soul or of a person."

2b. The Practice of the Perfections

4. Moreover, Subhuti, a Bodhisattva who gives a gift should not be supported by a thing, nor should he be supported anywhere. When he gives gifts he should not be supported by sight-objects, nor by sounds, smells, tastes, touchables, or mind-objects. For, Subhuti, the Bodhisattva, the great being should give gifts in such a way that he is not supported by the notion of a sign. And why? Because the heap of merit of that Bodhi-being, who unsupported gives a gift, is not easy to measure. What do you think, Subhuti, is the extent of space in the East easy to measure?—Subhuti replied: No indeed, O Lord.—The Lord asked: In like manner, is it easy to measure the extent of space in the South, West or North, downwards, upwards, in the intermediate directions, in all the ten directions all round?—Subhuti replied: No indeed, O Lord.—The Lord said: Even so the heap of merit of that Bodhi-being who unsupported gives a gift is not easy to measure. That is why, Subhuti, those who have set out in the Bodhisattva-vehicle, should give gifts without being supported by the notion of a sign.

2c. Buddhahood and the thirty-two marks

5. The Lord continued: "What do you think, Subhuti, can the Tathagata be seen by the possession of his marks?"—Subhuti replied: "No indeed, O Lord. And why? What has been taught by

the Tathagata as the possession of marks, that is truly a no-possession of no-marks." The Lord said: "Wherever there is possession of marks, there is fraud, wherever there is no-possession of no-marks there is no fraud. Hence the Tathagata is to be seen from no-marks as marks."

2d. Buddahood and the Dharmabody

2da. The Dharmabody as the body of teachings

6. Subhuti asked: Will there be any beings in the future period, in the last time, in the last epoch, in the last 500 years, at the time of the collapse of the good doctrine who, when these words of the Sutra are being taught, will understand their truth?—The Lord replied: Do not speak thus, Subhuti! Yes, even then there will be such beings. For even at that time, Subhuti, there will be Bodhisattvas who are gifted with good conduct, gifted with virtuous qualities, gifted with wisdom, and who, when these words of the Sutra are being taught, will understand their truth. And these Bodhisattvas, Subhuti, will not be such as have honoured only one single Buddha, nor such as have planted their roots of merit under one single Buddha only. On the contrary, Subhuti, those Bodhisattvas who, when these words of the Sutra are being taught, will find even one single thought of serene faith, they will be such as have honoured many hundreds of thousands of Buddhas, such as have planted their roots of merit under many hundreds of thousands of Buddhas. Known they are, Subhuti, to the Tathagata through his Buddha-cognition, seen they are, Subhuti, by the Tathagata with his Buddha-eye, fully known they are, Subhuti, to the Tathagata. And they all, Subhuti, will beget and acquire an immeasurable and incalculable heap of merit.

And why? Because, Subhuti, in these Bodhisattvas (1) no perception of a self takes place, (2) no perception of a being, (3) no perception of a soul, (4) no perception of a person. Nor do these Bodhisattvas have (5) a perception of a dharma, or (6) a perception of a no-dharma. (7) No perception or (8) non-perception takes place in them.

And why? If, Subhuti, these Bodhisattvas should have a perception of either a dharma, or a no-dharma, they would thereby seize on a self, a being, a soul, or a person. And why? Because a Bodhisattva should not seize on either a dharma or a no-dharma. Therefore this saying has been taught by the Tathagata with a hidden meaning: "Those who know the discourse on dharma as like unto a raft should forsake dharmas, still more so no-dharmas."

2db. The Dharmabody as the result of Gnosis

7. The Lord asked: What do you think, Subhuti, is there any dharma which the Tathagata has fully known as "the utmost, right and perfect enlightenment", or is there any dharma which the Tathagata has demonstrated?—Subhuti replied: No, not as I understand what the Lord has said. And why? This dharma which the Tathagata has fully known or demonstrated—it cannot be grasped, it cannot be talked about, it is neither a dharma nor a no-dharma. And why? Because an Absolute exalts the Holy Persons.

2dc. The Dharmabody as the result of Merit

8. The Lord then asked: What do you think, Subhuti, if a son or daughter of good family had filled this world system of 1,000 million worlds with the seven precious things, and then gave it as a gift to the Tathagatas, Arhats, Fully Enlightened Ones, would they on the strength of that beget a great heap of merit?—Subhuti replied: Great, O Lord, great, O Well-Gone, would that heap of merit be! And why? Because the Tathagata spoke of the "heap of merit" as a non-heap. That is how the Tathagata speaks of "heap of merit".—The Lord said: But if someone else were to take from this discourse on dharma but one stanza of four lines, and would demonstrate and illuminate it in full detail to others, then he would on the strength of that beget a still greater heap of merit, immeasurable and incalculable. And why? Because from it has issued the utmost, right and perfect enlightenment of the Tathagatas, Arhats, Fully Enlightened Ones, and from it have issued the Buddhas, the Lords. And why? For the Tathagata has taught that the dharmas special to the Buddhas are just not a Buddha's special dharmas. That is why they are called "the dharmas special to the Buddhas".

3. The Range of the Spiritual Life

3a. The four Great Saints

9*a*. The Lord asked: What do you think, Subhuti, does it occur to the Streamwinner, "by me has the fruit of a Streamwinner been attained"? Subhuti replied: No indeed, O Lord. And why? Because, O Lord, he has not won any dharma. Therefore is he called a Streamwinner. No sight-object has been won, no sounds, smells, tastes, touchables, or objects of mind. That is why he is called a "Streamwinner". If, O Lord, it would occur to a Streamwinner, "by me has a Streamwinner's fruit been attained", then that would be in him a seizing on a self, seizing on a being, seizing on a soul, seizing on a person.—*9b*. The Lord asked: What do you think, Subhuti, does it then occur to the Once-Returner, "by me has the fruit of a Once-Returner been attained"?—Subhuti replied: No indeed, O Lord. And why? Because there is not any dharma that has won Once-Returnership. That is why he is called a "Once-Returner".—*9c*. The Lord asked: What do you think, Subhuti, does it then occur to the Never-Returner "by me has the fruit of a Never-Returner been attained"?—Subhuti replied: No indeed, O Lord. And why? Because there is not any dharma that has won Never-Returnership. Therefore is he called a "Never-Returner".—*9d*. The Lord asked: What do you think, Subhuti, does it then occur to the Arhat, "by me has Arhatship been attained"?—Subhuti replied: No indeed, O Lord. And why? Because no dharma is called "Arhat". That is why he is called an Arhat. If, O Lord, it would occur to an Arhat, "by me has Arhatship been attained", then that would be in him a seizing on a self, seizing on a being, seizing on a soul, seizing on a person.—*9e*. And why? I am, O Lord, the one whom the Tathagata, the Arhat, the Fully Enlightened One has pointed out as the foremost of those who dwell in Peace. I am, O Lord, an Arhat free from greed. And yet, O Lord, it does not occur to me, "an Arhat am I and free from greed". If, O Lord, it could occur to me that I have attained Arhatship, then the Tathagata would not have declared of me that "Subhuti, this son of good family, who is the foremost of those who dwell in Peace, does not dwell anywhere; that is why he is called 'a dweller in Peace, a dweller in Peace indeed' ".

3b. The Bodhisattva's thought of Enlightenment

10*a*. The Lord asked: What do you think, Subhuti, is there any dharma which the Tathagata has learned from Dipankara, the Tathagata, the Arhat, the Fully Enlightened One? Subhuti replied: Not so, O Lord, there is not.

3c. The Bodhisattva and his Pure Land

10*b*. The Lord said: If any Bodhisattva would say, "I will create harmonious Buddhafields", he would speak falsely. And why? "The harmonies of Buddhafields, the harmonies of Buddhafields," Subhuti, as no-harmonies have they been taught by the Tathagata. Therefore he spoke of "harmonious Buddhafields".

3d. The Bodhisattva's Final Nirvana

10*c*. Therefore then, Subhuti, the Bodhisattva, the great being, should produce an unsupported thought, i.e. a thought which is nowhere supported, a thought unsupported by sights, sounds, smells, tastes, touchables or mind-objects.

Suppose, Subhuti, there were a man endowed with a body, a huge body, so that he had a personal existence like Sumeru, king of mountains. Would that, Subhuti, be a huge personal existence? Subhuti replied: Yes, huge, O Lord, huge, O Well-Gone, would his personal existence be. And why so? "Personal existence, personal existence," as no-existence has that been taught by the Tathagata; for not, O Lord, is that existence or non-existence. Therefore is it called "personal existence".

3e. The merit derived from Perfect Wisdom

11. The Lord asked: What do you think, Subhuti, if there were as many Ganges rivers as there are grains of sand in the large river Ganges, would the grains of sand in them be many?—Subhuti replied: Those Ganges rivers would indeed be many, much more so the grains of sand in them.—The Lord said: This is what I announce to you, Subhuti, this is what I make known to you—if some woman or man had filled with the seven precious things as many world systems as there are grains of sand in those Ganges rivers, and would give them as a gift to the Tathagatas, Arhats, Fully Enlightened Ones—what do you think, Subhuti, would that woman or man on the strength of that beget a great heap of merit?—Subhuti replied: Great, O Lord, great O Well-Gone, would that heap of merit be, immeasurable and incalculable.—The Lord said: But if a son or daughter of good family had taken from this discourse on dharma but one stanza of four lines, and were to demonstrate and illuminate it to others, then they would on the strength of that beget a still greater heap of merit, immeasurable and incalculable.

12. Moreover, Subhuti, that spot of earth where one has taken from this discourse on dharma but one stanza of four lines, taught or illumined it, that spot of earth will be like a shrine for the whole world with its gods, men and Asuras. What then should we say of those who will bear in mind this discourse on dharma in its entirety, who will recite, study, and illuminate it in full detail for others! Most wonderfully blest, Subhuti, they will be! And on that spot of earth, Subhuti, either the Teacher dwells, or a sage representing him.

4. The First Ending

13*a*. Subhuti asked: What then, O Lord, is this discourse on dharma, and how should I bear it in mind?—The Lord replied: This discourse on dharma, Subhuti, is called "Wisdom which has gone beyond", and as such should you bear it in mind!

5. Transcendentality

5a. The dialectical nature of reality

And why? Just that which the Tathagata has taught as the wisdom which has gone beyond, just that He has taught as not gone beyond. Therefore is it called "Wisdom which has gone beyond". 13*b*. What do you think, Subhuti, is there any dharma which the Tathagata has taught?—Subhuti replied: No indeed, O Lord, there is not.—13*c*. The Lord said: When, Subhuti, you consider the number of particles of dust in this world system of 1,000 million worlds—would they be many?—Subhuti replied: Yes, O Lord. Because what was taught as particles of dust by the Tathagata, as no-particles that was taught by the Tathagata. Therefore are they called "particles of dust". And this world-system the Tathagata has taught as no-system. Therefore is it called a "world system".—13*d*. The Lord asked: What do you think, Subhuti, can the Tathagata be seen by means of the thirty-two marks of the superman?—Subhuti replied: No indeed, O Lord. And why? Because those thirty-two marks of the superman which were taught by the Tathaggata, they are really no-marks. Therefore are they called "the thirty-two marks of the superman".

5b. The supreme excellence of this teaching

13*e*. The Lord said: And again, Subhuti, suppose a woman or a man were to renounce all their belongings as many times as there are grains of sand in the river Ganges; and suppose that someone else, after taking from this discouse on Dharma but one stanza of four lines, would demonstrate it to others. Then this latter on the strength of that would beget a greater heap of merit, immeasurable and incalculable.

14*a*. Thereupon the impact of Dharma moved the Venerable Subhuti to tears. Having wiped away his tears, he thus spoke to the Lord: It is wonderful, O Lord, it is exceedingly wonderful, O Well-Gone, how well the Tathagata has taught this discourse on Dharma. Through it cognition has been produced in me. Not have I ever before heard such a discourse on Dharma. Most wonderfully blest will be those who, when this Sutra is being taught, will produce a true perception. And that which is true perception, that is indeed no perception. Therefore the Tathagata teaches, "true perception, true perception".—14*b*. It is not difficult for me to accept and believe this discourse on Dharma when it is being taught. But those beings who will be in a future period, in the last time ,in the last epoch, in the last 500 years, at the time of the collapse of the good doctrine, and who, O Lord, will take up this discourse on Dharma, bear it in mind, recite it, study it, and illuminate it in full detail for others, these will be most wonderfully blest.—14*c*. In them, however, no perception of a self will take place, or of a being, a soul, or a person. And why? That, O Lord, which is perception of self, that is indeed no perception. That which is perception of a being, a soul or a person, that is indeed no perception. And why? Because the Buddhas, the Lords have left all perceptions behind.

14*d*. The Lord said: So it is, Subhuti. Most wonderfully blest will be those beings who, on hearing this Sutra, will not tremble, nor be frightened, or terrified. And why? The Tathagata has taught this as the highest (paramā) perfection (pāramitā). And what the Tathagata teaches as the highest perfection, that also the innumerable (aparimāṇa) Blessed Buddhas do teach. Therefore is it called the "highest perfection".

5c. Selfless Patience and perfect inner freedom

14*e*. Moreover, Subhuti, the Tathagata's perfection of patience is really no perfection. And why? Because, Subhuti, when the king of Kalinga cut my flesh from every limb, at that time I had no perception of a self, of a being, of a soul, or a person. And why? If, Subhuti, at that time I had had a perception of self, I would also have had a perception of ill-will at that time. And so, if I had had a perception of a being, of a soul, or of a person. With my superknowledge I recall that in the past I have for five hundred births led the life of a sage devoted to patience. Then also have I had no perception of a self, a being, a soul, or a person.

Therefore then, Subhuti, the Bodhi-being, the great being, after he has got rid of all perceptions, should raise his thought to the utmost, right and perfect enlightenment. He should produce a thought which is unsupported by forms, sounds, smells, tastes, touchables, or mind-objects, unsupported by dharma, unsupported by no-dharma, unsupported by anything. And why? All supports have actually no support. It is for this reason that the Tathagata teaches: By an unsupported Bodhisattva should a gift be given, not by one who is supported by forms, sounds, smells, tastes, touchables, or mind-objects.

5d. The existence and non-existence of beings

14*f*. And further, Subhuti, it is for the weal of all beings that a

Bodhisattva should give gifts in this manner. And why? This perception of a being, Subhuti, that is just a non-perception. Those all-beings of whom the Tathagata has spoken, they are indeed no-beings. And why? Because the Tathagata speaks in accordance with reality, speaks the truth, speaks of what is, not otherwise. A Tathagata does not speak falsely.

5e. Truth and Falsehood

14*g*. But nevertheless, Subhuti, with regard to that dharma which the Tathagata has fully known and demonstrated, on account of that there is neither truth nor fraud.

In darkness a man could not see anything. Just so should be viewed a Bodhisattva who has fallen among things, and who, fallen among things, renounces a gift. A man with eyes would, when the night becomes light and the sun has arisen, see manifold forms. Just so should be viewed a Bodhisattva who has not fallen among things, and who, without having fallen among things, renounces a gift.

5f. The Merit acquired, its presuppositions and results

14*h*. Furthermore, Subhuti, those sons and daughters of good family who will take up this discourse on Dharma, will bear it in mind, recite, study, and illuminate it in full detail for others, they have been known, Subhuti, by the Tathagata with his Buddha-cognition, they have been seen, Subhuti, by the Tathagata with his Buddha-eye, they have been fully known by the Tathagata. All these beings, Subhuti, will beget and acquire an immeasurable and incalculable heap of merit.—15*a*. And if, Subhuti, a woman or man should renounce in the morning all their belongings as many times as there are grains of sand in the river Ganges, and if they should do likewise at noon and in the evening, and if in this way they should renounce all their belongings for many hundreds of thousands of millions of milliards of aeons; and someone else, on hearing this discourse on Dharma, would not reject it; then the latter would on the strength of that beget a greater heap of merit, immeasurable and incalculable. What then should we say of him who, after writing it, would learn it, bear it in mind, recite, study and illuminate it in full details for others?

15*b*. Moreover, Subhuti, (1) unthinkable and (2) incomparable is this discourse on Dharma. (3) The Tathagata has taught it for the weal of beings who have set out in the best, in the most excellent vehicle. Those who will take up this discourse on Dharma, bear it in mind, recite, study and illuminate it in full detail for others, the

Tathagata has known them with his Buddha-cognition, the Tathagata has seen them with his Buddha-eye, the Tathagata has fully known them. All these beings, Subhuti, will be blest with an immeasurable heap of merit, they will be blest with a heap of merit unthinkable, incomparable, measureless and illimitable. All these beings, Subhuti, will carry along an equal share of enlightenment. And why? (4) Because it is not possible, Subhuti, that this discourse on Dharma could be heard by beings of inferior resolve, nor by such as have a self in view, a being, a soul, or a person. Nor can beings who have not taken the pledge of Bodhi-beings either hear this discourse on Dharma, or take it up, bear it in mind, recite or study it. That cannot be.

15*c*. (1) Moreover, Subhuti, the spot of earth where this Sutra will be revealed, that spot of earth will be worthy of worship by the whole world with its Gods, men and Asuras, worthy of being saluted respectfully, worthy of being honoured by circumambulation,—like a shrine will be that spot of earth.—16*a*. And yet Subhuti, those sons and daughters of good family, who will take up these very Sutras, and will bear them in mind, recite and study them, they will be humbled,—well humbled they will be! And why? The impure deeds which these beings have done in their former lives, and which are liable to lead them into the states of woe,—in this very life they will, by means of that humiliation, (2) annul those impure deeds of their former lives, and (3) they will reach the enlightenment of a Buddha.—16*b*. With my superknowledge, Subhuti, I recall that in the past period, long before Dipankara, the Tathagata, Arhat, fully Enlightened One, during incalculable, quite incalculable aeons, I gave satisfaction by loyal service to 84,000 million milliards of Buddhas, without ever becoming again estranged from them. But the heap of merit, Subhuti, from the satisfaction I gave to those Buddhas and Lords without again becoming estranged from them—compared with the heap of merit of those who in the last time, the last epoch, the last five hundred years, at the time of the collapse of the good doctrine, will take up these very Sutras, bear them in mind, recite and study them, and will illuminate them in full detail for others, it does not approach one hundredth part, not one thousandth part, nor a one hundred thousandth part, not a ten millionth part, nor a one hundred millionth part, nor a 100,000 millionth part. It does not bear number, nor fraction, nor counting, nor similarity, nor comparison, nor resemblance.—16*c*. (4) If moreover, Subhuti, I were to teach the heap of merit of those sons and daughters of good family, and how great a heap of merit they will at that time beget and acquire, beings would become frantic and confused. Since, however, Subhuti, the Tathagata has taught this discourse on Dharma as unthinkable, so just an unthinkable karma-result should be expected from it.

6. The Bodhisattvas

6a. *The Bodhisattva's Vow*

17*a*. [(Subhuti asked: How, O Lord, should one set out in the Bodhisattva-vehicle stand, how progress, how control his thoughts?—The Lord replied: Here, Subhuti, someone who has set out in the Bodhisattva-vehicle should produce a thought in this manner: "all beings I must lead to Nirvana, into that Realm of Nirvana which leaves nothing behind; and yet, after beings have thus been led to Nirvana, no being at all has been led to Nirvana". And why? If in a Bodhisattva the notion of a "being" should take place, he could not be called a "Bodhi-being". And likewise if the notion of a soul, or a person should take place in him.)] And why? He who has set out in the Bodhisattva-vehicle—he is not one of the dharmas.

6b. *The Bodhisattva's state of mind when he met Dipankara*

17*b*. What do you think Subhuti, is there any dharma by which the Tathagata, when he was with Dipankara the Tathagata, has fully known the utmost, right and perfect enlightenment?—Subhuti replied: There is not any dharma by which the Tathagata, when he was with the Tathagata Dipankara, has fully known the utmost, right and perfect enlightenment.—The Lord said: It is for this reason that the Tathagata Dipankara then predicted of me: "You, young Brahmin, will in a future period be a Tathagata, Arhat, fully Enlightened, by the name of Shakyamuni!"

6c. *The Bodhisattva at the end of his career*

17*c*. And why? "Tathagata," Subhuti, is synonymous with true Suchness (tathatā).—17*d*. And whosoever, Subhuti, were to say, "The Tathagata has fully known the utmost, right and perfect enlightenment", he would speak falsely. And why? [(There is not any dharma by which the Tathagata has fully known the utmost, right and perfect enlightenment. And that dharma which the Tathagata has fully known and demonstrated, on account of that there is neither truth nor fraud.)] Therefore the Tathagata teaches, "all dharmas are the Buddha's own and special dharmas". And why? "All dharmas," Subhuti, have as no-dharmas been taught by the Tathagata. Therefore all dharmas are called the Buddha's own and special dharmas.—17*e*. ([Just as a man, Subhuti, might be endowed with a body, a huge body.)]—Subhuti said: That man of whom the Tathagata spoke as "endowed with a body, a huge body", as a no-body he has been taught by the Tathagata. Therefore is he called, "endowed with a body, a huge body".

6d. The Bodhisattva's attitude to his tasks

17*f*. The Lord said: So it is, Subhuti. The Bodhisattva who would say, "I will lead beings to Nirvana", he should not be called a "Bodhi-being". And why? Is there, Subhuti, any dharma named "Bodhi-being"?—Subhuti replied: No indeed, O Lord.—The Lord said: Because of that the Tathagata teaches, "selfless are all dharmas, they have not the character of living beings, they are without a living soul, without personality".—17*g*. [(If any Bodhisattva should say, "I will create harmonious Buddhafields")], he likewise should not be called a Bodhi-being. [(And why? "The harmonies of Buddhafields, the harmonies of Buddhafields," Subhuti, as no-harmonies have they been taught by the Tathagata. Therefore he spoke of "harmonious Buddhafields".)]—17*h*. The Bodhisattva, however, Subhuti, who is intent on "without self are the dharmas, without self are the dharmas", him the Tathagata, the Arhat, the Fully Enlightened One has declared to be a Bodhi-being, a great being.

7. The Buddhas

7a. The Buddha's Five Eyes

18*a*. What do you think, Subhuti, does the fleshly eye of the Tathagata exist?—Subhuti replied: So it is, O Lord, the fleshly eye of the Tathagata does exist.—The Lord asked: What do you think, Subhuti, does the Tathagata's heavenly eye exist, his wisdom eye, his Dharma-eye, his Buddha-eye?—Subhuti replied: So it is, O Lord, the heavenly eye of the Tathagata does exist, and so does his wisdom eye, his Dharma-eye and his Buddha-eye.

7b. The Buddha's superknowledge of others' thoughts

18*b*. The Lord said: What do you think, Subhuti, has the Tathagata used the phrase, "as many grains of sand as there are in the great river Ganges"?—Subhuti replied: So it is, O Lord, so it is, O Well-Gone! The Tathagata has done so.—The Lord asked: What do you think, Subhuti, if there were as many Ganges rivers as there are grains of sand in the great river Ganges, and if there were as many world systems as there are grains of sand in them, would those world systems be many?—Subhuti replied: So it is, O Lord, so it is, O Well-Gone, these world systems would be many.—The Lord said: As many beings as there are in these world systems, of them I know, in my wisdom, the manifold trends of thought. And why? "Trends of thought, trends of thought," Subhuti, as no-trends have they been taught by the Tathagata. Therefore are they called "trends of thought". And why? Past thought is not got at; future thought is not got at; present thought is not got at.

7c. The Buddha's Merit is no Merit

19. What do you think, Subhuti, if a son or daughter of good family had filled this world system of 1,000 million worlds with the seven precious things, and then gave it as a gift to the Tathagatas, the Arhats, the fully Enlightened Ones, would they on the strength of that beget a great heap of merit?—Subhuti replied: They would, O Lord, they would, O Well-Gone!—The Lord said: So it is, Subhuti, so it is. On the strength of that this son or daughter of good family would beget a great heap of merit, immeasurable and incalculable. But if, on the other hand, there were such a thing as a heap of merit, the Tathagata would not have spoken of a "heap of merit".

7d. The Buddha's Physical Body

20*a*. What do you think, Subhuti, is the Tathagata to be seen by means of the accomplishment of his form-body?—Subhuti replied: No indeed, O Lord, the Tathagata is not to be seen by means of the accomplishment of his form-body. And why? "Accomplishment of his form-body, accomplishment of his form-body," this, O Lord, has been taught by the Tathagata as no-accomplishment. Therefore is it called "accomplishment of his form-body".—20*b*. The Lord asked: What do you think, Subhuti, is the Tathagata to be seen through his possession of marks?—Subhuti replied: No indeed, O Lord. And why? This possession of marks, O Lord, which has been taught by the Tathagata, as a no-possession of no-marks this has been taught by the Tathagata. Therefore is it called "possession of marks".

7e. The Buddha's teaching

21*a*. The Lord asked: What do you think, Subhuti, does it occur to the Tathagata, "by me has Dharma been demonstrated"? Whosoever, Subhuti, would say, "the Tathagata has demonstrated Dharma", he would speak falsely, he would misrepresent me by seizing on what is not there. And why? "Demonstration of dharma, demonstration of dharma," Subhuti, there is not any dharma which could be got at as a demonstration of dharma.

21*b*. Subhuti asked: Are there, O Lord, any beings in the future, in the last time, in the last epoch, in the last 500 years, at the time of the collapse of the good doctrine who, on hearing such dharmas, will truly believe?—The Lord replied: They, Subhuti, are neither beings nor no-beings. And why? "Beings, beings," Subhuti, the Tathagata has taught that they are all no-beings. Therefore has he spoken of "all beings".

7f. The Buddha's Dharma

22. What do you think, Subhuti, is there any dharma by which the Tathagata has fully known the utmost, right and perfect enlightenment?—Subhuti replied: No indeed, O Lord, there is not any dharma by which the Tathagata has fully known the utmost, right and perfect enlightenment.—The Lord said: So it is, Subhuti, so it is. Not even the least (aṇu) dharma is there found or got at. Therefore is it called "utmost (anuttara), right and perfect enlightenment".—

23. Furthermore, Subhuti, self-identical (sama) is that dharma, and nothing is therein at variance (vishama). Therefore is it called "utmost, right (samyak) and perfect (sam-) enlightenment". Self-identical through the absence of a self, a being, a soul, or a person, the utmost, right and perfect enlightenment is fully known as the totality of all the wholesome dharmas. "Wholesome dharmas, wholesome dharmas," Subhuti—yet as no-dharmas have they been taught by the Tathagata. Therefore are they called "wholesome dharmas".

7g. Once more about the Buddha's Merit

24. And again, Subhuti, if a woman or man had piled up the seven precious things until their bulk equalled that of all the Sumerus, kings of mountains, in the world system of 1,000 million worlds, and would give them as a gift; and if, on the other hand, a son or daughter of good family would take up from this Prajñāpāramitā, this discourse on Dharma, but one stanza of four lines, and demonstrate it to others, compared with his heap of merit the former heap of merit does not approach one hundredth part, etc., until we come to: it will not bear any comparison.

7h. The Buddha as a Saviour, and the nature of emancipation

25. What do you think, Subhuti, does it occur to a Tathagata, "by

me have beings been set free"? Not thus should you see it, Subhuti! And why? There is not any being whom the Tathagata has set free. Again, if there had been any being whom the Tathagata had set free, then surely there would have been on the part of the Tathagata a seizing of a self, of a being, of a soul, of a person. "Seizing of a self," as a no-seizing, Subhuti, has that been taught by the Tathagata. And yet the foolish common people have seized upon it. "Foolish common people," Subhuti, as really no people have they been taught by the Tathagata. Therefore are they called "foolish common people".

7i. The true nature of a Buddha

26*a*. What do you think, Subhuti, is the Tathagata to be seen by means of his possession of marks?—Subhuti replied: No indeed, O Lord.—The Lord said: If, Subhuti, the Tathagata could be recognized by his possession of marks, then also the universal monarch would be a Tathagata. Therefore the Tathagata is not to be seen by means of his possession of marks.—Subhuti then said: As I, O Lord, understand the Lord's teaching, the Tathagata is not to be seen through his possession of marks.

Further the Lord taught on that occasion the following stanzas:

Those who by my form did see me,
And those who followed me by voice
Wrong the efforts they engaged in,
Me those people will not see.

26*b*. From the Dharma should one see the Buddhas,
From the Dharmabodies comes their guidance.
Yet Dharma's true nature cannot be discerned,
And no one can be conscious of it as an object.

7k. The effectiveness of meritorious deeds

27. What do you think, Subhuti, has the Tathagata fully known the utmost, right and perfect enlightenment through his possession of marks? Not so should you see it, Subhuti. And why? Because the Tathagata could surely not have fully known the utmost, right and perfect enlightment through his possession of marks.

Nor should anyone, Subhuti, say to you, "those who have set out in the Bodhisattva-vehicle have conceived the destruction of a dharma, or its annihilation". Not so should you see it, Subhuti! For those who have set out in the Bodhisattva-vehicle have not conceived the destruction of a dharma, or its annihilation.

28. And again, Subhuti, if a son or daughter of good family had filled with the seven precious things as many world systems as there are grains of sand in the river Ganges, and gave them as a gift to the Tathagatas, Arhats, fully Enlightened Ones—and if on the other hand a Bodhisattva would gain the patient acquiescence in dharmas which are nothing of themselves and which fail to be produced, then this latter would on the strength of that beget a greater heap of merit, immeasurable and incalculable.

Moreover, Subhuti, the Bodhisattva should not acquire a heap of merit.—Subhuti said: Surely, O Lord, the Bodhisattva should acquire a heap of merit?—The Lord said: "Should acquire", Subhuti, not "should seize upon". Therefore is it said, "should acquire".

29. Whosever says that the Tathagata goes or comes, stands, sits or lies down, he does not understand the meaning of my teaching. And why? "Tathagata" is called one who has not gone anywhere, nor come from anywhere. Therefore is he called "the Tathagata, the Arhat, the fully Enlightened One".

8. Advice to The Imperfect

8a. The material world

30*a*. And again, Subhuti, if a son or daughter of good family were to grind as many world systems as there are particles of dust in this great world system of 1,000 million worlds, as finely as they can be ground with incalculable vigour, and in fact reduce them to something like a collection of atomic quantities, what do you think, Subhuti, would that be an enormous collection of atomic quantities? —Subhuti replied: So it is, O Lord, so it is, O Well-Gone, enormous would that collection of atomic quantities be! And why? If, O Lord, there had been an enormous collection of atomic quantities, the Lord would not have called it an "enormous collection of atomic quantities". And why? What was taught by the Tathagata as a "collection of atomic quantities", as a no-collection that was taught by the Tathagata. Therefore is it called a "collection of atomic quantities".

30*b*. And what the Tathagata taught as "the world system of 1,000 million worlds", that he has taught as a no-system. Therefore is it called "the world system of 1,000 million worlds". And why? If, O Lord, there had been a world system, that would have been a case of seizing on a material object, and what was taught as "seizing on a material object" by the Tathagata, just as a no-seizing was that taught by the Tathagata. Therefore is it called "seizing on a material object".—The Lord added: And also, Subhuti, that "seizing on a material object" is a matter of linguistic convention, a verbal expression without factual content. It is not a dharma nor a no-dharma. And yet the foolish common people have seized upon it.

8*b*. *Views and attitudes*

31a. And why? Because whosever would say that the view of a self has been taught by the Tathagata, the view of a being, the view of a living soul, the view of a person, would he, Subhuti, be speaking right?—Subhuti replied: No indeed, O Lord, no indeed, O Well-Gone, he would not be speaking right. And why? That which has been taught by the Tathagata as "view of self', as a no-view has that been taught by the Tathagata? Therefore is it called "view of self".—
31b. The Lord said: It is thus, Subhuti, that someone who has set out in the Bodhisattva-vehicle should know all dharmas, view them, be intent on them. And he should know, view and be intent on them in such a way that he does not set up the perception of a dharma. And why? "Perception of dharma, perception of dharma", Subhuti, as no-perception has this been taught by the Tathagata. Therefore is it called "perception of dharma".

8*c*. *The key to supreme knowledge*

32*a*. And finally, Subhuti, if a Bodhisattva, a great being had filled world-systems immeasurable and incalculable with the seven precious things, and gave them as a gift to the Tathagatas, the Arhats, the fully Enlightened Ones—and if, on the other hand, a son or daughter of good family had taken from this Prajñāpāramitā, this discourse on Dharma, but one stanza of four lines, and were to bear it in mind, demonstrate, recite and study it, and illuminate it in full detail for others, on the strength of that this latter would beget a greater heap of merit, immeasurable and incalculable. And how would he illuminate it? So as not to reveal. Therefore is it said, "he would illuminate".

As stars, a fault of vision, as a lamp,
A mock show, dew drops, or a bubble,
A dream, a lightning flash, or cloud,
So should one view what is conditioned.

9. The Second Conclusion

32b. Thus spoke the Lord. Enraptured, the Elder Subhuti, the monks and nuns, the pious laymen and laywomen, and the Bodhisattvas, and the whole world with its Gods, men, Asuras and Gandharvas rejoiced in the Lord's teaching.

THE "HEART OF PERFECT WISDOM"

THE "HEART OF PERFECT WISDOM" IN 25 LINES

Homage to the Perfection of Wisdom,
the Lovely, the Holy!

Thus have I heard at one time. The Lord dwelled at Rājagṛha, on the Vulture Peak, together with a large gathering of both monks and Bodhisattvas. At that time the Lord, after he had taught the discourse on dharma called "deep splendour", had entered into concentration.[1] At that time also the holy Lord Avalokita,[2] the Bodhisattva, the great being, coursed in the course of the deep perfection of wisdom, he looked down from on high,[3] and he saw the five skandhas, and he surveyed[3] them as empty in their own-being.

Thereupon the Venerable *Śāriputra*, through the Buddha's might, said to the holy Lord Avalokita, the Bodhisattva, the great being: "How should a son or daughter of good family train themselves if they want to course in the course of this deep perfection of wisdom?"

The holy Lord *Avalokita*, the Bodhisattva, the great being, then said to the Venerable Śāriputra: "The son or daughter of good family who wants to course in the course of this deep perfection of wisdom should thus consider:

"There are the five skandhas, and those he sees[3] in their own-being as empty. Here, O Śāriputra, form is emptiness and the very emptiness is form; emptiness is no other than form, form is no other than emptiness; whatever is form that is emptiness, whatever is emptiness that is form. The same is true of feelings, perceptions, impulses and consciousness. Thus, O Śāriputra, all dharmas are empty of own-being, are without marks; they are neither produced nor stopped, neither defiled nor immaculate, neither deficient nor complete. Therefore then, O Śāriputra, where there is emptiness there is no form, no feeling, no perception, no impulse, no consciousness; no eye, ear, nose, tongue, body or mind; no form, no sound, no smell, no taste, no touchable, no object of mind; no sight-organ element, etc., until we come to: no mind-consciousness element; there is no ignorance, no extinction of ignorance, etc., until we come to: there is no old age and death, no extinction of old age and death; there is no suffering, no origination, no stopping, no

[1] V.R. entered on a concentration called "deep splendour".
[2] Aryāvalokiteśvaro
[3] vyavalokayati

path; there is no cognition, no attainment and no non-attainment.[1]

"Therefore then, O Śāriputra, owing to a Bodhisattva's indifference to any kind of personal attainment[2] he dwells as one who has relied solely on the perfection of wisdom. In the absence of an objective support to his thought[3] he has not been made to tremble, he has overcome what can upset, in the end sustained by Nirvana.[4] All those who appear as Buddhas in the three periods of time—through having relied on the perfection of wisdom they fully awake to the utmost, right and perfect enlightenment.

"Therefore one should know the Prajñāpāramitā as the great spell, the spell of great knowledge, the utmost spell, the unequalled spell, allayer of all suffering, in truth—for what could go wrong? In the Prajñāpāramitā has this spell been uttered.[5] It runs like this: GONE, GONE, GONE BEYOND, GONE ALTOGETHER BEYOND, O WHAT AN AWAKENING, ALL HAIL![6] It is thus, O Śāriputra, that a Bodhisattva should train himself in the course of the deep perfection of wisdom."

Thereupon *the Lord* emerged from that concentration, and he applauded the holy Lord Avalokita, the Bodhisattva, the great being: "Well said, well said, son of good family! Just so, son of good family, just so should one course in the course of the deep perfection of wisdom. As you have explained it, so it is approved by all the Tathagatas."

Thus spoke *the Lord.* Enraptured the Venerable Śāriputra, the holy Lord Avalokita, the Bodhisattva, the great being, and those monks and those Bodhisattvas, great beings, and the whole world with its gods, men, asuras, garudas and gandharvas rejoiced in the Lord's teaching.

[1]nāprāptiḥ
[2]aprāptitvāt
[3]V.R. In the absence of any thought-coverings (or: "impediments" to thought).
[4]V.R. and he has attained to final Nirvana.
[5]V.R. This spell is joined (or devoted) to the Prajñāpāramitā.
[6]GATE GATE PĀRAGATE PĀRASAṂGATE BODHI SVĀHĀ.

THE "HEART OF PERFECT WISDOM", SHORT FORM

[1]Homage to the Perfection of Wisdom,
the Lovely, the Holy!

[2]Avalokita, the Holy Lord[3] and Bodhisattva, [4]was moving [5]in the deep course of the wisdom which has gone beyond.

I [6]He looked down from on high, [7]he beheld but five heaps, [8]and he saw that in their own-being they were empty.

II [9]Here, O Śāriputra,

II, 1 [10]form is emptiness, and the very emptiness is form,

II, 2 [11]emptiness does not differ from form, [12]nor does form differ from emptiness;

II, 3 [13]whatever is form, that is emptiness, [14]whatever is emptiness, that is form.

II, 4 [15]The same is true of feelings, perceptions, impulses and consciousness.

III [17]Here, O Śāriputra,

III, 1 [18]all dharmas are marked with emptiness,

III, 2*a* [19]they are neither produced nor stopped,

III, 2*b* [20]neither defiled nor immaculate,

III, 2*c* [21]neither deficient nor complete.

IV [22]Therefore, O Śāriputra, [23]where there is emptiness

IV, 1 [24]there is neither form, nor feeling, nor perception, nor impulse, nor consciousness,

IV, 2 [25]no eye, or ear, or nose, or tongue, or body, or mind,

IV, 3 [26]no form, nor sound, nor smell, nor taste, nor touchable, nor object of mind,

IV, 4 [27]no sight organ element, [28]etc. until we come to, [29]no mind-consciousness element;

IV, 5 [30]there is no ignorance, [31]no extinction of ignorance, [32]etc. until we come to, [33]there is no decay and death, nor extinction of decay and death;

IV, 6 [34]there is no suffering, nor origination, nor stopping, nor path;

IV, 7 [35]there is no cognition,

IV, 8 [36]no attainment and no non-attainment.

V, 1*a* [37]Therefore, O Śāriputra, [38]owing to a Bodhisattva's indifference to any kind of personal attainment,

V, 1*b* [39]and through his having relied on the perfection of wisdom,

V, 1*c* [40]he dwells without thought-coverings.

V, 2*a* [41]In the absence of thought-coverings [42]he has not been made to tremble,

V, 2*b* [43]he has overcome what can upset,

V, 2*c* [44]in the end sustained by Nirvana.

VI [46]All those Buddhas [45]who appear in the three periods of time, [47]through having relied on the perfection of wisdom [49]they fully awake [48]to the utmost, right and perfect enlightenment.

VII, 1 [50]Therefore one should know [51]the Prajñāpāramitā

VII, 2 [52]as the great spell, [53]the spell of great knowledge, [54]the utmost spell, [55]the unequalled spell, [56]allayer of all suffering, [57]in truth—for what could go wrong? [58]By the Prajñāpāramitā has this spell been delivered.

VII, 3 [59]It runs like this: [60]GONE, GONE, GONE BEYOND, GONE ALTOGETHER BEYOND, O WHAT AN AWAKENING, ALL HAIL!

THE PERFECTION OF WISDOM IN A FEW WORDS

Homage to all Buddhas and Bodhisattvas!

Thus have I heard at one time. The Lord dwelt at Rājagṛha, on the Vulture Peak, seated on the glorious Lion Throne, together with a large gathering of monks, with 1,250 monks, with hundreds of thousands of niyutas of kotis of Bodhisattvas, surrounded and revered by thousands of niyutas of kotis of gods, i.e. the World Guardians, and others.

Thereupon the holy Lord *Avalokita*, the Bodhisattva, the great being, rose from his seat, put his upper robe over one shoulder, placed his right knee on the earth, bent forth his folded hands towards the Lord, and with a smiling face said to the Lord:

"Demonstrate, O Lord, the Perfection of Wisdom in a Few Words which is of great merit: When they merely hear it, all beings will extinguish the obstacles (arising from their past) deeds, and they will definitely end up in enlightenment; and the Mantras of the beings who labour zealously at the evocation of Mantras will succeed without fail."

Thereupon *the Lord* gave his approval to the greatly compassionate holy Lord Avalokita, the Bodhisattva, the great being:

"Well said, well said, son of good family, you who have been engaged for a long time in furthering the weal of all beings, their welfare and their happiness.[1] Therefore, son of good family, listen and attend well! I will teach you the Perfection of Wisdom in a Few Words, which has great merit; when they merely hear it, all beings will extinguish the obstacles (arising from their past) deeds, and they will definitely end up in enlightenment. And the Mantras of those beings who labour zealously at the evocation of Mantras will succeed without fail."

Thereupon the holy Lord *Avalokita*, the Bodhisattva, the great being, said to the Lord: "Teach it then, O Sugata, for the weal of all beings, for their welfare and happiness!"

Thereupon the Lord at that time entered on the concentration called "The Liberation from all Suffering".[2] When he had entered

[1]The Sanskrit Ms, but not the Ch or Tib, adds: *prahāṇāya*, which in MDPL I explain as "their instruction". The meaning is more likely to be: "so as to make them forsake (their fetters)". It is fairly obviously a copyist's gloss.

[2]Ti, Ch: "The Liberation of all Sentient Beings".

into that concentration, many hundreds of thousands of niyutas of kotis of rays issued from the hair-tuft between His eye-brows, and all the Buddha-fields were filled with these rays, and all the beings who were touched by that radiance became fixed on the utmost, right and perfect enlightenment, even as far as the beings in the hells. And all the Buddha-fields shook in six ways, and showers of heavenly sandalwood powder rained down on the ground at the feet of the Lord.

Thereupon *the Lord* at that time taught the Perfection of Wisdom as follows: "The Bodhisattva, the great being, should have an even thought, he should have a friendly thought towards all beings, he should be thankful, he should be grateful, and he should desist in his heart from all evil."

[1]And this Heart of Perfect Wisdom should be repeatedly recited[1]: HOMAGE TO THE TRIPLE JEWEL! HOMAGE TO ŚĀKYAMUNI, THE TATHAGATA, THE ARHAT, THE FULLY ENLIGHTENED ONE! [2]i.e. OṂ MUNE MUNE, MAHĀMUNAYE SVĀHĀ.[3]

[4]Through having gained this Perfection of Wisdom [4]have I reached the utmost, right and perfect enlightment, and from it all the Buddhas have come into being. [5]I also have heard this very Perfection of Wisdom from Mahāśākyamuni, the Tathagata. Therefore then have you in front of all the Bodhisattvas been predicted to Buddhahood: "You, young man, will become in a future period a Tathagata, Samantaraśmisamudgata Śrīkūṭarājā by name, an Arhat, a fully enlightened One, perfect in knowledge and conduct, a Sugata, a World-knower, unsurpassed, a Tamer of men to be tamed, a Teacher of gods and men, a Buddha, a Lord!" And all those who will hear this his Name,[6] will bear it in mind, recite it, write it and explain it in detail to others, and who, when this has been made into a written book, will preserve and worship it, they will,

[1–1]Ch: he should have a thought (hsin = citta = hṛdaya) of perfect wisdom. And at that time the Lord said to the holy Avalokiteśvara, the Bodhisattva, the great being: "You all listen well! I now for your sake teach this mantra of the holy P.P. in a Few Words which is the Mother of the Buddhas".

[2]Ch. transliterates, Tib. translates.—Namaḥ Śākyamunaye tathāgata-arhate samyaksambuddhāya.

[3]Oṃ, O the Sage, O the Sage! Homage to the great Sage! All Hail!

[4]The Buddha said to the holy Avalokiteśvara, the Bodhisattva, the great being: "Through this holy Mantra which is the P.P. in a Few Words which is the Buddha's Mother".

[5]In the following Ch has many verbal differences.

[6]This subtle dharma.

even through learning just this little bit (*alpa*), become Tathagatas.[1] i.e.[2]

OṂ, JEYA JEYA PADMĀBHE, AVAME AVAME. SARASARAṆI. DHIRI DHIRI. DEVATĀ. ANUPĀLANI YUDDHĀT-TĀRIṆI PARA-CAKRA-NIVĀRIṆI. PŪRAYA PŪRAYA BHAGAVATI SARVA-ĀŚĀ, MAMA CA SARVA-SATTVĀNĀÑ CA SARVA-KARMA-ĀVARAṆĀNI VIŚO-HAYA, BUDDHA-ADHIṢṬHITE SVĀHĀ.

This, son of good family,[3] is the Perfection of Wisdom in the ultimate sense,[3] the genetrix of all the Buddhas, the mother of the Bodhisattvas,[4] donor of enlightenment, remover of all evil.[4] Even all the Buddhas are unable to express in words her advantages, even after hundreds of kotis of aeons. Where it is merely being recited, there all the Assemblies are consecrated, and all the Mantras are realized (face to face).

Thereupon the holy *Avalokiteśvara*, the Bodhisattva, the great being, said to the Lord: "For what reason, O Lord,[5] is this the Perfection of Wisdom in a Few (*alpa*) Words (*akshara*)?"[5]

The Lord said: "Because it is an easy[6] means. If there are beings who are dull and stupefied,[7] and if they will bear in mind this Perfection of Wisdom in a Few Words, will recite it, read it, cause it to be read, they will, through an easy means, end up in enlightenment. For this reason, son of good family,[8] has this Perfection of Wisdom been compressed into a Few Words."[8]

The holy *Avalokiteśvara*, the Bodhisattva, the great being, then said to the Lord: "It is wonderful, O Lord, it is greatly wonderful, O Sugata, how, O Lord, for the weal of all beings this discourse on

[1]Ch: And at that time all the Tathagatas will give you their stamp of approval. I now for your's sake will teach you furthermore the P.P. dhāraṇī, to wit:

[2]Ch transliterates, Tib. translates.—Oṃ, May I conquer, may I conquer! O you who are in the likeness of a lotus! Intimate, intimate! O You, the Path for going along! Possessor of Wisdom, Possessor of Wisdom! Goddess! Protectress! You who rescue us from strife, who ward off the hostile actions of others! Fulfill, fulfill, Lovely Lady, the hopes of all! Clean away all my karma-coverings and those of all beings! You who are sustained by the Buddhas! All Hail!

[3]Ch: is the supreme-subtle (or: saddharma)—P.P.-dhāraṇī.

[4]Ch: If there are sentient beings who hear this dharma then those karma-obstacles which have been made can all be abolished (gradually eroded).

[5]Ch: Why have you furthermore taught this dhāraṇī of the P.P.?

[6]*alpa, sla-ba*

[7]Ch: lazy, irresolute; Tib. *spro-ba chuṅ-ba*, with little energy.

[8]Ch: have I spoken this dhāraṇī of the P.P.

dharma has been pronounced, for the sake of dull people,[1] for their welfare, for their happiness."

Thus spoke the Lord. Enraptured the holy Lord Avalokita, the Bodhisattva, the great being, and the monks, and the Bodhisattvas, and the whole world with its gods, men, asuras and gandharvas rejoiced in the Lord's teaching.

[1]Tib. for the sake of beings of small merit; Ch: for the sake of sentient beings who are lazy and have need of an easy upāya.

(PERFECT WISDOM AND THE FIVE BODHISATTVAS:)

THE PERFECTION OF WISDOM FOR SŪRYAGARBHA

Homage to all Buddhas and Bodhisattvas!

Thus have I heard at one time. The Lord dwelled in Magadha, in a remote forest favourable to the practice of the Dharma,[1] together with a large gathering of monks, and with Bodhisattvas assembled from endless, immeasurable and innumerable Buddhafields. At that time a Bodhisattva called Splendour of the Sun[2] was present in the assembly. He rose from his seat, went to the Lord and said to Him: "I have come to ask the Tathagata a question." And he spoke to the Lord, confronting him with the Lord's consent.

The Lord said: "Ask me then what you want to ask! I will explain it to you."

Thereupon the Bodhisattva *Sun's Splendour* said to the Lord: "How, O Lord, should a Bodhisattva, skilled in means, train in the perfection of wisdom?"

The Lord said: "There is, son of good family, a concentration called 'skilled in means like the sun'. Therein should the Bodhisattvas train!"

He said to the Lord: "How should they train therein?"

The Lord said: "The concentration on 'skilled in means as the sun' is sevenfold. How? First, just as the sun ripens the sprouts, so the concentration of the Bodhisattva, like a sun, matures the sprout of enlightenment in beings. Secondly, as the sun never ceases to send out heat, so the concentration of the Bodhisattva establishes all beings in compassion. Thirdly, as the sun burns up foul matter, so the Bodhisattva, with his insight and wisdom, burns up the foul matter of the defilements. Fourthly, as the sun melts frozen things, so the concentration of the Bodhisattva who is endowed with a cognition of the antidotes, as it were melts the frost of the defilements. Fifthly, as the sun takes away the darkness, so the Bodhisattva, taken hold of by the contemplating cognition, takes away the darkness of grasping. Sixthly, as the sun turns round the four Continents, so the Bodhisattva, by the accomplishment of his labour, liberates from the four floods of suffering. Seventh, as the sun warms everything equally, so the Bodhisattva, by accomplishing his course, gladdens all beings, his skill in acting being like warmth.

[1] ? chos-kyi dgon-pa na

[2] ñi-ma rab-tu snaṅ-ba, sūryaprabhāsa

"Furthermore, son of good family, the Bodhisattva should train in the perfection of wisdom. He should train in all dharmas as without own-being, as signless, as devoid of all signs, as non-existence, as devoid of all existence, as impersonal, as devoid of all personality, and as empty in their own-being. A Bodhisattva, son of good family, should train in Dharmahood, in the Dharma-element, in Suchness, in the Reality-limit, in the Suchness which is free from falsehood, in the Suchness which is free from alteration, in the Truth, in what is truly real."

Thereupon *the Lord* again said to the Bodhisattva Sun's Splendour: "Moreover, son of good family, a Bodhisattva should train in all dharmas as not brought about, and as unproduced. He should, son of good family, train in the purity of the essential original nature of all dharmas. He should cognize all dharmas, form, etc., as empty in their essential original nature; he should cognize them as isolated in their own-being. Those people, son of good family, who will take up the Sutra on Perfect Wisdom—the obstacles from their past deeds will become extinct, they will produce an equipment with merit, they will become endowed with a measureless equipment with wisdom, they will be endowed with mindfulness, morality and concentration. Once more again, son of good family, Bodhisattvas should train in perfect wisdom!"

Thereupon *the Lord* at that time spoke the following verses:

"One who has learned much, who is devoted to the Dharma supreme,
Who is friendly to all beings,
Who has achieved the armour of vigour,
Who is intent on the weal of himself and of others,
Who is devoted to the development of trances and concentrations,
Who has no notion of himself and of beings,
Who has mounted on the path of the true vehicle,
Who courses like the Jina's sons in the past,
A wise one, he trains in that which is not false."

Thus spoke the Lord. The Bodhisattva Sun's Splendour, and the whole world with its gods and men rejoiced at the Lord's teaching.

THE PERFECTION OF WISDOM FOR CANDRAGARBHA

Homage to all Buddhas and Bodhisattvas!

Thus have I heard at one time. The Lord dwelled at Rājagṛha, on the Vulture Peak, together with a large gathering of monks, immeasurable and innumerable, and with a great many Bodhisattvas. At that time *Candragarbha*, the Bodhisattva, the great being, was present in that assembly. He rose from his seat, and said to the Lord: "How, O Lord, should Bodhisattvas train in the perfection of wisdom?"

The Lord replied: "The fact, Candragarbha, that all dharmas are devoid of existence, that is the perfection of wisdom. i.e. Just as the disk of the moon indiscriminately turns round[1] the four Continents and removes the darkness, just so the Bodhisattva, the great being, coursing in the perfection of wisdom, indiscriminately moves round[2] the four perverted views with his compassion, removes the defilements in the very core of their essential nature, and that by way of non-discrimination."

Candragarbha asked: "What, O Lord, is the perfection of wisdom of the Bodhisattva?"

The Lord replied: "Son of good family, the perfection of wisdom of a Bodhisattva is twofold, with and without outflows. The wisdom with outflows takes place on the station of the stage of the course in resolute faith,[3] and one there imagines that it should be taken up and seized upon; but that attitude should be given up. So much about the perfection of wisdom with outflows. The perfection of wisdom without outflows is the non-discriminating cognition on the path of vision, on account of the fact that the cognition is devoid of all imagination. It is a wisdom which has gone beyond[4] because it is not supported on either of the two extremes, i.e. not on this[5] and not on the other shore.[6]

"The perfection of wisdom should be cognized as without own-being because form, etc., to the knowledge of all modes, are without own-being. Because all dharmas, form, etc., are not apprehended in the three periods of time, she should be cognized as neither bound nor freed. The perfection of wisdom is sameness because all dharmas are sameness. The perfection of wisdom is not stopped because all dharmas are not stopped. The perfection of wisdom is signless because all dharmas are signless. The perfection of wisdom is unproduced because all dharmas are unproduced. The perfection of wisdom is not annihilated because all dharmas are not annihilated. The perfection of wisdom does not come because all dharmas do not come. The perfection of wisdom does not go because all dharmas do

[1]'khor-bar byed ciṅ, parivartate
[2]? 'khor shiṅ, bhramati
[3]adhimukti-caryā-bhūmer avasthā
[4]pāram-itā, also "perfection"
[5]āram
[6]pāram

not go. The perfection of wisdom is not eternal because all dharmas are not eternal. The perfection of wisdom is unbroken because all dharmas are unbroken. The perfection of wisdom has just one single meaning because all dharmas have just one single meaning. The perfection of wisdom has non-existence for own-being because all dharmas have non-existence for own-being. Briefly, the perfection of wisdom has transcended all signs, all essential nature, all own-being.

"Therefore then, the perfection of wisdom is a mantra, i.e. OṂ, PRAJÑE PRAJÑE, MAHĀPRAJÑE, CANDRAPRAJÑE, SARVAŚĀ SAGARI[1], SVĀHĀ![2]

"That all dharmas are brought about by a cause
That is conventional truth.
That they are without own-being, unimpeded (*niṣprapañca*),
That is the range of ultimate reality."

Thus spoke the Lord. The Bodhisattva Candragarbha, and the whole world with its gods, men, asuras and gandharvas, rejoiced at the Lord's teaching.

THE PERFECTION OF WISDOM FOR SAMANTABHADRA

Homage to all Buddhas and Bodhisattvas!

Thus have I heard at one time. The Lord dwelt in Magadha, in a remote forest called the "Pith of Dharma",[3] together with Bodhisattvas who had assembled from countless Buddhafields in the ten directions, Buddhafields which are as numerous as the atomic particles (in the universe). All the Bodhisattvas dwelt in the ambrosial course of Samantabhadra's Vow.

Thereupon the Bodhisattva Samantabhadra entered on a concentration called "the firm non-discrimination of all dharmas". Through the power of that concentration all the Buddhafields in the world systems as numerous as the atomic particles (in the universe) were shaken. Thereupon the Lord touched the head of the Bodhisattva Samantabhadra with his hand, and in consequence all the Buddhafields trembled once more. And through the power of the *gods* the following verses were sung:

"Light of the world, you who surpass the gods and men,
Ocean of virtues, perfection for the sons of gods,
You have crossed over the flood of worldly becoming,
Let us seek protection from you as the caravan leader!"

[1]Peking: Sarvaśāsa-kari

[2]Om, Oh Wisdom, Oh Wisdom! Oh you, Great Wisdom! Oh you Moon of Wisdom! Universal Ocean! All Hail!

[3]? yul ma-ga-lha'i dgon-pa chos-kyi sñiṅ-po

Thereupon the Bodhisattva *Samantabhadra* said to the Lord: "What is the wisdom like in which one should train, and in what kind of wisdom should one train?"[1]

The Lord replied: "The true wisdom, Samantabhadra, is like the wisdom of wayfarers among the troubles of the world.[2] The wisdom in which (one should train) is the wisdom which begins with the first stage."

Thus spoke the Lord. The Bodhisattva Samantabhadra, and the whole world with its gods, and men rejoiced at the Lord's teaching.

THE PERFECTION OF WISDOM FOR VAJRAPĀṆI

Homage to all Buddhas and Bodhisattvas!

Thus have I heard at one time. The Lord dwelt at Rājagṛha. At that time the Bodhisattva *Vajrapāṇi* was present in that assembly. He rose from his seat, and said to the Lord: "How should a Bodhisattva train in the perfection of wisdom?"

The Lord said: "The Bodhisattva, Vajrapāṇi, should train in perfect wisdom through the non-production of all dharmas. Furthermore, he should train in perfect wisdom through the fact that all dharmas, form, etc., are devoid of own-being, devoid of signs, devoid of existence, and cannot be apprehended. He should train in perfect wisdom through the emptiness of the subject, etc., to: through the emptiness of non-existence.

"The perfection of wisdom, Vajrapāṇi, is the mother of all the Buddhas in the three periods of time. She has been taught as a mantra of great lore, i.e. OṂ, MUNE MUNE, MAHĀMUNAYE, SVĀHĀ! Those who take up this perfection of wisdom, they take up the dharmas of the Buddhas in the three periods of time, they acquire a recollection of their (previous) births, they leave all inauspicious rebirths behind, they obtain a measureless fruit from their merit, they will always and at all times meet with the Buddhas, the Lords, and they will become endowed with the thought of enlightenment."

Thus spoke the Lord. The Bodhisattva Vajrapāṇi, and the whole world with its gods, men, asuras and gandharvas rejoiced at the teaching of the Lord.

THE PERFECTION OF WISDOM FOR VAJRAKETU

Homage to all Buddhas and Bodhisattvas!

Thus have I heard at one time. The Lord dwelt at Rājagṛha, together

[1] ? 'ji-ltar bslab-par bya-ba'i don śes-rab 'dra-ba daṅ, śes-rab yin-pa-la bslab-par bya.

[2] ? śes-rab 'dra-ba ni, 'jig-rten tshegs-kyi lam-pa rnams-kyi śes-rab gaṅ yin-pa'o

with the usual assembly. At that time the Bodhisattva *Vajraketu* was present in that assembly. He rose from his seat and said to the Lord: "With which dharmas, O Lord, is the perfection of wisdom endowed?"

The Lord said: "It is, Vajraketu, endowed with four kinds of dharmas. Which four? i.e. All dharmas should be seen from emptiness; all conditioned things should be cognized as impermanent and ill; it is endowed with a dharmic nature which is devoid of all impediments (*prapañca*); in every way it should be developed free from imagination and apprehension.

"Moreover, the endowment with four dharmas is the reason for the production of wisdom. Which four? i.e. First, the tending of the person who is the preacher of Dharma and the instructor; secondly, to hear from him the supreme Dharma; thirdly, the reflection on it and the entering into its meaning; fourthly, the desire to wisely (*yoniśas*) show it also to others. These are the reasons for the production of wisdom.

"Furthermore, Bodhisattvas should train in the perfection of wisdom as follows: All dharmas should be cognized as pure in their essential original nature, as empty, as without self, as having non-existence for own-being, as signless, as neither bound nor freed, as in their essential original nature neither light nor darkness.

"Therefore then should Bodhisattvas train in perfect wisdom. One should train in perfect wisdom by way of (considering) all dharmas as non-production, by way of not taking one's stand anywhere.

"A development in what has non-existence for own-being,
A longing for what causes the production of wisdom—
One should train in the meaning of a wisdom
Which is devoid of all signs."

Thus spoke the Lord. The Bodhisattva Vajraketu, etc., and the whole world with its gods, men, asuras and gandharvas rejoiced at the teaching of the Lord.

THE HOLY AND BLESSED PERFECTION OF WISDOM IN 50 LINES

Homage to all Buddhas and Bodhisattvas!

Thus have I heard at one time. The Lord dwelt at Rājagṛha, on the Vulture Peak, together with a large gathering of monks,[1] and with Śakra, Brahmā and the World Guardians, with gods, nāgas, yakshas, gandharvas, asuras, garudas, kinnaras and mahoragas, and with monks, nuns, laymen and laywomen.[1]

Thereupon *the Lord* said to the Venerable Subhuti: "If someone wants to train in Discipleship or Pratyekabuddhahood, they should hear this Perfection of Wisdom, should take it up, bear it in mind, recite and master it. For from the Bodhisattva who is skilled in means have all the dharmas of the Buddhas and Bodhisattvas been brought about. One should make endeavours in this Perfection of Wisdom. And why? The Bodhisattva, the great being should train and make endeavours therein because all the dharmas of the Buddhas and Bodhisattvas are expounded in detail in this Perfection of Wisdom.

"Also one who wants to train for full enlightenment should hear this perfection of wisdom, should take it up, bear it in mind, recite and master it. Because from the Bodhisattva who is skilled in means have all the dharmas of the Buddhas and Bodhisattvas been brought about. One should make endeavours in this perfect wisdom. Subhuti, whatever wholesome dharmas there are, or dharmas leading to enlightenment, be they Disciple-dharmas, or Pratyekabuddha-dharmas, or Bodhisattva-dharmas, or Buddha-dharmas, since they are all included in the perfection of wisdom, contained and embodied in it, one should apply oneself diligently to it."

Subhuti said: "One should, O Lord, train in the perfection of wisdom and make endeavours about it, if one wants to train in Discipleship or Pratyekabuddhahood. This perfection of wisdom, and all the Buddha-dharmas and Bodhisattva-dharmas should be heard, should be taken up, borne in mind, recited and mastered. Which then are those wholesome dharmas, or dharmas leading to enlightenment, be they Disciple-dharmas, or Pratyekabuddha-dharmas or Bodhisattva-dharmas, or Buddha-dharmas, which are included in the perfection of wisdom, contained and embodied in it, and to which one should diligently apply oneself?"

[1]Ch: 1,250 of them, who had all attained Arhatship, with all their outflows dried up, etc., to: in perfect control of their whole minds.—This is the usual opening, as in *A*.

The Lord said: "Subhuti, they are the perfection of giving, the perfection of morality, the perfection of patience, the perfection of vigour, the perfection of meditation, the perfection of wisdom. Emptiness of the subject, emptiness of the object, emptiness of both subject and object, the emptiness of emptiness, the great emptiness, the ultimate emptiness, conditioned emptiness, unconditioned emptiness, infinite emptiness, emptiness without beginning or end, the emptiness of non-repudiation, the emptiness of the essential original nature, the emptiness of all dharmas, the emptiness of own-marks, the emptiness of non-apprehension, the emptiness of non-existence, the emptiness of own-being, the emptiness of the non-existence of own-being. The four applications of mindfulness, the four right efforts, the four bases of psychic power, the five faculties, the five powers, the seven limbs of enlightenment, the Holy eightfold path, the four Holy truths, the four trances, the four boundless states, the four formless attainments, the eight emancipations, the nine successive stations, the doors of emancipation, i.e. emptiness, the signless, the wishless, the superknowledges, the concentrations, all dharani-doors, the ten powers of a Tathagata, the four grounds of self-confidence, the four analytical knowledges, the great friendliness, the great compassion, the eighteen special Buddha-dharmas, the fruit of a Streamwinner, the fruit of a Once-Returner, the fruit of a Never-Returner, Arhatship, Pratyekabuddhahood, all-knowledge, the knowledge of the modes of the path, the knowledge of all modes. Subhuti, these are the wholesome dharmas, or dharmas leading to enlightenment, be they Disciple-dharmas, or Pratyekabuddha-dharmas, or Bodhisattva-dharmas, or Buddha-dharmas, which are included in the perfection of wisdom, contained and embodied in it, and to which one should diligently apply oneself."

Subhuti said: "If, O Lord, these are the wholesome dharmas, the dharmas leading to enlightenment, the Disciple-dharmas, the Pratyekabuddha-dharmas, the Bodhisattva-dharmas, the Buddha-dharmas, which are included in the perfection of wisdom, contained and embodied in it, and to which one should apply oneself diligently, then, O Lord, aye, alas, it is difficult to get to the bottom of this perfection of wisdom."

The Lord said: "Because, Subhuti, the perfection of wisdom is absolutely isolated."

Subhuti said: "Aye! Alas! O Lord, this perfection of wisdom is hard to fathom."

The Lord said: "Because, Subhuti, the perfection of wisdom is absolutely pure."

Subhuti said: "Aye! Alas, O Lord, is not the perfection of wisdom like unto space?"

The Lord said: "Because, Subhuti, the perfection of wisdom is absolutely clear. In consequence the perfection of wisdom is like unto space."

Subhuti said: "Alas, alas, O Lord, is not the perfection of wisdom difficult to understand for someone who does not practice?"

The Lord said: "So it is, Subhuti, so it is, as you say. It is difficult for one to gain confidence in this perfection of wisdom, if he has only limited wholesome roots, is of little mental power, aimless, has learned little, has little wisdom, relies on bad spiritual teachers, has intercourse with bad spiritual teachers, is taken in hand by bad spiritual teachers, is endowed with little faith, a mere beginner, one unworthy, who is not inclined to ask questions, is stupid, lazy, of little vigour, with little power of compassion, of inferior resolve, and unpractised in these wholesome dharmas. That is why it is difficult to gain confidence in this perfection of wisdom. Subhuti, any son or daughter of good family who has heard this deep perfection of wisdom, taken it up, borne it in mind, recited and mastered it, and who explains it in full detail to others, he will obtain[1] the enlightenment of the past, future and present Buddhas and Lords. Therefore then, Subhuti, the son or daughter of good family, who is full of resolute intention, who wants to quickly fully know the utmost, right and perfect enlightenment, should constantly hear this perfection of wisdom, take it up, bear it in mind, recite and master it. Thereby they will fully know the utmost, right and perfect enlightenment."

Thus spoke the Lord. Enraptured the Venerable Subhuti, and those monks and Bodhisattvas, and the whole world with its gods, men, asuras and gandharvas rejoiced at the Lord's teaching.

[1]*bzuṅ-ba;* Ch: "hold", *dhṛ*, *ch'ih*

THE PERFECTION OF WISDOM FOR KAUŚIKA

Homage to all the Buddhas and Bodhisattvas!

Thus have I heard at one time. The Lord dwelt at Rājagṛha, on the Vulture Peak, together with a large congregation of monks, and with many hundreds of thousands of Bodhisattvas, all of them Crown Princes. At that time the Lord said to Śakra, Chief of Gods:

(I) This, Kauśika, is the meaning of the perfection of wisdom: the perfection of wisdom should not be viewed from duality or non-duality; not from a sign, or the signless; not through bestowal or withdrawal; not through subtracting something or adding something; not from defilement or non-defilement; not from purification or non-purification; not through abandoning or non-abandoning; not from taking one's stand or not taking one's stand; not through junction or no-junction; not through a connection or a non-connection; not through a condition or a non-condition; not from dharma or no-dharma; not from Suchness or no-Suchness; not from the reality-limit or the no-reality limit.

(II) This is the meaning of the perfection of wisdom, Kauśika: i.e. the perfection of wisdom is self-identical because all dharmas are the same. The perfection of wisdom is deep because all dharmas are deep. The perfection of wisdom is isolated because all dharmas are isolated. The perfection of wisdom is immobile because all dharmas are immobile. The perfection of wisdom is devoid of mental acts because all dharmas are devoid of mental acts. The perfection of wisdom is free from fear because all dharmas are free from fear. The perfection of wisdom is fearless because all dharmas are fearless. The perfection of wisdom has but one single taste because all dharmas have one and the same taste. The perfection of wisdom is non-production because all dharmas are non-production. The perfection of wisdom is non-stopping because all dharmas are not stopped. The perfection of wisdom is fashioned like the firmament because all dharmas are fashioned like the firmament. The perfection of wisdom is boundless because form is boundless. Likewise is the perfection of wisdom boundless because feeling, perception, impulses and consciousness are boundless. The perfection of wisdom is boundless because the element of earth is boundless. Likewise is the perfection of wisdom boundless because the elements of water, fire, air, ether and consciousness are boundless. The perfection of wisdom is boundless as Sumeru is boundless. The perfection of wisdom is boundless as the ocean is boundless. The perfection of wisdom is self-identical as the thunderbolt, just as the thunderbolt is self-identical. The perfection of wisdom is undifferentiated because all dharmas are undifferentiated. The perfection of wisdom is non-apprehension because the own-being of all dharmas cannot be apprehended. The perfection of wisdom remains the same whatever it may surpass because all dharmas remain the same whatever they may surpass. The perfection of wisdom is powerless to act, because all dharmas are powerless to act. The perfection of wisdom is unthinkable because all dharmas are unthinkable.

(III) Likewise, the perfection of wisdom is boundless because of the boundlessness of the triple purity of the perfections of giving, morality, patience, vigour, meditation, wisdom (skill in means, vow, power and cognition).[1]

(IV) One speaks of the perfection of wisdom, i.e. the eighteen kinds of emptiness. As follows: emptiness of the subject, emptiness of the object, emptiness of both subject and object, emptiness of emptiness, the great emptiness, emptiness in the ultimate sense, conditioned emptiness, unconditioned emptiness, absolute emptiness, emptiness without beginning and end, emptiness of non-repudiation, emptiness of essential nature, emptiness of all dharmas, emptiness of own-marks, emptiness of the absence of a basis, emptiness of non-existence, emptiness of own-being, emptiness of the non-existence of own-being. These are in short the emptinesses. This is the perfection of wisdom.

(V) As stars, a fault of vision, as a lamp,
A mock show, hoar frost, or a bubble,
A dream, a lightning flash, or cloud,
So should one view what is conditioned.

(VI) HOMAGE TO THE PERFECTION OF WISDOM, THE LOVELY, THE HOLY! OṂ DHĪ, HRĪ ŚRĪ, ŚRUTI SMṚTI MATI GATI VIJAYE, SVĀHĀ![2]

(VII) Non-stopping and non-production,
No cutting off and no everlastingness,
Neither single nor manifold,
Neither coming nor going.
That conditioned co-production is
The Bliss of the cessation of the differentiated world,
That the fully Enlightened One has demonstrated.
I salute Him, the best of all preachers!

[1]Only in the Tibetan.
[2]See the Preface on page V.

Thus spoke the Lord. Enraptured the Venerable Śāriputra, as well as Śakra, Chief of Gods, and the Bodhisattvas, the great beings, and the entire assembly, and the world with its gods, gandharvas and asuras rejoiced at the Lord's teaching.

THE QUESTIONS OF NĀGAŚRĪ

(I) The Bodhisattva Mañjuśrī went one morning into the city of Śrāvastī to practise seeking for alms. He placed his yellow robe in order, took his begging bowl and sieve, and, following the example of the Buddha, though imperfectly, his walk was quiet and beautiful . . . (II) The Bodhisattva *Nāgaśrī* (who was learning the perfection of wisdom from Mañjuśrī) saw him enter the city, accompanied by an enormous crowd, and asked him, "What are you doing?"

Mañjuśrī answered: I enter this city in order to beg, full of thoughts of compassion. Great will be the advantage produced by wisdom. I will practice begging in order to save all gods and men in the world, and to become the great guide of beings.

Nāgaśrī asked Mañjuśrī: How is it that you have not yet forsaken the notion of seeking for alms?

Mañjuśrī: I have forsaken that notion from the point of view of existence; from the point of view of non-existence there is no forsaking, nor anything that could be forsaken. This is what is called the pure seeking for alms on the part of the Bodhisattvas.

(III) *Mañjuśrī:* When one practises the seeking for alms, one must have no thought of lifting the feet, nor of putting them down, nor of standing, going forward, going backward, bending and straightening the body, nor of a place, nor of walking. One must not have the notion of a town, road, path, house or door, of men or women, of young people or weak people, (IV) nor of form or figure, of production or extinction.

(V) *Nāgaśrī:* Son of good family, seek for alms (in Śrāvastī) in the East!

Mañjuśrī: East, west, south and north, do they exist in a way any more real than a magically created will o' the wisp?

(VI) *Nāgaśrī:* I will go away (from Śrāvastī) because there is no Bodhisattva who is a Crown Prince to accompany me.—*Mañjuśrī:* I neither come nor do I go away. I have no companion, no associate. Why is this? It is because the Path has no companion.

(VII) *Nāgaśrī:* This is the proper time prescribed by the Vinaya for us to go together and seek for alms in the city. I am aware of the time of the day in order to go on time and not be too late.—*Mañjuśrī:* Dharmas are not in time; and so one cannot let (the opportune moment) pass. Those who dwell in the practice of perceptions have the perceptions of time and of the absence of time. How could Bodhisattvas who have comprehended the incomprehensibility of empty dharmas, speak of time or its absence? The absence of an opportune or inopportune time makes the Discipline and Dharma of the Buddha, whereas the other dharmas admit of an opportune and inopportune time. Those who calculate and consider the divisions of time have the perception of letting the opportune moment pass. The Disciples of the Exalted one satiate themselves always on the wisdom of the Path—(VIII) they have neither a perception of food, nor of the fact of a food which exists. This food (without perception) is called the food without admixture; those who eat it are called "holy" and "good". If one always eats such food as this, then this is the surpassing deathless (ambrosial) Dharma-food, and by the power which comes from eating that food they can live for an aeon or more. They have no longer the perception of seeking for food. (IX) They only desire to free (all beings) from the sufferings of the five destinies, and because of this they appear entering a country, district, town or village, begging and receiving alms. But these holy ones are detached from all food; they do not eat any food. They are always satiated by the concentration of wisdom. Those who continue to eat the mixed food experience transmigration in numerous births and deaths. (X) From the first thought of enlightenment onwards the Buddhas lose all perceptions of hunger and thirst.

(XI) *Nāgaśrī:* Well said, well said. The Dharma which is taught by Mañjuśrī is very subtle. There I am already satiated by this superior kind of food, although I have done nothing except listening to your sermon on this food of the Dharma. How much more so must those who mature by eating this unmixed food cease to eat all food (mixed with) reflection and sense desire!—*Mañjuśrī:* How could that of which the substance is empty, feed on mixed food and be satisfied?—*Nāgaśrī:* Emptiness does not exist.—*Mañjuśrī:* Can one satiate a magician's creation?—*Nāgaśrī:* No.—*Mañjuśrī:* Can one satiate an illusion?—*Nāgaśrī:* No.—*Mañjuśrī:* Is the ocean satiated by the rivers?—*Nāgaśrī:* No.—*Mañjuśrī:* So also the dharmas are not satiated, since they are like the Void, and yet you have said that the perception of saturation exists. (XII) Dharmas are always without sense-desire, because of concentration and liberation; they have neither form nor appearance. (XIII) How could one have a perception of satiation?

Nāgaśrī: If this is so, O Mañjuśrī, the one who possesses such a practice would no longer eat any food; and yet you say that emptiness is the basis (or: root) of food.—*Mañjuśrī:* If this were so, then all beings do not eat. As in the case of the Exalted One by magically creating innumerable people, who would use food to feed all these magically created persons. Is there any food which these people who were created by magic, eat, or are there any who eat it?—*Nāgaśrī:* The state of magical creation has no perception, no consciousness, it does not exist, and it has no food. How much less can one say that the eaters exist!—*Mañjuśrī:* In this way all dharmas, concerned with a view of existence or a view of non-existence, are like magical creations.

(XIV) *Nāgaśrī:* This is the proper time for us to return together to Jetavana in Anāthapiṇḍada's garden. My hunger and my thirst have been (for ever) eliminated.—*Mañjuśrī:* This is as if a man conjured up by a magician would say that "hunger and thirst have been eliminated". What then is the dharma of a hungry will o' the wisp? And the same is the case with everything; for all dharmas are like those will o' the wisps. The sons of good family who understand this say that "we have eliminated hunger and thirst". They will eat this food which is similar to dharmas that can be neither eliminated or destroyed and that are without hunger or thirst; this is how the basis (or: root) of all dharmas has been satiated. The common people who do not understand this basis say, "we are hungry and thirsty; we have been satiated". But the holy men and the good men, who understand this basis of dharmas, have neither hunger or thirst, nor the conception of being satiated.

(XV) *Mañjuśrī* said to Śāriputra: I invite you to eat the pure food.—*Śāriputra:* At what place will that food be given to me? What kind of food are you about to prepare and give me?—*Mañjuśrī:* As far as that is concerned which is eaten, there is no food, no swallowing and nothing which is swallowed. And as for the thing swallowed, there is no form, nor sound, smell or taste, nor a mucous or fine substance. The place of this food is found neither within the triple world, nor outside it. This is the place of the food of all the Buddhas and Lords (a food which is invisible to the carnal eye, inner or outer, to the heavenly eye, and even to the eye of wisdom).

(XVI) *Myōshin* asked Mañjuśrī: What food should be eaten? By eating what food have Subhuti, Śāriputra and others entered into the attainment of cessation?—*Mañjuśrī:* By eating the food without outflows, the food which has no attachments and is not ordinary. (XVII) They eat no more food in the triple world.

At that moment Subhuti and Śāriputra awakened from their trance (of cessation), and went to beg for alms. Subhuti entered the house of a householder whose wife was a *lay-sister*. (XVIII) She asked him: Do you still have the perception of seeking for alms? Have you not yet destroyed it?—*Subhuti:* From the very beginning

I have destroyed the perception of seeking for alms.—*The lay-sister:* At the beginning, was it destroyed or not yet destroyed?—*Subhuti:* The future is empty like the past, quite like the original emptiness.—*Lay-sister:* Then, everything being empty, how can one talk of "destroyed" and "not yet destroyed"? Stretch out your hand, I will give you some alms!—Subhuti held out his hand.—*Lay-sister:* But that is the hand of an Arhat who (as different from a Bodhisattva) does not understand this original emptiness, and realizes cessation; or is that not so?—*Subhuti:* The hand of an Arhat does not have form, it is not visible, it can be neither stretched nor withdrawn. As a magician makes a mock show, so a man (created by) magic pronounces these words. Where then could the hand of that illusory man be found? How can one say that he stretched out his hand? The illusory hand, is it visible? Can one stretch it out?—*The lay-sister* replied: No.—*Subhuti:* Thus the Lord says that all dharmas are, like a mock show, originally empty.—*The lay-sister* asked: If everything is empty, why do you continue to seek for food? —And at that moment she was not yet willing to give alms to Subhuti (i.e. before he had performed a miracle to prove the Void). She said: Hold out your bowl!—Suddenly the bowl disappeared. She used her hand to search for it, but it was not to be found, and her hands did not come near Subhuti.—She said: This is a pure body, without attachment, a dweller in Peace, praised by the Lord.—After these words the bowl reappeared spontaneously. Subhuti held out the bowl, the lay-sister took it, filled it with food and handed it back to him, saying: This is truly the bowl of the foremost dweller in Peace, praised by the Buddha Śākyamuni, or is it not?—*Subhuti:* The dwellers in Peace of whom the Buddha speaks have no bowl.—*Lay-sister:* If the dwellers in Peace have no bowl, what means do they have to receive their food?—*Subhuti* said: The dwellers in Peace (who are the object of a prediction to Buddhahood) must not be Arhats who realize cessation.—*Lay-sister:* After they have eaten this food, they understand that the eater is like a mock show, and that which is eaten is like a magical creation; it is like a man created by magic who feeds others created by the power of magic; or it is like the stilling of the thirst of a will o' the wisp. Those who understand this penetrate like the Tathagata into the practice of seeking for alms in the original Void, of past, future and present. Those who have the perception of giving or receiving fabricate numerous divisions of becoming, have the erroneous view of dualism and, along with the common people, transmigrate in the five destinies. (XIX) According to the Dharma of the Buddha, not only those who receive food, but also those who give it, must understand that it is just like a magical creation, (XX) that dharmas are pure, do not exist at all, that there is no gift or receiving of it, no moral rule or transgression of it, no patience or quarrel. no energy or laziness, no concentration or distraction, no wisdom or stupidity. (XXI) The disciples who practise the Dharma and who understand the practice of seeking for alms in that manner do not have the perception of of food mixed with the triple world; but, on the other hand, they also do not dwell in the Ease of Nirvana.

THE SUTRA ON PERFECT WISDOM WHICH EXPLAINS HOW BENEVOLENT KINGS MAY PROTECT THEIR COUNTRIES

CHAPTER I: PREFACE

1. *Description of the Assembly* (Ku (=T245)—825a: 7, Am (=T246) —834c: 10)

Thus have I heard at one time. The Lord dwelt on the Vulture Peak near Rājagṛha with a large crowd of monks, all of them Arhats, their outflows dried up, etc., with Rishis, Bodhisattvas, sages, devout women, hermits, the kings of the six heavens of the plane of sense-desire, i.e. Śakra and others, with sixteen great kings of countries, i.e. king Prasenajit, and others, and innumerable other living beings of the five places of rebirth.

2. *Cosmic Wonders* (Ku—825b: 1, Am—835a: 1)

Further, in a miraculous way the "Pure Lands" of the ten directions were made visible, as well as a hundred kotis of lion seats, upon which Buddhas were seated, broadly expounding the main points of the Dharma. Before each seat one flower was seen, and each of these flowers was adorned with a precious stone. Further there were innumerable Buddhas and Bodhisattvas, monks and beings of the eight classes (devas, nāgas, yakshas, gandharvas, garuḍas, asuras, kinnaras and mahoragas). Among them the Buddhas all explained the Prajñāpāramitā to all sides. And the whole crowd bowed before the Buddha's feet and retired to their seats on one side.

At that time on the eighth day of the fourth lunar month the Lord had entered the great, silent, quiet, wonderful concentration, and his body emitted a great, brilliant light over all the Buddha Lands of the ten directions. And the innumerable Devalokas caused wonderful flowers to rain, and the gods of the world of form also sent down a rain of heavenly flowers, as well as those of the formless world. These fragrant flowers descended like a cloud and covered the great crowd, and all the Buddha Lands shook in six ways.

Then king Prasenajit of Śrāvastī and the large crowd all asked in vain, why the Tathagata emitted such a brilliant light, what lucky sign this might be. And king Prasenajit and the other kings, having received the Buddha's divine power, made a far-sounding music, and all the devas of the worlds of sense-desire and form did the same, causing it to resound all over the great trichiliocosm.

3. *Appearance of ten Bodhisattvas from the ten directions* (Ku—825b: 29, Am—835a: 25)

Then the Tathagata again emitted numberless rays of mixed colours, and in each ray he caused a precious, thousand-leaved, golden coloured lotus flower to appear, upon each of which a Buddha was seated, preaching the Law. This Light of the Buddha shone over all the Buddha Lands of the ten directions. And from these Buddha Lands ten Bodhisattvas, each with a retinue of innumerable Bodhisattvas, came to the assembly, holding all kinds of incense, scattering all kinds of flowers, making immeasurable music, which they all offered to the Tathagata. They bowed before his feet, then silently retired to their seats, joined their hands and gazed at the Buddha, reverently and with their whole heart.

(Am) These ten Bodhisattvas were:

East	Universal Light	Samantaprabhā
South-East	Lotus-Hand	Padmapāṇi
South	Free from Sorrow	Vigatāśoka
South-West	Brilliant Light	Raśmiprabhāsa
West	He who is disposed to good conduct	Cāritramati (?)
North-West	Precious Conqueror	Ratnajaya (jina)
North	Receiver of Victory	Jayapratigraha (?)
North-East	Free from Dust	Vigatarajas (?)
Upper Region	Receiver of Joy	Tuṣṭigrāhin
Lower Region	Lotus Conqueror	Padmajina

Ku gives only the names of the Bodhisattvas of the four quarters:

South	Hero of the Law	Dharmaśūra
East	Precious Pillar	Ratnasthunā (?)
North	Nature of Space	Ākāśamaya
West	Maintainer of Virtue	Supratishṭha

CHAPTER II: CONTEMPLATING EMPTINESS (KU)
CONTEMPLATING THE TATHAGATA (AM)

1. *Protection of the Buddha-fruit* (Ku—825c: 13, Am—835b: 10)

(Am) Then the Tathagata awoke from His concentration and rising from His lion seat he spoke to the large crowd: "I know that the sixteen kings all have this thought: 'The Tathagata's Great Compassion everywhere spreads benefits and joy'. We, the Kings say: 'How shall we protect our countries?' But I shall first explain on behalf of the Bodhisattvas, how to protect the Buddha-fruit and how to protect the actions of the ten stages. You must all listen attentively, and virtuously think about it."

Then the large crowd, king Prasenajit, etc., on hearing the Buddha's words, all praised Him, saying: "How virtuous! How virtuous!" And they spread innumerable flowers, wonderful and precious, into the air, and made them into precious parasols which covered the large crowd on all sides. Then king Prasenajit rose from his seat, made a prostration before the Buddha's feet, joined his hands, and, kneeling down, spoke to the Buddha, saying: "Tathagata, the Bodhisattvas, the great beings say: 'How shall we protect the Buddha-fruit? How shall we protect the actions of the ten stages?' "

(Ku) *The Lord:* I know that the kings of the sixteen great countries in their thoughts wish to ask about the cause and condition of protecting their countries. I now first will explain for all the Bodhisattvas the cause and condition of protecting the Buddha-fruit, and the cause and condition for protecting the practice of the ten stages. Listen carefully, and attend well, I will now explain it . . . practise in accordance with dharma!

King Prasenajit: Good! Because of causes and conditions in the great affair (*vastu*=the preaching of the perfection of wisdom, cy) billions of various-coloured blossoms were scattered (=*pūjā*, cy), and changed into millions of jewelled parasols covering all the great assemblies (refers to ch. 1).

The great king arose, made his reverence, and said to the Buddha: How do all the Bodhisattvas protect the Buddha-fruit? Which causes and conditions protect the practice of the ten stages?

2. *Emptiness* (Ku—825c: 26, Am—835b: 20)

The Lord: Here the Bodhisattva does not review the four kinds of living beings; nor the Suchness of the skandhas, the Suchness of a being, a self, a person, or of permanence, ease, self and attractiveness, the Suchness of awareness, the Suchness of a Bodhisattva, the Suchness of the six perfections, of the four means of conversion and of all practices, or the Suchness of the double truth. Therefore the nature of all dharmas in its true reality is empty. It does not come or go; it is not produced or stopped. It is the same as the Reality-limit, the same as the true nature of Dharma, non-dual, not discriminated, like unto space. Therefore the skandhas, sense-fields and elements are without self, and have non-existence for their mark. This is the perfection of wisdom which demonstrates to the Bodhisattvas the practice of the ten stages.

The King: If all dharmas are such as this, what about the teaching of the beings whom the Bodhisattva is said to protect and teach?

The Lord: The nature of dharmas, O great king, concerns form, feeling, perception, impulse, consciousness; permanence, ease, self and attractiveness. It does not abide in form, it does not abide in no-form, it does not abide in what is not no-form, etc., to: it does not abide in not non-abiding. And why? Because form is not Suchness, no-form is not Suchness, on account of (their belonging to) worldly truth (only). On account of the three falsehoods are beings said to be seen. They are seen because of the true nature of all dharmas, etc., to: they are said to be seen because of all Buddhas, the triple vehicle, the seven auspicious things and the eight holy men. They are said to be seen because the sixty-two kinds of false views. Great king, if all dharmas are said to be seen by name(s only), etc., to: all Buddhas, the triple vehicle, the four kinds of birth (are), this is then not a non-vision of all dharmas.

The King: If the perfection of wisdom possesses a dharma which is not a non-dharma, then how does the great vehicle become manifest?

The Lord: The great vehicle, Great King, sees that which is not a no-dharma. As for a dharma, if it is (a dharma that is a) not no-dharma, this can be called the emptiness of non-non-dharmas.

Then there are eighteen kinds of emptiness. They are:

(1) The emptiness of the nature of dharmas; (2) the emptiness of form, feeling, perception, impulses and consciousness; (3) the emptiness of the twelve sense-fields and the eighteen elements; (4) the emptiness of the six great (physical) elements; (5) the emptiness of the four truths and of the twelve links.

This dharma is produced, abides, and is stopped. What is existence, just that is emptiness. Just this dharma is production, abiding, stopping, existence, emptiness. From moment to moment it takes place, like that. A dharma arises, a dharma abides, a dharma is stopped. And why? Ninety moments make up one thought. In one moment of one thought there pass nine hundred rises and falls; and so on, even so: form, all dharmas are like that. On account of the emptiness of perfect wisdom the links are not seen, the truths are not seen. And so we come to:

(6) The emptiness of all dharmas; (7) the emptiness of the subject; (8) the emptiness of the object; (9) the emptiness of both subject and object; (10) the conditioned emptiness; (11) the unconditioned emptiness; (12) the beginningless emptiness; (13) the emptiness of (essential) nature; (14) the emptiness of ultimate reality; (15) the emptiness of perfect wisdom; (16) the emptiness of the cause;

(17) the emptiness of the Buddha-fruit, and (18) the emptiness of emptiness.

Because of all these they are empty. They take place only because dharmas come together, and because of the conjunction of feelings, names, causes and fruits, because of the ten practices, because of the Buddha-fruit, etc., to: because of all those who exist in the six destinies. Son of good family, if a Bodhisattva is aware of dharmas and beings, of self, of persons, of one who sees, then he courses in the world, and is not separate from it. All dharmas are unshakeable, and they do not come, have not been stopped, are without marks, and without no-marks, with one mark only. Thus are all dharmas. Buddha, Dharma and Saṁgha are also like this. This is the first stage of one-pointedness of thought which is endowed with the eight-four thousand (dharmas of the) perfection of wisdom.

This then is called "the great vehicle". Cessation then become adamantine (*vajra*), which is also called transic concentration, and is also called all-practices. So it is explained in "The Prajñāpāramitā which emits light" (i.e. Mokshala's translation of the Version in 25,000 Lines in A.D. 291).

Great King, one hundred Buddhas, one thousand Buddhas, one thousand million Buddhas have preached the words, syllables and sentences of this Sutra. If all sentient beings in the great trichiliocosms countless as the sands of the Ganges would complete the giving of the innumerable precious substances and thereby attain the seven auspicious things and the four fruits, their merit would not be such as that of the production of one single thought of serene faith in this Sutra. How much more so the one who understands one single sentence! This may refer to a sentence, or a non-sentence, or what is neither a sentence or a non-sentence. Wisdom is not a verbal statement, and a verbal statement is not wisdom. Moreover, the perfection of wisdom is empty and in consequence the Bodhisattva is also empty. And why? Because the ten stages and the thirty rebirths are empty. It cannot be attained at beginning, middle or end. In stage after stage each of the thirty rebirths is empty. Wisdom also is neither all-knowledge nor the great vehicle. Because it is empty.

Great king, if the Bodhisattva sees his range, if he sees his cognition, if he sees his preaching or if he sees its reception, then that is not a holy seeing, but it is the perverted viewing of things by ordinary common people. This seeing of the triple world is in fact the karmic retribution of sentient beings. The innumerable arisings of desire in the six consciousnesses are said to be inexhaustible. All of them are deeds and fruits of deeds delineated and stored up in the world of sense desire, the world of form and the formless world,—and they are all empty. As the triple world is empty, so is the ignorance on which it is based. The holy stages are without outflows and without birth and death. In the three realms the remaining residues of ignorance and the karmic retribution which is evolved are also empty. The Bodhisattva who is enlightened to sameness attains to the adamantine concentration. The fruit of birth and death is empty, and so is the fruit of becoming. Their cause also is empty. Because of their emptiness. All-knowledge also is empty. The fruit of cessation also is empty. And so is the fruit of the all-knowledge which encompasses the three unconditioned fruits of a Buddha,—i.e. the cessation which results from intellectual comprehension, the cessation which is effected without intellectual comprehension (and which results from the incompleteness of the necessary conditions) and space.

If there is a teaching of the practice of perfect wisdom and if there is a hearing of it, it is just like a magically created man. There is in fact no speaking, no listening. The dharma is the same as the Dharma-nature which is like space. All dharmas are such. Great King, a Bodhisattva cultivates the protection of the Buddha-fruit. To protect the perfection of wisdom is to protect all-knowledge, as well as the ten powers, the eighteen special dharmas of a Buddha, the five eyes, the five-divisioned Dharma-body, the four boundless thoughts and all the virtuous fruits. When the Buddha preaches, then countless men and gods obtain the purity of the Dharma-eye, the natural stage and the stage of faith. And one hundred thousand men all obtain the great practice of the great emptiness of a Bodhisattva. (Am. 836a: 22–836b:). Finally King Prasenajit explains his ideas about Buddhahood, which are approved by the Buddha.

CHAPTER III: INSTRUCTION AND CONVERSION OF BODHISATTVAS (KU) THE COURSE OF A BODHISATTVA (AM)

1. *Fourteen kinds of patience* (Ku—826b: 20, Am—836b: 11)

King Prasenajit: What are the practices of the ten stages on the part of the Bodhisattvas? How do they convert beings? What are the marks of those to be converted (*vineya*)?

The Lord: The five kinds of Patience are the dharmas of a Bodhisattva. They are:

1. Patience of Submission: (1) lower, (2) middle, (3) upper. (Precedes the stages (*bhūmi*).)
2. Patience of Faith: (4) lower, (5) middle, (6) upper. (=Belief, stages 1–3.)

3. Adaptable (*anulomikī*) Patience: (7) lower, (8) middle, (9) upper. (Following the Buddha-road, stages 4–6.)

4. Patient acceptance of that which fails to be produced (*anutpattika*): (10) lower, (11) middle, (12) upper. (No-rebirth; stages 7–9.)

5. Patience of Calm Cessation: (13) lower, (14) upper. (Nirvana; 10th stage.)

This is called the practice of the perfection of wisdom by all the Buddhas and Bodhisattvas.

1. When the son of good family first puts forth the thought of faith, living beings countless like the sands of the Ganges practise the *Patience of Submission.* In the triple jewel they practise kindliness, as well as the following ten thoughts, i.e. faith, vigour, mindfulness, concentration, wisdom, giving, morality, protecting, the Vow and the dedication (of merit). So they help to convert living beings, having transcended the level of the two vehicles. All Bodhisattvas nourish these ten thoughts which are the holy womb. In succession they rouse up the dry vision (cf. PDc p. 174 *sukkhavipassaka*) which makes them one of the clan. They then have ten further thoughts, which means the four applications of mindfulness, i.e. to (1–4) body, feelings, thoughts and dharmas, or to impurity, ill, impermanence and not-self; (5–7) three applications of mindfulness, i.e. the three wholesome roots of kindness, generosity and wisdom; (8–10) three applications of mindfulness, i.e. to the three times, or the three patiences, the patience with regard to the past causes, the patience with regard to present causes and effects, and the patience with regard to future effects. This Bodhisattva also is able to convert all living beings, and he has transcended (the notions of) self, person, awareness and living beings, and the perverted notions of the outsiders which cannot crush him. Again there are the ten paths of the lineage-stages, which are the contemplations of form, etc., and the attaining of the patience of morality, the patience of insight, the patience of concentration, the patience of wisdom, the patience of deliverance, the concentration of contemplating both cause and effect in the triple world, the emptiness patience, the signless patience, the wishless patience, the patience of the contemplation of the two truths as respectively false and real. The impermanence of all the dharmas is called the patience of impermanence. The emptiness of a dharma is the patience of that which fails to be produced, which obtains the emptiness of all dharmas. With the ten firm thoughts this

Bodhisattva turns the royal wheel; he also converts the four Continents, and arouses the roots of goodness in all living beings.

2. Moreover, *the Patience of Faith* is the Bodhisattva's perceiving and understanding well the bonds and defilements of the triple world and his cutting himself off from them, and his being able to transport himself to one hundred, one thousand or ten thousand Buddha-fields, and therein to exhibit ten, one thousand or ten thousand bodies. His magical proficiencies are innumerable, and his virtues are constant, with fifteen thoughts at their head, i.e. the four means of conversion, the four boundless thoughts, the four vast vows and the three doors to deliverance. From this good stage the Bodhisattva advances to all-knowledge, and takes these fifteen thoughts to be the seeds of the roots of all the practices.

3. Moreover, *the Adaptable Patience*, which is the Bodhisattva's overcoming, or conquering, of the seeming appearance of dharmas, and his ability to cut off all thoughts of the triple world and of the bonds and defilements. And therefore there is the exhibition of one (single) body (simultaneously) in the Buddha-fields of the ten directions. With countless inexplicable magical proficiencies he converts living beings.

4. Moreover, *the patient acceptance of that which fails to be produced* is the Bodhisattva's contemplation and insight which goes far without moving (=*dūrāṅgama*, the 7th stage). He also has cut off both the thoughts and the forms of the triple world. He has cut off both the defilements and their residues from these thoughts and forms. Therefore he manifests inexplicable virtues and magical proficiencies.

5. Moreover, *the Patience of Calm Cessation.* The Buddhas and Bodhisattvas alike use this patience when they enter into the adamantine concentration. Here the practice of the lower patience (No. 13) is said to belong to the Bodhisattva, whereas in the higher (No. 14) it is called all-knowledge. Both alike contemplate ultimate reality. They have truly cut off the thoughts, residues and ignorance with regard to the triple world. Their exhaustion of all signs is adamantine (*vajra*). Their exhaustion of both signs and no-signs is all-knowledge. It transcends both the conventional and the ultimate truth (of the outsiders). As all-knowledge, enlightenment, it becomes the eleventh stage. It is neither existent nor non-existent, profoundly pure, constantly abiding and not changing, the same as the Reality-limit, equal to the true nature of Dharma, without conditions, greatly

compassionate and, riding in the vehicle of all-knowledge, it comes to convert the beings of the triple world.

2. *Sequel to this teaching* (Ku—827b: 4, Am—837b: 4)

Then all those present rose from their seats, spread innumerable flowers and burned incense as an offering to the Buddha, and reverently praised Him. And king Prasenajit, standing before the Tathagata, spoke a long hymn in praise of Him and of the fourteen royal Bodhisattvas who represent the fourteen kinds of forbearance just explained by the Buddha.

And the Lord said to all those present: "Ten thousand aeons ago this king Prasenajit was king Nāgaprabhā, a Bodhisattva of the fourth stage. And now, standing before Me, he has uttered a lion's roar like this, like this!" Furthermore the Buddha digressed upon the wonderful blessing power of the fourteen kinds of forbearance, practised by the Bodhisattvas of the ten stages. And by this preaching numberless men and gods among the audience reached one of the ten stages of Bodhisattvahood, and numberless Bodhisattvas were advanced on their way to Buddhahood.

CHAPTER IV: THE TWO KINDS OF TRUTH

1. *The two truths* (Ku—829a: 4, Am—837a: 3)

At king Prasenajit's request the difference is explained between the "conventional truth" (which only refers to the outer appearance of the world), and the "ultimate truth" (which is free from errors and consists of the views of the Sages concerning the nature of things). The subject is dealt with in verse and prose.

2. *Blessings derived from perfect wisdom* (Ku—829c: 2, Am—839a: 28)

The Tathagata then praises the immeasurable blessing power of the Prajñāpāramitā, which, being expounded by the Buddhas, causes countless sentient beings to reach Buddhahood. Whoever in reading this Sutra can form one thought of pure belief, thus passes over ten thousands of aeons of birth and death and suffering. How much greater is its blessing power to those who copy and keep and read it, thus obtaining salvation and protection from all the Buddhas and speedily reaching full enlightenment. By these words of the Tathagata many myriads among the audience reached different stages of Bodhisattvahood.

3. *Ku: Name of the Sutra, and assurance of its power to protect*

Here the fourth chapter of Am is concluded. In Ku (829c: 16) the Buddha goes on to speak about the name of the Sutra and its blessing power as regards the protection of countries, of houses, and of the bodies of all living beings. "Great kings, the name of this Sutra is: Prajñāpāramitā (in answer to) the questions of benevolent kings". It may be called the Medicine of the Law for all kings of countries; when they use it, it will be very useful in protecting their homes and all that lives; this Prajñāpāramitā shall protect them as walls and swords and shields (see at end of ch. 8).

CHAPTER V: PROTECTING THE COUNTRY

1. *The Prajñāpāramitā protects from calamities* (Ku—829c: 29, Am—840a: 10)

The Buddha said to the great kings: "Listen attentively, listen attentively! Now I shall explain on your behalf the Law of Protecting the Country. In all countries, when riots are imminent, calamities are descending, or robbers are coming in order to destroy (the houses and possessions of the inhabitants), you, the kings, ought to receive, keep and read this Prajñāpāramitā, solemnly to adorn the place of worship, to place (there) a hundred Buddha images, a hundred images of Bodhisattvas, a hundred lion-seats, and to invite a hundred Dharma-masters (priests) that they may explain this Sutra. And before the seats you must light all kinds of lamps, burn all kinds of incense, spread all kinds of flowers. You must liberally offer clothes, and bedding, food and medicine, houses, beds and seats, all offerings, and every day you must read this Sutra for two hours. If kings, great ministers, monks and nuns, male and female lay-members of the community listen to it, receive and read it, and act according to the Law, the calamities shall be extinguished. Great Kings, in the countries there are innumerable demons and spirits, each of them with innumerable relatives (followers); if they hear this Sutra, they shall protect your countries. If riots are imminent, the demons and spirits are uproarious beforehand, and it is for this reason that the people revolt; then robbery arises, and the hundred families (the people) perish; the Kings and the crown princes, the princes and the hundred magistrates mutually do right and wrong. If unnatural things happen in heaven and on the earth: the sun, the moon and the stars lose their times and their courses, and great fires, inundations and storms are prevalent, if all these calamities arise, all people must receive, keep and read this Prajñāpāramitā. If they receive, keep and read this Sutra, all their desires shall be fulfilled: they shall obtain rank and wealth, sons and daughters, wisdom and intelligence, success in their actions, human and heavenly rewards. The dangers of disease and pestilence shall be removed from them, and if fetters, the cangue and chains restrain and bind their bodies, they shall be released. Even if they have broken the four important commandments, committed the five evils and violated all the precepts, even immeasurable crimes shall all be wiped out."

2. *Story about Śakra* (Ku—830a: 21, Am—840b: 1)

Thereupon the Buddha relates how in olden times Śakra, Chief of Gods, caused the four armies of king Mūrdhajarājā, who came to attack his heavenly abode and to destroy Śakra himself, to retire only by the power of the Prajñāpāramitā Sutra, read by a hundred priests at his request. Śakra thus followed the Dharma of the former Buddhas, and peace and joy returned among the gods.

3. *Story of the conversion of a thousand kings* (Ku—830a: 24, Am—840b: 5)

In the second tale, related by the Buddha, the conversion of a thousand kings is described. When the Crown-prince of Devala ascended the throne, he was consecrated by a heterodox priest, who ordered him to take the heads of a thousand kings in order to sacrifice them to Mahākāla Deva in the grave (of his father). After he had caught 999 kings, he went ten thousand miles to the North, and found there a king called "Universal Light" (Samantaprabhāsa). This king asked him to allow him to hold, one day, a service in honour of the Triple Jewel and to give drink and food to the monks. When he had obtained the conqueror's permission, he followed the doctrine, as preached by the Buddhas of the past (Ku: "the seven Buddhas"), had a hundred high seats prepared and invited a hundred priests to explain eight thousand milliards of Verses on Prajñāpāramitā one day during two hours.

Then the first of those priests explained a hymn on behalf of king Samantaprabhāsa who, on hearing the Dharma, achieved, with all his relatives, a high degree of enlightenment. When they arrived in Devala, he caused the other 999 kings, whom he addressed as "Benevolent Ones", to read the Verses on Prajñāpāramitā, whereupon they all reached the same degree of "Concentration on Emptiness". Then the king of Devala asked, which doctrine they were reading. When he heard king Samantaprabhāsa recite the Verses, explained to him by the priest, he too was converted, and danced with joy. He then said to the one thousand kings: "I was deceived by a heterodox priest. Return to your countries, and invite Buddhist priests to explain the Prajñāpāramitā." And he himself became a monk, and obtained the patient acceptance of that which fails to be produced (see pp. 171-2), representing the 7th, 8th and 9th stages of a Bodhisattva.

4. *Advice to the kings* (Ku—830b: 27, Am—840c: 9)

The Tathagata continued: "Great Kings, there were in former times five thousand kings of countries, who always read this Sutra, and who in their present life have got their reward. In the same way you, sixteen great kings, must practise the Rite of Protecting the Country, and you must keep, read and explain this Sutra. If in future ages the kings of countries wish to protect their kingdoms and to protect their own bodies, they too must act in the same way."

5. *Rewards of hearing this teaching* (Ku—830c: 4, Am—840c: 13)

When the Buddha explained this teaching, numberless men obtained the irreversible stage, Asuras obtained rebirth in a heaven, and numberless gods of the worlds of sense-desire and form won the patient acceptance of non-production.

CHAPTER VI: SPREADING FLOWERS (KU), MIRACLES (AM)

1. *Flower miracles* (Ku—830c: 13, Am—840c: 18)

Then the kings of the sixteen countries and the whole large crowd, on hearing the Buddha explain the very profound meaning of this Prajñāpāramitā, danced with joy and scattered innumerable precious flowers in the air. These flowers became precious lotus seats, upon which the numberless Buddhas of the ten directions were seated, explaining the Prajñāpāramitā. Thus various flower miracles took place in the air, and the Prajñāpāramitā was expounded by Buddhas and the great Bodhisattvas.

2. *Praise of Prajñāpāramitā* (Ku—830c: 27, Am—841a: 3)

King Prasenajit and the whole crowd joined their hands and said to the Buddha: "We wish that in the past, present and future the Buddhas may always explain the Prajñāpāramitā, and that the living beings may always see and hear what we see and heard today." The Buddha answered: "Great Kings, this Prajñāpāramitā is the mother of the Buddhas and Bodhisattvas, and the origin of blessing and supernatural power. As the Buddhas by explaining it in the same way can create much benefit, you must always receive and keep it."

3. *Five miracles of the Tathagata* (Ku—831a: 4, Am—841a: 10)

Then the Tathagata in front of the great crowd showed his wonderful supernatural power by means of five miracles: (1) He changed one flower into numberless flowers, and these again into one; (2) one Buddha-land into innumerable Buddha-lands, and vice-versa; (3) one of the countries, numerous as the particles of dust, into innumerable such countries, and vice-versa; (4) an immeasurable sea into a hair-pore, and the immeasurable Mount Sumeru into a mustard seed; (5) one Buddha body into innumerable bodies of living beings, and vice-versa. Thus he caused large things to appear as small things, and small things as large, pure things as dirty, and dirty ones as pure. At the sight of these miracles the thousand women became men and obtained the trance of supernatural power, numberless gods and men obtained the patient acceptance of non-production, innumerable asuras attained the Bodhisattva-road and the Bodhisattvas became Buddhas.

CHAPTER VII: RESPECTFULLY RECEIVING AND KEEPING THIS SUTRA

1. *The practice of the Dharma* (Ku—831c: 19, Am—841c: 23)

After having explained how virtuous men can get the clear insight mentioned in this Sutra by practising the different kinds of forbearance up to the adamantine concentration and always performing the ten ways of wholesome action, the Buddha speaks in prose and verse about the Bodhisattvas of the ten stages. These stages are, as usually, called "the joyous stage", "the immaculate stage", etc. All these Bodhisattvas receive ,keep and explain the Dharma and, going to the Buddha-Lands, obtain perfect enlightenment. He also speaks about practising the 84,000 perfections, i.e. the numberless ways leading to Nirvana.

2. *Prediction of seven calamities* (Ku—832b: 20, Am—843a: 6)

Then the Tathagata states that at the time when after his death the Dharma shall be about to be extinguished, and all sentient beings shall commit evil deeds, in the countries all kinds of calamities shall arise. Then all the kings, crown-princes, queens and their relatives, the hundred officials and the hundred families of all the countries must receive and keep this Prajñāpāramitā, in order to protect themselves; and peace and joy shall be their reward. The Buddha commits this Sutra to the kings of the countries, and not to the monks and nuns, or laymen or laywomen, because these kings alone have the royal majesty and power necessary to establish the Dharma (in those times). Therefore these kings must receive, keep, read and explain this text, in order to drive away the seven calamities which may descend upon the sixteen large, 500 middle and 100,000 small countries of Jambudvīpa.

These seven calamities are:

1. The sun and moon lose their courses, or their colours change, or they are eclipsed, or surrounded by several halos.
2. The stars lose their courses, comets appear, the five planets change or appear in the day time.
3. Nāga fire, demon fire, human fire and tree fire, the four great fires, arise and burn down everything.
4. The seasons change. It rains and thunders in winter. There is hoar-frost, ice and snow in summer. It rains earth and stones, sand and pebbles. It hails at wrong times. It rains red or black water. The rivers swell and overflow, carrying stones and rocks along.
5. Heavy storms arise, clouds cover the sun and moon, houses are destroyed and trees uprooted. Sand and stones fly about.
6. Excessive heat causes ponds to dry up, grass and trees to wither and die, and the hundred cereals to remain in a state of unripeness.
7. From all sides enemies come to attack the country. Internal and external wars break out, and the hundred families go to ruin and death.

In all calamities of heaven and earth this Prajñāpāramitā must be received, kept, read and explained.

On hearing the Buddha's words, the sixteen kings were all terrified, and king Prasenajit asked the Tathagata for what reasons these numberless calamities of heaven and earth took place. Then the Buddha answered that they were caused by the impiety of the people towards their parents, by irreverence towards their teachers and elders, recluses and Brahmins, kings and ministers, and by not acting according to the True Dharma.

3. *The Prajñāpāramitā protects from calamities* (Ku—, Am—843b: 10)

And again the Buddha enumerated the blessing powers of this Prajñāpāramitā with regard to Buddhas and Bodhisattvas, kings and all sentient beings. Like a precious jewel it gives them all kinds of virtues, it can protect them from poisonous Nāgas and from the evil demons and spirits; it can fulfil the desires of human hearts and give them the title of a king, or a wishing gem. It can cause the great Nāga kings to send down a sweet and beneficient rain upon grasses and trees. It is like a brilliant light, placed upon a high standard in the darkness of the night.

4. *Description of the Ceremony* (Ku—832c: 26, Am—843b: 17)

Ku: Great Kings, you must (order to) make nine-coloured flags, nine *chang* (90 feet) long, and nine-coloured flowers, two *chang* high, and a thousand lamps, five *wan* high, and nine boxes of jade, nine covers of jade and tables (or, a table) made of the seven precious things, and thereupon place the Sutras (apparently nine copies of this Sutra, preserved in nine boxes and covers). If a king celebrates the ceremony, he must always distribute (the offering) one hundred steps in front of these tables (or, this table). This Sutra always emits a thousand brilliant rays, and prevents the seven calamities from arising within a radius of a thousand miles. If a king is in residence he must have curtains made of the seven precious things, and inside these curtains a high seat, also consisting of the seven precious things, on which the Sutra must be placed. Day after day he must make offerings, spread flowers, and burn incense, as if he served his father and mother, or king Śakra, chief of the gods.

Am: You kings must order precious flags and canopies to be made, must light lamps and spread flowers, make extensive offerings, precious boxes and splendid Sutras, and place these upon precious tables. When you are about to perform the ceremony, you always must lead (the performing rites) before these tables, and around the place of worship curtains made of the seven precious things should be hung. Seats should be made of all kinds of precious things, and the Sutras should be placed on these seats, and all kinds of offerings should be made, as if serving your parents, or the gods or Śakra, their ruler.

Great Kings, I see that all human beings have obtained this rank because in former ages they have served the five hundred Buddhas and respectfully made offerings to them, and that all holy men and those who obtained the fruit of the Dharma are reborn in their countries and cause great blessings. But if the felicity of those kings is exhausted and they do not walk in the Dharma, the holy men go away and violent calamities arise.

5. *The five Bodhisattvas* (Ku—833a: 8, Am—843b: 24)

(Ku) If in future ages a king of a country receives and keeps the Triple Jewel, I shall cause the five Great-Power Bodhisattvas to go there and to protect the country;

1. Vajra-nāda	Adamantine-Roar
2. Nāgarāja-nāda	Nāga-king-Roar
3. Abhaya-daśabala-nāda	Fearless-ten-power-Roar
4. Meghadundhubhi-nāda (?)	Thunder-and-Lightning-Roar
5. Amita-bala-nāda	Immeasurable-Power-Roar

(Am) Great Kings, if in future ages the kings of the countries establish the Good Dharma and protect the Triple Jewel, I order the crowds of Bodhisattvas, of great beings, from five directions to go and protect their countries.

The first Bodhisattva shall come, holding a "thousand-treasures-wheel". The second shall come carrying a "golden-wheel lamp". The third shall come holding a "thunderbolt-club". The fourth shall come carrying a "thousand-treasure-net". The fifth shall come carrying a "fifty-swords-wheel".

These "Five Great Officers" are the kings of the five thousand Great Spirits, and they shall produce great blessings in your countries. You must erect their images and make offerings to them. Great Kings, I now commit the Triple Jewel to you all. (The sixteen countries are then enumerated.)

From the East the Bodhisattva Vajrapāṇi, the great being, shall come to protect those countries, carrying a vajra-club (or: vajra-pestle) in his hand and emitting a red lustre. He shall be accompanied by four kotis of Bodhisattvas.

From the South Vajraratna shall come, holding a vajra-gem in his hand, and emitting a sun-coloured lustre. He too shall be accompanied by four kotis of Bodhisattvas.

From the West Vajratīkshṇa shall come, carrying a vajra-sword in his hand, and emitting a golden lustre. He also shall be accompanied by the same retinue of Bodhisattvas.

From the North Vajrayaksha shall come, carrying a vajra-bell in his hand, and emitting a vaiḍūrya-coloured lustre. He also shall be accompanied by four kotis of Bodhisattvas.

From the Centre Vajrapāramitā shall come, carrying a vajra-wheel, and emitting a five-coloured lustre. He also shall be accompanied by four kotis of Bodhisattvas.

All these Bodhisattvas shall give great blessings to your countries. You should erect their images and make offerings to them.

Then Vajrapāṇi and the other Bodhisattvas rose from their seats, prostrated themselves before the Buddha's feet, went to one side, and said to the Tathagata:

"Venerable of the World, it is our original vow to receive the Buddha's divine power and, if in the worlds of the ten directions and in all the Buddha-Lands there are spots where this Sutra is received and kept, read and explained, to arrive there within a moment with all these followers in order to protect and erect the True Dharma, to cause those countries to be free from all calamities, war as well as pestilence, and to remove them all."

6. *The Dharanis* (Ku—833a: 27, Am—843c: 13)

"Lord, we possess dhāraṇīs, which can maintain, embrace and protect (those who use them). This is what all the Buddhas originally have practised and which causes a speedy salvation. If a man once hears this Sutra, all obstacles derived from his past deeds are taken away; how much greater is its blessing power if he reads and studies it! By means of the majestic power of the Dharma we shall cause the countries to be always free from all kinds of calamities."

Then, with different mouths but one sound, they pronounced the Dharanis before the Buddha.

Am here (843c: 20–844a: 9) gives the thirty-six Dharanis, absent in Ku.

On hearing them the Tathagata praised the Bodhisattvas and said: "If there are persons who read and keep these Dharanis, I and all the Buddhas of the ten directions shall always protect them. The bad demons and spirits shall revere them like Buddhas, and soon they shall obtain perfect enlightenment. Great Kings, I commit this Sutra to you, kings of the sixteen countries (here their names are enumerated: Vaiśālī, Kośala, Śrāvastī, Magadha, Vārāṇaśī, Kapilavastu, Kuśinagara, Pātaliputra, Campā, Sāmkāsya, Gāndhāra, etc.), you must receive and keep the Prajñāpāramitā."

7. *Results of this teaching* (Ku—833a: 23, Am—844a: 10)

Then all the big crowds, the Asuras, etc., on hearing the Buddha's words regarding the calamities, were excited; the hair of their bodies stood erect, and with loud voices they exclaimed: "We vow that henceforth we shall not be reborn in those countries."

And the sixteen kings forthwith threw away their thrones and became monks, and won the eight deliverances, the ten all-bases, and the patience of submission, the patience of faith, and the patient acceptance of non-production.

Then all the gods, Asuras, etc., spread four kinds of flowers as an offering to the Buddha and reached the three doors to deliverance. And innumerable Bodhisattvas also spread flowers and immediately reached the third and fourth of the five kinds of patience, or, developing a great compassion in the numberless Buddha-Lands, they brought extensive blessings to the living beings, and in their present life reached Buddhahood.

CHAPTER VIII: THE BUDDHA COMMITS THIS SUTRA AND THE TRIPLE JEWEL TO THE BENEVOLENT KINGS

1. *Prophecies of disasters to come* (Ku—833b: 13, Am—844b: 6)

The Buddha then predicts to the kings that 50,500 and 5,000 years after his death (in Ku: 80,800,8000 years) there will be no Buddha, no Dharma, no Samgha (and, according to Ku, no devout man or woman). Then this Sutra and the Triple Jewel shall be committed to the kings of the countries and to the four classes of Saints (Streamwinners, etc.)—to the former that they may erect and protect them, to the latter that they may receive, keep and read the Sutra, explain its meaning and, on behalf of the living beings, extensively expound the essential points of the Dharma.

Then He prophecies the extinction of the Doctrine and the ruin of the states at the time when all kings and royal princes and ministers shall be self-confident and haughty, and when they shall destroy the Buddha's doctrine and promulgate rules and laws in order to restrain his disciples, monks and nuns, when they shall not allow (their subjects) to become monks, to walk in the correct path, to build Stupas and to make Buddhist images, white robes and high seats, etc. He warns the kings that, at the time when after his death the four classes of Saints, and the kings, royal princes and officials who all have the task of maintaining and protecting the Triple Jewel, shall destroy it, like worms within the body of a lion devouring its flesh, all kinds of calamities shall fall upon them and they shall be reborn in hell, or as hungry ghosts, or as poor and mean men. He warns them that the extinction of the Dharma shall be near when wicked monks hanker after fame and gain, and, without relying on the Buddha's Law, cause the kings to set up rules and laws, and not to depend on the Buddha's commandments.

The sixteen kings, on hearing this prophecy, were deeply distressed, and the sound of their crying moved the 3,000 heavens: darkness fell upon the earth, and there was no light to be seen. All the kings decided to receive and keep the Buddha's words, to follow his instructions, and not to restrain the four classes of his followers from leaving their homes and from studying the doctrine. But the numberless crowd of gods lamented the approaching emptiness of the world, the Buddha-less age.

2. *Name of the Sutra* (Ku—, Am—844c: 19)

King Prasenajit then said to the Buddha: "Lord, how shall we call this Sutra?" And the Tathagata answered: "Great King, this Sutra's name is Prajñāpāramitā on benevolent kings protecting their countries." It also has the name 'Sweet Dew (*amṛita*), Medicine of the Dharma'. If one obeys it, it can cure all diseases. Great King, the blessing power of the Prajñāpāramitā is as immeasurable as empty space. If it is received, kept and read, its blessing power can protect the benevolent kings and all living beings, like a fence or the wall of a castle. Therefore you ought to receive and to keep it!"

When the Buddha had ended explaining this Sutra, then Maitreya, Simhacandra, and all the numberless Bodhisattvas, the Disciples, gods, monks and nuns, laymen and laywomen rejoiced greatly and received his word devoutly.

THE PERFECTION OF WISDOM IN 150 LINES

Homage to the Perfection of Wisdom!

Introduction

Thus have I heard at one time. The Lord *Mahāvairocana* had obtained the various kinds of omniscience from all the Tathagatas. With the jewelled crown of a Tathagata He had achieved the ten sovereignties over the triple world. He had won the cognition of all-knowledge which is the genetrix of all the Tathagatas. A great master of Yoga, He had taken to heart the Seal of all the Tathagatas, which is the sameness of all dharmas. He had performed manifold deeds, and had through them fulfilled the hopes of all beings in the world without exception. Greatly compassionate, He dwelled perpetually in the sameness of the triple world, a Tathagata whose (actions of) body, speech and mind were all Adamantine.

Now he had taken up his abode among the Paranirmitavaśavartin gods who still belong to the plane of sense-desire. It is bedecked with all kinds of fine and precious jewels, ensigns of various colours and bells on fine threads flutter in the breeze, and it abounds in garlands of flowers, diadems, necklaces and pendants, all as beautiful as the moon. When Tathagatas visit it, they all laud it as full of all blessings. And He dwelt together with 8,000 koṭis of great Bodhisattvas, headed by Vajrapāṇi, Avalokiteśvara, Ākāśagarbha, Vajramuṣṭi, Mañjuśrī, Sacittotpādadharmacakrapravartin, Gaganagañja and Sarvamārapramardin. Surrounded and accompanied by them, He demonstrated the Dharma—lovely in the beginning, lovely in the middle, lovely in the end, salutary, well expressed, uncontaminated, perfect and quite pure.

I. The word "Bodhisattva"

"The word 'Bodhisattva' is a word for the purity of Rapture. (It is a word for the purity of signs, and therefore of greed, hate, delusion, conceit and envy.) It is a word for the purity of views, of Delight, of craving, of arrogance, of Adornment, of mental satisfaction, of Light, and of physical happiness. It is a word for the purity of visual forms, sounds, smells, tastes and touchables." And why? Because all dharmas are pure in their own-being. It is because of the fact that all dharmas are empty in their own-being that there is this purity of the perfection of wisdom.

I. A. If someone, Vajrapāṇi, has once only heard this Method of the perfection of wisdom, which is the consummation of the purity of the own-being of all dharmas, then, until the time that he reaches the terrace of enlightenment, all his coverings will be removed—the covering of the defilements, the covering of the dharmas, and the covering of his (past) deeds—however thickly they may have piled up. He will never again be reborn in the places of woe, i.e. in the hells, and so on. Even when he had done evil he will immediately become free from suffering and pure. Whosoever bears it in mind, and for even one single day recites and studies it, and attends to it methodically, he will in this very life already, after he has attained the Adamantine concentration of the sameness of all dharmas, become the sovereign of all dharmas, and in all dharmas he will experience happiness, contentment and supreme bliss. After sixteen rebirths as a great Bodhisattva he will become a Tathagata, a Holder of the Thunderbolt.

I. B. Thereupon the Lord *Vajrapāṇi* who has won Reunion with the great vehicle of all the Tathagatas, who (combines) all the Mandalas, who is the best of all the beings who hold the Thunderbolt, who is the conqueror of all the triple worlds without exception, the discipliner of all the inhabited worlds without exception, who brings all things to Success, great in Sacraments, the great Essence of the Adamantine Secret, surrounded by a manifold retinue, demonstrated the meaning of this method of perfect wisdom. He smiled, made the Thunderbolt-yawn, brandished in his left hand the great Original Thunderbolt and held it raised to his own heart. Thereafter He uttered this Quintessence of the Inner Reality which is called the Adamantine fruitful Sacrament of the Great Bliss, i.e. Hūṃ.

II. The Great Enlightenment

Thereupon the Lord *Vairocana*, the Tathagata, demonstrated the method of the perfection of wisdom which is called the Consummation of awakening to the calm true nature of all the Tathagatas:

"Where one has awoken to the sameness of the Thunderbolt, there is the great enlightenment, because the Thunderbolt is exceedingly compact;

where one has awoken to the sameness of the meaning, there is the great enlightenment, because there is only one single meaning;

where one has awoken to the sameness of Dharma, there is the great enlightenment, because it is pure in its own-being;

where one has awoken to the sameness of everything, there is the great enlightenment, because everything remains undiscriminated."

II. A. If, Vajrapāṇi, someone will hear these four consummate dharmas, bear them in mind, recite and develop them, he will, although he may practise all kinds of evil, until the time that he is established on the terrace of enlightenment, escape all the places of woe. Though his sins be vast, he will soon awake to the supreme enlightenment.

II. B. Thereupon, when this had been said, *the Lord* here explained in further detail the acquisition of the Fist of Cognition, and with a smiling face he taught this Quintessence of the sameness of all dharmas. A.

III. Non-obsession

Thereupon the Lord *Sarvaduṣṭavinayaśākyamuni*, the Tathagata, demonstrated the consummation of the perfection of wisdom called the Assembling of the conquest achieved through the sameness of all dharmas:

"From non-obsession with greed should non-obsession with hate be known;
from non-obsession with hate non-obsession with delusion;
from non-obsession with delusion non-obsession with all dharmas;
from non-obsession with all dharmas non-obsession with the perfection of wisdom."

III. A. If someone, Vajrapāṇi, will listen to this method of the perfection of wisdom, bear it in mind, recite and develop it, then, even though[1] he may kill all the beings born in the triple world, he will not fall into the places of woe. Though his sins be vast, he will soon awake to the supreme enlightenment.

III. B. Thereupon the Lord *Vajrapāṇi* demonstrated in further detail the meaning of this Dharmahood. He made the gesture[2] called the Thunderbolt which conquers the triple world, he frowned and raised his eye-brows, his eyes flamed and he showed his eye-teeth, stretched out his left foot and taught the Quintessence of the doctrine called Vajra hūṃ. Huṃ.

IV. The state of purity

Thereupon the Lord *Svabhāvaśuddha*, the Tathagata, demonstrated the method of the perfection of wisdom called the Seal of the sovereign cognition which surveys the sameness of all dharmas:

[1]+'dul-ba'i dbaṅ-gi phyir,="by means of the discipline", or "for the sake of enforcing the discipline"?

[2]or: Seal.

"The state of purity from all greed leads in the world to the state of purity from hate;
the state of purity from all taints leads in the world to the state of purity from all evil;
the state of the purity from (of) all dharmas leads in the world to the state of purity of (from) all beings;
the state of purity of all cognition leads in the world to the state of purity of the perfection of wisdom."

IV. A. If, Vajrapāṇi, someone will listen to this method of the perfection of wisdom, bear it in mind, recite and develop it, then, although he may find himself in the midst of all kinds of stains and passions, like a lotus he will not be stained by the adventitious defilements, the stains and faults of the passions. Though his sins be vast, he will soon awake to the supreme enlightenment.

IV. B. Thereupon the Bodhisattva *Avalokiteśvara*, the great being, with a smiling face explained the meaning of this (method) in greater detail. He saw that, like a lotus with wide open petals (a Bodhisattva) is not stained by the stains of passion, etc., and for the sake of the whole world he taught this Quintessence (of the doctrine) called "the Variegated Lotus". Hrīḥ.

V. The gift

Thereupon the Lord *Sarvatraidhātukādhipati*, the Tathagata, demonstrated the method of the perfection of wisdom called the Womb of the cognition which has as its Source the Consecration of all the Tathagatas:

"The gift of Consecretion leads to the acquisition of kingship over everything in the triple world;
the gift of Meaning leads to the fulfilment of all hopes;
the gift of Dharma leads to the attainment of the sameness of all dharmas;
the fleshly gift leads to the acquisition of all happiness in body, speech and thought."

V. B. Thereupon the Bodhisattva *Akāśagarbha*, the great being, gave a smile. He tied on to his head the Rosary of the Adamantine and precious Consecration, explained the meaning of this (method) in greater detail, and taught the Quintessence (of the doctrine) which is called "the precious Sacrament of all Consecrations". Trāṃ.

VI. The Seal

Thereupon the Lord *Śāśvatasarvatathāgatajñānamudrāprāptasarvatathāgatamuṣṭidhara*, the Tathagata, demonstrated the method of the perfection of wisdom called the Thunderbolt of the Sustaining Power of the Seal of the cognition of all the Tathagatas:

"The Assumption of the Seal of the body of all the Tathagatas leads to all Tathagatahood;
the Assumption of the Seal of the speech of all the Tathagatas leads to the acquisition of all dharmas;
the Assumption of the Seal of the thought of all the Tathagatas leads to the acquisition of all concentrations;
the Assumption of the Adamantine Seal (of all the Tathagatas) leads to the highest Success of all, (the accomplishment of the) Adamantine Essence in all (acts of) body, speech and thought."

VI. A. If someone hears this method of the perfection of wisdom, bears it in mind, recites it, gives advice on it and develops it, he will, after he has attained all possible spiritual successes, accomplishments, cognitions and activities, including the highest spiritual success, i.e. (the accomplishment of) the Adamantine Essence in all (acts of) body, speech and mind, soon awake to the supreme enlightenment, even though his sins be vast.

VI. B. Thereupon the great Bodhisattva *Vajramuṣṭi* took hold of the Seal of the great Adamantine Sacrament and explained the meaning of this (method) in greater detail. With a smiling face he taught the Quintessence (of the doctrine) called the Sacrament of the Adamantine and Compact Seal of all (kinds of) spiritual Success. Aḥ.

VII. Emptiness

Thereupon the Lord *Sarvadharmāprapañca*, the Tathagata, demonstrated the method of the perfection of wisdom called the imperishable revolving of the wheel[1]:

"Empty are all dharmas, in consequence of the absence of own-being;
signless are all dharmas, on account of their signlessness;
wishless are all dharmas, because no plans are made for the future;
translucent in their essential original nature are all dharmas, because of the perfect purity of the perfection of wisdom."

VII. B. Thereupon the Lord *Mañjuśri*, the Crown Prince, explained the meaning of this (method) in greater detail. With a smiling face he offered his sword to all the Tathagatas and taught this supreme Quintessence of the perfection of wisdom, i.e. A.

[1]But Tib: 'khor-lo ltar yi-ge bskor-ba shes bya-ba, =called the revolving of the letters like a wheel?

VIII. The Entrance

Thereupon the Lord *Sarvatathāgatacakrāntargata*, the Tathagata, demonstrated the method of the perfection of wisdom called Entrance into the great Wheel:

"The Entrance into the Adamantine sameness leads to the Entrance into the Wheel of all the Tathagatas;
the Entrance into the sameness of the Meaning leads to the Entrance into the Wheel of the great Bodhisattvas;
the Entrance into the sameness of all dharmas leads to the Entrance into the Wheel of the true Dharma;
the Entrance into the sameness of everything leads to the Entrance into all Wheels."

VIII. B. Thereupon the Bodhisattva *Sacittotpādadharmacakra-pravartin* explained the meaning of this dharmic truth in greater detail. Smiling he revolved the Adamantine Wheel and taught the Quintessence (of the doctrine) called "the Entrance into all Adamantine Wheels". Hūṃ.

IX. Worship.

Thereupon the Lord *Sarvapūjāvidhivistarabhājana*, the Tathagata, demonstrated the method of the perfection of wisdom called the foremost of all acts of worship:

"The fact of raising one's thought to enlightenment is the prosperity-promoting Ritual for the worship of all the Tathagatas;
the fact of sheltering the whole world of beings is the prosperity-promoting Ritual for the worship of all the Tathagatas;
the Assumption of the true Dharma is the prosperity-promoting Ritual for the worship of all the Tathagatas;
the effecting of the writing of the perfection of wisdom, of dictating it, bearing it in mind, of teaching, reciting, developing and worshipping it is the prosperity-promoting Ritual for the worship of all the Tathagatas."

IX. B. Thereupon the great Bodhisattva *Gaganagañja* explained the meaning of this (method) in greater detail. Smiling he taught the Quintessence (of the doctrine) called "the fruitful Sacrament of all deeds". Oṃ.

X. Frenzy

Thereupon the Lord *Sarvavinayasamartha*, the Tathagata, demonstrated the method of the perfection of wisdom called the

Womb of the cognition for the disciplining of all beings, which is the Assumption of the Fist of cognition:

"From the sameness of all beings the sameness of Frenzy;
from the fact of disciplining all beings the fact of the disciplining of Frenzy;
from the true dharmic nature of all beings the true dharmic nature of Frenzy;
from the Adamantine nature of all beings the Adamantine nature of Frenzy.
And why? Because enlightenment consists in the disciplining of all beings."

X. B. Thereupon the Bodhisattva *Sarvamārapramardin* explained the meaning of this (method) in greater detail. Smiling he taught the Quintessence (of the doctrine) called "the Laughter of Vajrabhairava in his shape as the Adamantine Yaksha and the Seal of the Adamantine Eye-tooth". Ha.

XI. The true dharmic nature of everything

Thereupon the Lord *Sarvadharmasamatāpratiṣṭhita*, the Tathagata, demonstrated the method of the perfection of wisdom called the foremost of all dharmas:

"From the sameness of everything (should) the sameness of the perfection of wisdom (be known);
from the Meaningness of everything the Meaningness of the perfection of wisdom;
from the Dharmahood of everything the Dharmahood of the perfection of wisdom;
from the Doingness of everything the Doingness of the perfection of wisdom."

XI. B. Thereupon the Lord *Vajrapāṇi*, the Tathagata, and *all the Bodhisattvas* entered into the concentration called "the Sustaining Power of the Mandala of the fruitful Sacrament" and taught the Quintessence (of the doctrine) called "the Sacrament of all that is fruitful". Hūṃ.

XII. Samantabhadra

Thereupon the Lord *Vairocana*, the Tathagata (spoke) once more (and) demonstrated the method of the perfection of wisdom called the Power which Sustains all beings:

"Tathagatas in embryo are all beings, because they all have the self-nature of Samantabhadra, the great Bodhisattva;

Thunderbolts in embryo are all beings, because they are Consecrated with the Thunderbolt-Womb;
Dharma in embryo are all beings, because they all use speech[1];
Karma is potentially present in all beings, because they exert themselves in doing deeds."

XII. B. Thereupon the outside Adamantine families raised a clamour and (to them) this Quintessence (of the doctrine) was offered, and the meaning of this Dharmahood was explained in greater detail. Thereupon the great Adamantine Ruler of his own offered this very same Quintessence. Trī.

Thereupon all the heavely Mothers paid homage to the Lord, and of their own offered this very same Quintessence (of the doctrine) called "the Sacrament of the accomplishment of the gathering, taking up and examining all harmonious sayings". Bhyoḥ.

Thereupon, beginning with the Bees, the three Brothers paid homage to the Lord and, speaking harmoniously, on their own offered this very same Quintessence. Svā.

Thereupon the four Sisters paid homage to the Lord, and of their own offered this very same Quintessence. Hā.

XIII.

Thereupon the Lord *Anantāparyantāniṣṭha*, the Tathagata, who is in his dharmic nature infinite, boundless and endless, again for the sake of (establishing) the final Sustaining Power of this Body of Ritual Rules,[2] demonstrated the method of the perfection of wisdom which is called the Thunderbolt of the Final Sustaining Power of the sameness of all dharmas:

"Because of the infinitude of perfect wisdom the infinitude of all the Tathagatas;
because of the boundlessness of perfect wisdom the boundlessness of all the Tathagatas;
because of the manifoldness of perfect wisdom the manifoldness of all dharmas;
because of the Non-finality of perfect wisdom there is the Non-finality of all dharmas."

XIII. A. If someone hears this method of the perfection of wisdom, learns it, bears it in mind, copies it out, teaches, recites and develops it, he will reach the final end of the practice of the Buddhas and Bodhisattvas, which is, however, really non-final, and he will,

[1](?) sarvavākpravartanatayā; ṅag thams-cad rab-tu 'byuṅ-bas

[2](?) asya kalpasya; chos 'di

once all his coverings have become extinct, soon become a Tathagata or a Holder of the Thunderbolt.

XIII. B. Thereupon *all the Tathagatas* who were assembled, so that this discourse on dharma might soon come to a fruitful and unobstructed fulfilment, gave their approval to Vajrapāṇi:

"Fine is the great being, fine! Fine is the great bliss, fine!
Fine is the great vehicle, fine! Fine is the great insight, fine!
This Ordinance has been well preached by all the Buddhas, Holders of the Thunderbolt.
It is the supreme fruit of Discipline, Blessed in the Adamantine Sūtrāntas.
Those who take up this unsurpassed king of Ordinances,
No Māra, or anyone else, will be able to slay or to hurt them.
As it is taught by Buddhas, Bodhisattvas, and the supreme Perfected Ones,
And by all the Buddhas, he will reach it before long.
When it has thus been taught, when, for the sake of the Secret Success, an Adamantine teacher demonstrates it,
All the precious Buddhas in their wisdom rejoice (at the teaching)."

XIV. Success

Thereupon the Lord *Vairocana*, who has attained the Secret Dharmahood of all the Tathagatas and who is not obsessed by any dharma, furthermore demonstrated the most excellent door to the perfection of wisdom, which is without beginning, end or middle, which concerns its fruitful Adamantine Dharmahood and is called the Adamantine fruitful Sacrament of the Great Bliss:

"The supreme Success of the great Passion on the part of the great Bodhisattvas leads to the supreme Success of the Great Bliss (of all the Tathagatas);

the supreme Success of the Great Bliss on the part of the great Bodhisattvas leads to their supreme Success in winning the great enlightenment of all the Tathagatas;

the supreme Success of the great enlightenment of all the Tathagatas on the part of the great Bodhisattvas leads to their supreme Success in crushing all the great Māras;

the supreme Success of the great Bodhisattvas in crushing all the great Māras leads to their supreme Success in winning the sovereignty over the entire triple world;

the supreme Success of the great Bodhisattvas in winning the sovereignty over the entire triple world leads to their supreme Success in winning the most excellent, absolute Great Bliss, which brings happiness and benefit to all beings, and provides shelter for beings in all the worlds without exception."

XV.

And why?
"As long as the best of heroes reside in becoming,
So long are they able to effect the peerless weal of beings, for they do not escape into the Blessed Rest.
Having achieved perfect wisdom and skill in means, as well as the Sustaining Power of Cognition,
From the purity of all their deeds they become pure in (the world of) becoming. Haṃ.
The disciplining of greed, etc., goes on steadily in the world until the end of becoming;
So as to purify the world of these evils, do exert discipline until the end of becoming!
As a well-coloured red lotus is not sullied by any faults in its hues,
So those who are well-disposed towards the world are never sullied by the faults of residing in becoming.
But pure in their great Passion, immensely happy and affluent,
Having attained to the sovereignty of the triple world, let them steadily work its weal!" Hā.

XV. A. If, Vajrapāṇi, someone gets up early in the morning and for one single day only repeats this discourse on dharma dealing with the door to the method of the most excellent perfection of wisdom, hears it, learns, copies and develops it, he will gain all kinds of mental and physical bliss. In this very life already he will gain the supreme Success of the Adamantine and fruitful Sacrament of the Great Bliss. And he will also progress to the supreme Secret of all the Tathagatas. He will become a great Holder of the Thunderbolt, or a Tathagata.

XV. B. (*The 25 doors to Perfect Wisdom*).[1] Thereupon *the Lord* said to Vajrapāṇi, the Regent of the Guhyaka Clan:

"Regent of the Guhyaka Clan, there are twenty-five Mantras which express the doors to the method of perfect wisdom. (They are:)

(1) Oṃ, the Adamantine thought of enlightenment! (2) Oṃ, the conduct of Samantabhadra! (3) Oṃ, the wishing jewel! (4) Oṃ, non-stopping! (5) Oṃ, the obstruction of production! (6) Oṃ, all consciousness! (7) Oṃ, the great Dharmahood of dispassion! (8) Oṃ, the armour of vigour! (9) Oṃ, to go everywhere! (10) Oṃ,

[1]See pp. 199–200.

the Adamantine and exceedingly Solid Thought, hūṃ! (11) Oṃ, all the Tathagatas! (12) Oṃ, the purity of own-being! (13) Oṃ, the purity of the cognition of the true nature of Dharma! (14) Oṃ, likewise the purification of deeds, hūṃ! (15) Oṃ, Adamantine Slayer, phaṭ! (16) Oṃ, to be Passionate in sense-desire! (17) Oṃ, Adamantine forsaking! (18) Oṃ, hūṃ, the disciplining of all! (19) Oṃ, hrīḥ! (20) Oṃ, the door which is called A! (21) Oṃ, perfect wisdom! (22) (Oṃ), A Vaṃ hūṃ! (23) Oṃ, the supreme excellence of the body of all the Tathagatas! (24) Oṃ, the purity of the speech of all the Tathagatas! (25) Oṃ, the Thunderbolt of the mind of all the Tathagatas.[1]

XV. C. Oṃ, A, free us from all the bonds of evil, liberate us from all rebirth in the places of woe! Oṃ, Thunderbolt of all Sacraments, hūṃ ṭat!

This is the Mantra and Seal which suppress all evil, the Secret Success of all the Tathagatas, (and through it) one shall become a great Holder of the Thunderbolt and a Tathagata.

XV. D. (*Advantages*). Beings, Vajrapāṇi, who have not planted wholesome roots cannot come to hear of this. It is impossible that beings who have planted no wholesome roots can hear of it, write, dictate or recite it, bear it in mind, develop, honour, esteem or worship it. Those beings who hear even one single syllable of this discourse on dharma (which deals with) the method of the perfection of wisdom, they have elsewhere under many Buddhas planted wholesome roots, not to speak of their having perfected them.

Those, Vajrapāṇi, who have not honoured *niyutas* of *koṭis* of Buddhas, equal in number to the sands of eighty Ganges rivers, have not revered, adored and worshipped them, they cannot hear this discourse on dharma which deals with the door to the method of the perfection of wisdom. The spot of earth where this discourse on dharma is practised will be like a true shrine. The person who practises this discourse on dharma—whether he has heard it from someone or read it in a book—is worthy of reverence. He will remember his births over many *koṭis* of aeons. To him Māra the Evil One cannot cause any obstacle. The four great (Lokapāla) Kings, and the other gods also will follow closely behind him, in order to guard, defend and protect him. He will not die an untimely death. He will be brought to mind by all Buddhas and Bodhisattvas. Finally, he will be reborn in whichever Buddhafield he wishes to be

[1]The numbering is that suggested by the *Āryapañcaviṃśati(kā) prajñāpāramitā-mukha nāma mahāyāna-sūtra*. It may be that here 23–25 should be taken as one item, and then the two extra items of XV, C would be 24 and 25 respectively.

reborn. In that way the advantages of this discourse on dharma which deals with the door to the method of perfect wisdom, are numerous, although I have stated them only by way of outline.

XV. E. Thus spoke the Lord. Enraptured the great Bodhisattva Vajrapāṇi, and the (other) Bodhisattvas (who were present), and the whole world with its gods, men, asuras and gandharvas rejoiced at the Lord's teaching.

THE 108 NAMES OF THE HOLY PERFECTION OF WISDOM

Homage to the Blessed Perfection of Wisdom!

The Jinas of the past, future and present,
To them all you are a lovely mother.
The Jinas, O Goddess, are your sons.
To have no own-being is your own-being.
Of the names of the lovely Mother of the Buddhas
I will now speak.
If you want ample merit, listen![1]

The Perfection of Wisdom is:

(1) All-knowledge, (2) Knowledge of the modes of the Path, (3) Knowledge of all modes,

(4) Reality-limit, (5) Suchness, (6) Non-falseness, (7) Unaltered Suchness, (8) True Reality, (9) What truly is, (10) unpervertedness, (11) emptiness, signlessness, wishlessness, (12) the state of non-existence, (13) absence of own-being,[2] (14) having non-existence for own-being, (15) Dharmahood, (16) the Dharma-element, (17) the stability of Dharma, (18) the fixed sequence of Dharma, (19) the mark of Dharma, (20) absence of self in dharmas (and absence of own-being in them),[3] absence of (21) a being, (22) a living soul, (23) a person, (24) a personality, (25) and of individuality,

(26) inexpressible, (27) not to be talked about, (28) bereft of thought, mind and consciousness, (29) unequalled, (30) equal to the unequalled, (31) without sense of ownership, (32) without self-conceit, (33) unimpeded, (34) free from impediments,[4] (35) absolutely beyond all impediments,

(36) Mother of all the Buddhas, (37) genetrix of all Bodhisattvas, (38) support of all Disciples, nurse of all Pratyekabuddhas, (39) support of the entire world, (40) inexhaustible store of equipment with merit, (41) a torrential descent of cognitions,

[1]The Chinese has, in verse:
Homage to the Victorious Mother of all the Buddhas, the Prajñāpāramitā-dharma!
From her all the past, future and present Buddhas are born.
Because she is able to give birth to all Buddhas she is their mother.
Her own-being is to have no own-being.
The Buddha proclaimed it for Subhuti,
And as it was proclaimed by him,
So I now summarize it.

[2]So Narthang *Rgyud. Sna-tshogs* and Chinese: own-being.

[3]Tibetan only.

[4]*spros-pa=prapañca*

achievements of (42) the various wonderworking powers, (43) the purification of the heavenly eye, (44) the clarification of the heavenly ear, (45) the cognition of the thoughts of others, (46) the recollection of previous lives, (47) the extinction of the outflows,

(48) holy, pure and immaculate, (49) sacred and majestic,[1]

(50) firmly established in the applications of mindfulness, (51) associated with the strength of the right exertions, (52) associated with the four roads to psychic power, achievement of (53) the purification of the faculties, (54) of the powers, (55) of the unblemished jewel of the seven limbs of enlightenment, (56) of the gift of the seven prizes, (57) exhibition of the holy eightfold path, (58) achievement of the exhibition of the attainment of the nine successive stations, (59) acquisition of the ten sovereignties, (60) achievement of the dwelling on the ten stages, (61) perfect achievement of the ten powers, (62) adornment of the ten All-bases, (63) acquisition of the ten cognitions, (64) achievement of the destruction of the ten inimical evil tendencies, (65) perfect accomplishment of the trances, (66) achievement of the transcending of the formless world, (67) praised by all the fully enlightened Buddhas, (68) achievement of all cognitions,

(69) emptiness of the subject, (70) emptiness of the object, (71) emptiness of subject and object, (72) emptiness of emptiness, (73) great emptiness, (74) ultimate emptiness, (75) conditioned emptiness, (76) unconditioned emptiness, (77) infinite emptiness, (78) emptiness without beginning or end, (79) emptiness of non-repudiation, (80) emptiness of the essential original nature, (81) emptiness of all dharmas, (82) emptiness of own-marks, (83) emptiness of non-apprehension, (84) emptiness of non-existence, (85) emptiness of own-being, (86) emptiness of the non-existence of own-being,

(87) No-birth, (88) Non-production, (89) Non-stopping, (90) non-annihilation, (91) non-eternity, (92) not one thing, (93) not many things, (94) not coming, (95) not going away, (96) the full meditational development of conditioned co-production,

absence (97) of thought-constructions, (98) of all inclination towards entities or their signs, (99) of something to be known, (100) from the very beginning unsupported by any foundation, (101) non-dual, (102) undivided, (103) entrance into the quiet calm of purified understanding, (104) identical with the unobstructed and stainless ether, (105) neither existing nor expressible in words, (105) her own-being like a dream, her true nature like an illusion, (107) like unto a fiery circle, (108) the one single taste of all dharmas.

[1]Ch: śrī-lakṣmī

Anyone who recites these 108 names of the perfection of wisdom is freed for ever from all the states of woe. All the Buddhas bring him to mind, and all the Bodhisattvas constantly and always protect, guard and defend him.

And also by the uttering of the following mantra should she repeatedly be recalled in mindfulness:

"Homage, homage to the perfection of wisdom, the lovely, the holy; who is adorable and endowed with immeasurable virtues! Homage to the knowledge of all modes of all the Tathagatas,[1] and to all the Buddhas and Bodhisattvas!" i.e.:

OṂ PRAJÑE PRAJÑE, MAHĀPRAJÑE, PRAJÑĀVABHĀSE, PRAJÑĀLOKAKARE, AJÑĀNAVIDHAMANE, SIDDHE SUSIDDHE SIDDHAMANE, BHAGAVATI SARVĀNGA-SUNDHARI BHAKTIVATSALE PRASARITAHASTE SAMĀŚVĀSAKARI, TIṢṬHĀ TIṢṬHĀ, KAMPA KAMPA, CALA CALA, RĀVA RĀVA, GACCHA GACCHA, ĀGACCHA ĀGACCHA, BHAGAVATI, MĀ VILAMBA, SVĀHĀ.[2]

When someone has learned this perfection of wisdom, he will thereby bear in mind the Perfection of Wisdom in One Hundred Thousand Lines. He should always murmur it. All the obstacles (arising) from (his past) deeds will then be extinguished. Deceased from here he will be reborn as one who is mindful, self-possessed and of matchless wisdom. He will bear in mind of all the Tathagatas of the three times all the dharmas without exception, and he will have taken hold of all the mantras and spells. Deceased from here he will be reborn as one who is mindful, self-possessed and of great wisdom.

[1]The reading is here uncertain.

[2]This mantra has been transmitted in a highly corrupt form. I have consulted Narthang Sna-tshogs and Rgyud, as well as Lhasa and the Chinese for this text. The same mantra also occurs elsewhere, and I have compared R. Toganoo, *Rishukyō no kenkyū*, 1930, p. 396, the *pañcaviṃśatisāhasrikā-prajñāpāramitā-mantra* edited by R. O. Meisezahl in *Tribus* 7, 1957, pp. 50, 102, the *Kauśika-prajñāpāramitā* No. IX, and *Sādhanamālā* No. 156. From this material I have tried to construe what appears to me to be a sensible text, but the result is, of course, pretty speculative. And here is a translation: O*ṃ*, O Wisdom, O Wisdom! O Great Wisdom! O Wisdom, the illuminator! Wisdom, the giver of light! Remover of ignorance! Success, Good Success, Help me succeed! Blessed Lady, Beautiful in all your limbs, Loving mother! Your hand is held out to me! Give courage! Stand, stand! Tremble, tremble! Shake, shake! Yell, yell! Go, go! Come, come! Blessed Lady! Do not delay your coming! All Hail!

THE 25 DOORS TO PERFECT WISDOM

Homage to all the Buddhas and Bodhisattvas!

Thus have I heard at one time. The Lord dwelt on the summit of Mount Sumeru, which is at night the abode of all the Gods, together with hundreds of thousands of niyutas of kotis of Bodhisattvas. Thereupon the Lord demonstrated Dharma in front of an assembly of 250 monks, surrounded by gods, sons of gods, asuras, marutas, garudas, nagas, yakshas, kinnaras, rakshasas, all the Fairies who are the holders of magical lore, ghosts, misleading ghosts, piśaca demons, phantoms and invisible demons, assembled in an exceedingly large circle extending to 500 miles.

Thereupon Vajrapāṇi, the Bodhisattva, the great being, surrounded by all the Families, and by the hosts of wise spirits and Fairies, and by niyutas of kotis of the Fairies who are the holders of magical lore, came to where the Lord was. Descending from the intermediate space he thrice circumambulated the Lord, and sat down on one side. Thereupon the Lord said to Vajrapāṇi, the great Regent of the Guhyaka clan:

"There are her twenty-five doors. They are the doors to Perfect Wisdom. Homage to all Buddhas and Bodhisattvas!

"(1) Oṃ. The adamantine thought of enlightenment is a door to perfect wisdom. (2) Oṃ. Wholly auspicious conduct is a door to perfect wisdom. (3) Oṃ. The wishing jewel is a door to perfect wisdom. (4) Oṃ. Non-stopping is a door to perfect wisdom. (5) Oṃ. Turning away from birth is a door to perfect wisdom. (6) Oṃ. All consciousnesses are a door to perfect wisdom. (7) Oṃ. The true nature of the Great Passion is a door to perfect wisdom. (8) Oṃ. The armour of vigour is a door to perfect wisdom. (9) Oṃ. To go everywhere is a door to perfect wisdom. (10) Oṃ. Firm adamantine thought, hūṃ! is a door to perfect wisdom. (11) Oṃ. All Tathagatas are a door to perfect wisdom. (12) Oṃ. The purity of own-being is a door to perfect wisdom. (13) Oṃ. The purity of the cognition of the true nature of dharmas is a door to perfect wisdom. (14) Oṃ. The purification of karma, hūṃ! is a door to perfect wisdom. (15) Oṃ. Adamantine slayer, phaṭ! is a door to perfect wisdom. (16) Oṃ. (Purity of) sense-desire and greed is a door to perfect wisdom. (17) Oṃ. Adamantine renunciation is a door to perfect wisdom. (18) Oṃ. Hūṃ, what leads everywhere is a door to perfect wisdom. (19) Oṃ. Hrīḥ! is a door to perfect wisdom. (20) Oṃ. The letter A is a door to perfect wisdom. (21) Oṃ. Perfect Wisdom, oṃ vaṃ hūṃ! is a door to perfect wisdom. (22) Oṃ. Aṃ is a door to perfect wisdom.

(23) Oṃ. The supreme excellence of the body of all Tathagatas is a door to perfect wisdom. (24) Oṃ. The purity of the speech of all Tathagatas is a door to perfect wisdom. (25) Oṃ. The thunderbolt of the mind of all Tathagatas, āḥ! is a door to perfect wisdom."

Thus spoke the Lord. Vajrapāṇi, the Bodhisattva, the great being, and the whole world with its gods, men, asuras and gandharvas rejoiced at the Lord's teaching.

THE BLESSED PERFECTION OF WISDOM, THE MOTHER OF ALL THE TATHAGATAS, IN ONE LETTER

Homage to the Perfection of Wisdom!

Thus have I heard at one time. The Lord dwelt at Rājagṛha, on the Vulture Peak, together with a large congregation of monks, with 1,250 monks, and with many hundreds of thousands of niyutas of kotis of Bodhisattvas. At that time the Lord addressed the Venerable Ānanda, and said:

"Ānanda, do receive, for the sake of the weal and happiness of all beings, this perfection of wisdom in one letter, i.e. A."

Thus spoke the Lord. The Venerable Ānanda, the large congregation of monks, the assembly of the Bodhisattvas, and the whole world with its gods, men, asuras and gandharvas rejoiced at the teaching of the Lord.

NAMES

Abhayadaśabalanāda, a Bodhisattva 180
Airāvaṇa, a nāga-king 77
Ākāśagarbha, a Bodhisattva 184, 187
Ākāśamaya, a Bodhisattva 166
Amitabalanāda, a Bodhisattva 180
Ānanda, a disciple of the Buddha Śākyamuni 18sq., 92, 101, 201
Anantāparyantāniṣṭha, a Buddha 191
Anāthapiṇḍada, a lay supporter of the Buddha Śākyamuni 79, 122, 162
Anavatapta, a lake 19, 70, 73
Anikṣiptadhura, a Bodhisattva 79
Arāḍa Kālāma, a yogin, Śākyamuni's first teacher 64
Asaṅgapratibhāna, a Bodhisattva 79
Avalokiteśvara, a Bodhisattva 140–147, 184, 187
Bamboo Grove (Veṇuvana), a place in Rājagṛha 1
Bhadrapāla, a Bodhisattva 75
Candragarbha, a Bodhisattva 149–151
Cāritramati, a Bodhisattva 164
Devala, a kingdom 175–176
Dharmaśūra, a Bodhisattva 166
Dīpaṅkara, a Buddha 126, 131, 132
Gaganagañja, a Bodhisattva 184, 189
Guhyaka, a clan 193, 199
Jambudvīpa, India 178
Jayapratigraha, a Bodhisattva 166
Jeta Grove (Jetavana) 79, 122, 162
Kauśika, a Buddhist name for Indra 157–159
Magadha, a country in North-East India 148, 151, 181
Maitreya, a Bodhisattva 79, 183
Mahākāla Deva, a Hindu deity 175
Mahākāśyapa, a great disciple 79, 96; also Kāśyapa 96sq.
Mahākātyāyana, a great disciple 79
Mahākauṣṭhila, a great disciple 79
Mahāmaudgalyāyana, a great disciple 79
Mahāvairocana, a Buddha 184
Mahāśākyamuni, a Tathagata 145
Mañjuśrī, a Bodhisattva 79sq., 160sq., 184, 188
Māra, the Evil One 1–3, 7, 54, 58–65, 76–77, 192, 194
Meghadundubhināda, a Bodhisattva 180
Mokshala, a Khotanese translator into Chinese 169

TOPICS

accomplishment 12, 31, 35, 51, 60, 69, 104, 107, 188, 191
analytical knowledges (four) 55
annihilation (1) meditational, vibhāvanā, opp. development 11, 12, 17, 47, 49–51, 56, 61, 116; (2) uccheda, opp. eternity 24, 54, 56, 58, 66, 100, 115, 150, 158 (cutting off)
Arhat 47, 79, 87–89, 104, 106, 126, 162, 165
attainment 141, 143
austerities 2
basis 15, 20, 21, 48, 54, 67, 82, 84, 86 (baseless), 94, 102, 107, 161, 162
beings (living) 11, 12, 14–16, 48, 49, 57, 70, 80, 81, 88, 99, 104, 105, 115, 123, 124, 129, 130, 132, 133, 135, 136, 144, 161, 167–169, 184, 187, 189, 193, 196, 201
beyond 10, 17, 23, 67, 70, 128, 150
Bodhisattva 11–16, 20, 21, 70, 71, 100, 103, 123, 132, 133, 184
—course 14 —Pitaka 22 —pledge of 131
—qualifications of 36–38, 61 —stage of 13
Buddha 17, 87, 129
—cognition 70, 95
—dharmas 13, 17, 37, 46, 62, 69, 81–85, 97, 100, 103–107, 116, 125, 132, 152, 154
—'s domain 81, 88, 90, 100
—field 20, 51, 69, 80, 100, 116, 126, 133, 145, 148, 151, 172, 194
—fruit 167, 169; —three 170
—lands 165, 166, 177, 181
—lineage of the 61 —mark of 13
calm 68, 109, 112, 120, 121, 171, 185, 197
cognition of extinction 8, 10
compassion 38, 61, 70, 116, 148, 150, 156, 160, 166, 173, 182, 184
conceit 18, 19, 54, 84, 90, 184
—5 kinds 113, 114
concentration(s), various 144, 148, 151, 165, 190
—adamantine 7, 170, 172, 177, 185
—"One Single Array" 101sq.
—five kinds 118 —on emptiness 175
conditioned co-production 8–9, 49, 158, 197
consecration 146, 187, 191
contradictions 51, 130, 137
coverings 192; three kinds 185
deathless 161, 183

GLOSSARY

ADEPT (*a-śaikṣa*). One who has ceased learning, because he knows enough already.

ANALYTICAL KNOWLEDGES (*pratisaṃvid*). Four: The full knowledge of meanings, of dharmas, of languages, of ready speech. They are needed for success in preaching and for removing the doubts of others.

ALL-BASES (*kṛtsnāyatana*). Ten: Earth-device, water, fire, wind, space, blue, yellow, red, white, consciousness.

ANNIHILATION. (1) *Vibhāvanā*, the reversal and undoing of meditational development (*bhāvanā*) which is in fact its consummation. (2) *Uccheda*, the view that events are cut off, annihilated, after having existed; this is an extreme view often condemned; its opposite is the assumption of eternity (*śāśvata*).

ARHAT. Literally: "worthy of respect". The perfect Hinayana saint. He is exempt from further rebirth.

ASURAS. Titanic beings, forever at war with the gods.

ASSEMBLIES. Four: Monks, nuns, laymen, laywomen.

AUSPICIOUS THINGS. Seven: Gold, silver, lapis lazuli, crystal, agate, rubies, cornelian.

AUSTERITIES. Twelve kinds: Ascetic practices of special severity by which the more zealous monks purify themselves, e.g. they sleep in a sitting position, live in burial grounds, do not eat after midday, and so on.

BIRTH-AND-DEATH (*saṃsāra*). Undergoing transmigration.

BODHISATTVA. Literally: "enlightenment-being". The Mahayana ideal, who seeks the enlightenment of others as well as his own. He is not content with anything less than the full enlightenment of a Buddha.

BOUNDLESS STATES. Four: Boundless friendliness, compassion, sympathetic joy and impartiality. Also = Unlimited, Brahma-dwellings, stations of Brahma.

BRAHMĀ. A very high deity. Reputed creator of the world in the Hindu tradition.

BRAHMA-DWELLINGS. Boundless states.

BRAHMA, STATIONS OF. Boundless states.

BRAHMINS. A caste traditionally regarded as the repositors and communicators of sacred knowledge.

BUDDHADHARMAS. (1) (Eighteen) qualities or attributes peculiar to a Buddha. (2) Teachings of a Buddha.

BUDDHA-FIELD (*buddha-kṣetra*). A "kingdom of God" in which a Buddha teaches the Dharma and brings sentient beings to spiritual maturity.

BUDDHA LANDS. Buddha-fields.

COGNITION (*jñāna*). Knowledge which aims at salvation. Also "gnosis".

COGNITIONS. Ten: Of suffering, origination, stopping, path; of extinction, non-production; of dharma; subsequent; conforming to worldly convention; of mastery.

CONDITIONED CO-PRODUCTION (*pratītya-samutpāda*). Twelve conditions (cf. links), beginning with ignorance and ending with decay and death, which explain the mechanism behind individual rebirth.

CONSCIOUSNESSES. Six: Acts of awareness associated with the six kinds of contact, i.e. between visual form and eye, sound and ear, smells and nose, tastes and tongue, touchables and body, mind-objects (*dharmā*) and mind.

CONTINENTS (*dvīpa*). Four: The terrestrial world is divided in Hindu geography into seven, four or thirteen continents. The Buddhists adopted the fourfold division.

CROWN PRINCE (*kumārabhūta*). (1) A candidate to Buddhahood. (2) One ever youthful.

DEADLY SINS (*ānantaryāni*). Five: Killing mother, father, or an Arhat; causing dissension in the Order; deliberately causing the Tathagata's blood to flow. The Sanskrit term indicates that their retribution is an immediate one.

DELIVERANCES. Eight: (1) Having form, he sees forms. (2) Not perceiving inward form he sees outward forms. (3) He becomes resolved on emptiness (or: on loveliness). (4–7) The four formless attainments. (8) The trance of the cessation of perception and feeling.

DESTINIES (*gati*). Six classes of animate beings, i.e. gods, men, asuras, animals, ghosts and beings in the hells.

DEVAS. Gods.

DEVALOKAS. The heavens inhabited by the 28 classes of gods.

DHARANIS. Short formulas designed to enable us to remember the basic doctrines of Mahayana Buddhism.

DHARMA, DHARMAS. (1) The one ultimate Reality. (2) As reflected in life: righteousness, virtue. (3) As interpreted in the Buddha's teaching: doctrine, Scripture, Truth. (4) An ultimately real event. (5) Object of the sixth sense-organ, i.e. of mind. (6) Property. (7) Mental state. (8) Thing. (9) Quality.

DHARMA-VINAYA. The oldest division of the Scriptures into (1) Sutras devoted to doctrine (*dharma*), and (2) Vinaya devoted to monastic discipline.

DIRECTIONS. Ten: The four cardinal, the four intermediate directions, and above and below.

DISCIPLES (*śrāvaka*). Literally: "one who listens", i.e. to the Buddha. A term for the followers of the "Hinayana" in Mahayana texts.

DOORS TO DELIVERANCE. Three (1) Emptiness. (2) The signless. (3) The wishless.

DOUBLE TRUTH. (1) Conventional, verbalized truth. (2) Ultimate truth, conforming to true reality as it actually is.

DWELLER IN PEACE (*araṇā-vihārin*), often said of the Ven. Subhuti. It indicates inward peace of mind, peacefulness towards others, and the ability to bring peace to them.

ELEPHANT-LOOK. This refers to the occasion when the Buddha cast a last look at Vaiśalī before he left that city to go to his Parinirvana. He then turned round his entire body, as an elephant does when he gazes at something, always looking straight before him, not glancing round this way or that.

FACULTIES (*indriya*). Five: Faith, vigour, mindfulness, concentration and wisdom.

FAIRIES (*yakṣa*). Semi-divine, generally benevolent "gnomes", very often tree spirits.

FLOODS (*ogha*). Four: Greed for sense-objects, greed for becoming, wrong views, ignorance.

FOUR GREAT KINGS. The lowest level of gods, the world-guardians (*lokapāla*), corresponding to the four directions.

FOUR KINDS OF LIVING BEINGS. Egg-born, born from a womb, moisture-born, miraculously born.

GANDHARVA. (1) A heavenly musician. (2) A being about to enter the womb.

GARUDA. A mythical bird of prey, traditionally an enemy of the serpents.

GHOSTS. (1) Demons in a general sense. (2) *Preta*, hungry ghosts.

GODS (*deva*). Happy and blissful angels, inhabiting 28 kinds of heaven.

GODS OF THE THIRTY-THREE. Associated with Indra and dwelling on Mount Sumeru.

GROUNDS OF SELF-CONFIDENCE. Four: The self-confidence (*vaiśāradya*) of the Tathagata which comes from (1) having fully known all dharmas; (2) having dried up all outflows; (3) having correctly described the impediments to emancipation, and (4) having shown how one must enter on the path which leads to deliverance.

HEAVENS. Twenty-eight different abodes of the gods, rising on successive levels from the plane of sense-desire to the summit of existence.

HINDRANCES (*nīvaraṇa*). Five obstacles to the attainment of transic concentration, i.e. sense-desire, ill-will, sloth and torpor, excitedness and sense of guilt, doubt.

HOLY (*ārya*) MEN, or PERSONS (*pudgala*). Eight: The four saints when they enter their paths, and when they reap their fruits.

JAMBUDVĪPA. Buddhist name for India. *Jambu* means "rose-apple tree" and *dvīpa* "island", "continent".

JINA. "Conqueror", "Victor", epithet of the Buddha.

KARMA-RESULT (*vipāka*). The reward or punishment of actions, good or bad.

KARSHAPANA COIN. A coin, of gold, silver or copper, "which weighs a karsha", or 280 grains troy.

KINNARAS. Fabulous beings, human in the upper part of their bodies, and birds in the lower part.

KOTI. A very high number.

KOVIDĀRA TREE. A tree that "can be split only with difficulty", one of the trees of paradise.

LINKS (*nidāna*). The 12 members of the chain of conditioned co-production, i.e. ignorance, karma-formations, consciousness, name-and-form, six (inner and outer) sense-fields, contact, feelings, craving, grasping, becoming, birth, old age and death.

LOKAPĀLA. World guardians.

MAHORAGA. "Great serpents", a group of demons.

MANTRAS. Spells, incantations. Words of power which work wonders.

MĀRA. (1) Death. (2) The "Tempter". (3) The personification of all evil.

MEANS OF CONVERSION (*saṃgraha-vastu*). Four: Through generous giving, kind words, helpfulness, consistency between words and deeds.

NĀGA. (1) Serpent or dragon. (2) Water spirit. (3) Elephant.

NAME-AND-FORM. The psycho-physical organism.

NEVER-RETURNER (*anāgāmin*). A saint who after death will no more return to this world, but win Nirvana "elsewhere".

NIRVANA. The ultimate goal of all Budhhist endeavour, the

extinction of craving and separate selfhood, a life which has gone beyond death.

NIYUTA. A large number.

ONCE-RETURNER (*sakṛd-āgāmin*). Destined to have just one more reincarnation.

OUTFLOWS (*āsrava*). Four: Sense-desire, desire for becoming, ignorance, false views. When they are extinguished the result is Arhatship.

PARADISE. Heaven.

PARANIRMITAVAŚAVARTIN GODS. The highest gods of the plane of sense-desire. The name means that they control (enjoyments) magically created by others.

PARINIRVANA. Complete Nirvana, or final Nirvana.

PATH. Eightfold: Right views, intentions, speech, conduct, livelihood, effort, mindfulness, meditation.

Fourfold: Streamwinner, Once-Returner, Never-returner, Arhat.

PERFECTIONS (*pāramitā*). Six: Giving, morality, patience, vigour, meditation, wisdom.

PIŚĀCA DEMONS. Impish devils.

PLACES OF REBIRTH. Five: The six destinies, minus the Asuras.

PLACES OF WOE. States of woe.

POWERS (*bala*). Five: As the five faculties, but quite firmly established.

Ten: Of a Buddha. They describe his unique intellectual powers by which he comprehends what others cannot comprehend.

PRAJÑĀPĀRAMITĀ. The perfection of wisdom. Literally: "The wisdom which has gone beyond", to the other shore, to the Unconditioned, to Nirvana. Also: "transcendental wisdom".

PRATYEKABUDDHA. A self-enlightened Buddha who is unwilling or unable to teach others.

PREDICTION. At one stage in the career of a Bodhisattva a Buddha predicts of him that he will be a Buddha at some predestined time in the future and that such and such will be his name.

PRIZES (*dhana*). Seven: Faith, morality, sense of shame, dread of blame, learning, renunciation, wisdom.

"PURE LAND". Buddhafield = Buddha Land.

RĀKSHASAS. Malignant demons.

RISHIS, "seers". Legendary wise men, raised to heaven and comparable to the gods in stature.

ROOT OFFENCES (*mūla-āpatti*). Four: Fornication, theft, killing a human being, and falsely claiming spiritual attainments. They are also called "unforgivable" because they lead to automatic expulsion from the Order of monks.

(SACRED) KNOWLEDGE (*vidyā*). Triple knowledge, see s.v.

SAINTS (*ārya*) are the eight holy men who are moving straight towards Nirvana, since they have won the Path. The opposite are the "foolish common people".

ŚAKRA. Indra, "Chief of the gods" of the Thirty-three.

SAMGHA. The community of monks and nuns.

SAMSARA. Birth-and-death.

SEAL (*mudrā*). (1) The imprint left by a seal guarantees the authenticity of what has been said and "fixes" the efficacy of the rites based on it. It shows that it bears the stamp of divine authority and eliminates any possibility of lie or error. (2) Magic gesture of the hands. (3) The consort (matrix) of a deity.

SENSE-PLEASURES. Five: Derived from sight, sound, smell, taste, touch.

SIGN (*nimitta*). (1) Object of attention. (2) Basis of recognition of an object. (3) An occasion for being led astray by objects.

SOVEREIGNTIES (*vaśitā*). Ten: Over the lifespan, over thought, over the requisites of life, over karma, over rebirth, over determination, over resolve, over the miraculous powers, over cognition, over dharma.

ŚRAMAṆA. A religious mendicant.

STAGES. Ten: This is a standard division of the career of a Bodhisattva, beginning with his resolve to win a Buddha's enlightenment and ending with his actually winning it.

STATES OF WOE: Rebirth in hell, as an animal, as a ghost, as an Asura.

STREAMWINNER (*srota-āpanna*). One who has entered, or won, the Path, thereby detaching himself from mundane existence. The first of the holy men. He will return to this world no more than seven times.

STŪPA. A reliquary, cairn, tope, often bell-shaped and built in the open to contain relics of the Buddha or his disciples, or to commemorate the scene of their acts.

SUCCESSIVE STATIONS, ATTAINMENTS OF. Nine: Four trances, plus four formless attainments, plus the trance of the cessation of perception and feeling.

SUCHNESS (*tathatā*). To take a given datum such as it is, with nothing added on to it or subtracted from it.

SUGATA. "Well-Gone", an epithet of the Buddha.

SUMERU. A gigantic mountain located in the centre of the universe.

SUMMIT OF EXISTENCE (*bhavāgra*). The part of the universe which corresponds to the trance marked by the cessation of perception and feeling.

SUPERKNOWLEDGES (*abhijñā*). Six: (1) Psychic powers. (2) Heavenly ear. (3) Cognition of others' thoughts. (4) Recollection of past lives. (5) Heavenly eye. (6) Cognition of the extinction of the outflows.

SUPERMAN (*mahā-puruṣa*). An extraordinary human being whose body is characterized by (32) special marks.

SŪTRĀNTA. A doctrinal text which claims to have been spoken by the Buddha himself; also the doctrine contained in it.

TATHAGATA. Epithet of the Buddha. "The Truth-finder".

TERRACE OF ENLIGHTENMENT (*bodhi-maṇḍa*). The spot under the sacred fig tree on which the Buddha sat when he became enlightened.

TRICHILIOCOSM, great: A universe which comprises 1,000 million suns, moons, heavens, hells, etc.

TRIPLE JEWEL (*tri-ratna*). The Buddha, the Dharma, the Samgha.

TRIPLE KNOWLEDGE (*tri-vidyā*). The last three superknowledges, i.e. the recollection of previous lives, the knowledge of the rise and fall of living beings, the knowledge of the extinction of the outflows.

TRIPLE VEHICLE (*yāna*). Three methods of salvation noted in the *Prajñāpāramitā* Scriptures. They are those of Disciples, Pratyekabuddhas and Bodhisattvas.

TRIPLE WORLD (*traidhātuka*): The worlds of (1) Sense-desire; (2) Of form; (3) The formless world.

TRUTHS, HOLY. Four: Ill, origination of ill, stopping of ill, path that leads to the stopping of ill.

UNEFFECTED (*anabhisaṃskāra*). That which is not brought about by conditions of any kind.

UNIVERSAL MONARCH (*cakravartin*). A "wheel-turning king" who has gained over the entire earth a sovereignty which is his by right (*dharma*) and not by the use of force.

UTTARAKURU. One of the four continents. It lies in the north, and is a country of great beatitude.

VAIḌURYA. Lapis lazuli.

VIEWS, FALSE. Sixty-two: A standard list, found in *Dīgha Nikāya*, of heretical views, or groundless opinions, e.g. that the world is eternal, that the Buddha exists after death, etc.

VINAYA. Monastic discipline.

VOW (*praṇidhāna*). (1) The original vow of a Bodhisattva takes place at the beginning of his career when he resolves to rescue many beings by showing them the way out, after he himself has understood how reality works. (2) Any further benevolent resolve is also described as a "vow".

WAYS OF WHOLESOME ACTION (*kuśalakarmapatha*). Ten: Abstention from: taking life, taking what is not given, sexual misconduct, false speech, slander, harsh speech, frivolous talk, covetousness, ill will, and wrong views.

WHEEL. Jewel of: One of the seven precious things, or royal treasures, which are the prerogatives of a universal monarch, i.e. the perfect wheel, elephant, horse, pearl, minister, wife and general.

WINGS OF ENLIGHTENMENT (*bodhipakṣa*). Thirty-seven: A list of practices which carry us to salvation, i.e. four applications of mindfulness, four right efforts, four bases of psychic power, five faculties, five powers, seven limbs of enlightenment, eight limbs of the path.

WORLD GUARDIANS. Four Great Kings.

YAKSHAS. Fairies.

OTHER BPG PUBLICATIONS

EXPERIENCE BEYOND THINKING

A Practical Guide to Buddhist Meditation

Diana St.Ruth

A simple, practical, guide on how to begin meditating — the Buddhist way — as well as a good look at what lies behind the method and the thinking mind. For those who wish to experience the richness of meditation without getting caught up in too much intellection about it, this is an ideal first reader
0-946672-26-1

AN INTRODUCTION TO BUDDHISM

Ed. Diana St.Ruth

A comprehensive account of Buddhism and its teachings. Advice on treading the Buddhist path, with easy-to-follow instructions on how to meditate, also make this a practical guide for those who wish to experience the truth of what the Buddha taught.
0-946672-22-9

TEACHINGS OF A BUDDHIST MONK

Ajahn Sumedho Foreword by Jack Kornfield

Ajahn Sumedho invites us all, ordained and lay people alike, to enjoy the freedom beyond all conditions, a freedom from fears, from gain and loss, from pleasure and pain.
0-946672-23-7

THE ZEN TEACHING OF INSTANTANEOUS AWAKENING

Hui Hai Trans. John Blofeld

An eighth-century T'ang Dynasty Zen Text. Zen Master Hui Hai was of the same spiritual tradition as Hui Neng, Ma Tsu and Huang Po. His style of teaching is very direct and just as pertinent today in the West as it was twelve hundred years ago in China. 'When things happen,' says Hui Hai, 'make no response: keep your minds from dwelling on anything whatsoever: keep them for ever still as the void and utterly pure (without stain): and thereby spontaneously attain deliverance.'

0-946672-03-2

FINGERS AND MOONS

Trevor Leggett

A collection of humorous and instructive Zen stories and incidents pointing directly to the truth in ourselves. Humorous and profound. Trevor Leggett spent many years as both a student and teacher of Judo and its Zen background. Many of his stories are drawn from this period in his life.

0-946672-07-5

ZEN GRAFFITI

Azuki

A book of aphorisms and robust line drawings which point to the practice and fruits of Buddhism. They can nudge one out of apathy, dullness and habit into a direct awareness of the

moment's reality. Each reader will respond to different sayings according to individual need and development.
0-946672-24-5

THE BUDDHA'S LAW AMONG THE BIRDS
Translated by Edward Conze

Some three hundred years ago an unknown lama wrote this charming little book describing how the birds of the Himalayas met on a holy mountain under the leadership of the great Bodhisattva Avalokiteśvara who had taken the form of a cuckoo and who taught them how to live a Buddhist way of life.
0-946672-29-6

BUDDHISM NOW

For all kinds of Buddhists
by all kinds of Buddhists.

A quarterly Buddhist journal — interviews, practical advice on living a Buddhist way of life, translations, stories, verse, letters, news, book reviews etc. Indeed, something for everyone.
(Send £1 or $2 for a sample issue.)